GOOD
HOUSEKEEPING
Glut
Cookery
Book

GOOD HOUSEKEEPING
Glut Cookery Book

by Good Housekeeping Institute

Illustrated by Hilary Evans

EBURY PRESS
LONDON

Published by Ebury Press
National Magazine House
72 Broadwick Street
London W1V 1BP

First impression 1979

ISBN 0 85223 143 1

Designer Derek Morrison
Home economist Janet Marsh
Colour photography by Paul Kemp

Jacket photograph shows

Front Apple glazed bacon with herb stuffed apples (page 24),
Apple nut appetiser (page 24), Apple gingerbread ring (page 25),
Apple jelly (page 26), Apple jam (page 25)

Back Apple jelly (page 26), Spicy mincemeat (page 26), Apple
chutney (page 26)

Filmset in Great Britain by
Typesetting Services Ltd, Glasgow
Printed and bound in Great Britain by
Cambridge University Press, Cambridge

Contents

How to Use this Book

Good Housekeeping GLUT COOKERY BOOK is a shopping guide and recipe file combined. We hope it will enable you to take advantage of those all too brief drops in price when suddenly the shops and market stalls seem full of courgettes, for instance, and you can't think what to do with them. (Or when the garden's bursting with beans, or the family troops in with pounds of blackberries.) We've planned it to be as easy as possible to use. This is how it works.

You notice that a certain food item – say, tomatoes – are cheaper today, so you look up 'Tomato' in Part 1, *A–Z Shopper's Guide*. This is arranged in the form of a table. Here you will find, along with advice on choosing and storing, a list of the recipes featuring tomatoes as a main ingredient that are included in Part 2, *Recipe File*. You decide you like the sound of Tomato quiche, or Tomato fish bake for supper and you just turn to the page number indicated in the *Recipe File*.

If it's a really big glut of that particular food item, and you want advice on freezing, bottling, etc., you will also find in the '*A–Z*' tables the page number in Part 3, *Freezing and other Methods of Preserving*, where this information is given.

The foods included are mainly vegetables and fruit – simply because these are most subject to price fluctuation – but we have also covered certain other foods which you may find you have accumulated in the refrigerator from time to time. Such things as milk, cheese, eggs, bacon and chicken are versatile items in the diet and worth taking advantage of when occasionally they are available at a cheaper price than usual.

Good Housekeeping Institute

A–Z Shopper's Guide

	PRIME CONDITION	TIME FOR SEASONAL GLUT	STORAGE	METHODS OF PRESERVING
Apple, cooking	Fresh looking and sweet smelling. Firm to the touch. Without bruises or marks on the skin	September– October	3–7 days in the salad drawer of the refrigerator; 3–7 days lightly wrapped in cool dark place	Freezing Bottling Jam Jelly Chutney Drying

Basic preparation and cooking page 24; Apple gingerbread ring page 25; Apple glazed bacon with herb stuffed apples page 24; Apple and mint stuffed lamb page 69; Baked blackberry and apple loaf page 39; Chicken en cocotte with apples and cream page 57; Red cabbage with apple page 47.
Preservation: Apple chutney page 26; Apple jam page 25; Apple jelly page 26; Blackberry and apple jam page 40; bottling page 118; drying page 116; freezing page 111; Green tomato and apple chutney page 105; Spicy mincemeat page 26.

	PRIME CONDITION	TIME FOR SEASONAL GLUT	STORAGE	METHODS OF PRESERVING
Apple, eating	Fresh looking and sweet smelling. Firm to the touch. Without bruises or marks on the skin	September– October	3–7 days in the salad drawer of the refrigerator: 3–7 days lightly wrapped in cool dark place	Freezing Drying

Apple and almond tart page 25; Apple nut appetiser page 24; Fish fillets Normandy style page 24; Grapefruit, apple and mint cocktail page 65; Jellied beetroot and apple salad page 38; Spanish onion salad page 80.
Preservation: drying page 116; freezing page 111.

	PRIME CONDITION	TIME FOR SEASONAL GLUT	STORAGE	METHODS OF PRESERVING
Apricot	Fruits should be firm. Skin should be unwrinkled and without bruises and blemishes	May–August December– February	1–3 days in a covered container in the refrigerator	Freezing Bottling Jam Drying

Basic preparation and cooking page 26; Apricot oat pudding page 27; Apricot stuffed veal rolls page 27.
Preservation: Apricot jam page 27; bottling page 118; drying page 116; freezing page 111.

	PRIME CONDITION	TIME FOR SEASONAL GLUT	STORAGE	METHODS OF PRESERVING
Artichoke, globe	Leaves should be closely folded, without dry edges, and have a slight bloom. There should be no swelling at the base of the globe.	July– September	1–2 days in the salad drawer of the refrigerator	Freezing

Basic preparation and cooking page 28; Ham-stuffed artichokes page 28.
Preservation: freezing page 113.

	PRIME CONDITION	TIME FOR SEASONAL GLUT	STORAGE	METHODS OF PRESERVING
Artichoke, Jerusalem	Free from dirt and not too knobbly or twisted in shape. Creamy coloured and an unwrinkled skin	January– February	2–3 days in the vegetable rack; 5–8 days in the bottom of the refrigerator	

Basic preparation and cooking page 28; Artichokes and button onions in tomato sauce page 28.

	PRIME CONDITION	TIME FOR SEASONAL GLUT	STORAGE	METHODS OF PRESERVING
Asparagus	The heads should be well-formed and tightly packed. Avoid woody or wilting stems	May–June	1–2 days in the salad drawer of the refrigerator	Freezing Bottling

Basic preparation and cooking page 29; Asparagus Stilton pizza page 30; Prawn and asparagus mousse page 29.
Preservation: freezing page 113.

Aubergine	Skin should be shiny and unwrinkled. Fruit should feel firm when gently squeezed. Avoid any blemishes	November–December	1–3 days in the salad drawer of the refrigerator	Freezing Chutney

Basic preparation and cooking page 30; Aubergine au gratin page 31; Aubergines in yogurt dressing page 31; Bean and aubergine curry page 30; Egg stuffed aubergines page 62.
Preservation: freezing page 113.

Avocado	Skin will be smooth or knobbly according to variety – avoid wrinkled skin. Buy fruit that is firm rather than soft	November–December	2–3 days at room temperature; 4–5 days in the refrigerator	Freezing

Basic preparation page 31; Avocado shrimp creams page 32; Dressed tomato with avocado page 32; Veal sauté with avocados page 32.
Preservation: freezing page 113.

Bacon	Select bacon rashers or joints with firm moist flesh and white or creamy fat. Avoid 'sweaty' bacon or yellow-tinged fat	November and January	5–7 days in a covered container in the refrigerator	Freezing

Basic preparation and cooking page 33; Apple glazed bacon with herb stuffed apples page 24; Bacon and spinach quiche page 34; Bacon toad in the hole page 77; Cabbage stuffed with bacon page 46; Cauliflower and cheese bake page 53; Cheese and bacon pudding page 52; Cumberland bacon page 34; Leek and bacon pinwheels page 70; Midweek bacon stew page 33; Sweetcorn and bacon fritters page 103; Turnips braised with bacon page 106.
Preservation: freezing pages 108–110.

Banana	Skin should be yellow better to buy when slightly green. Avoid marked skins or squashy fruits	All year	5–7 days in a cool dark place—larder	Chutney

Basic preparation and cooking page 35; Baked banana and fig pudding page 35; Cauliflower, date and banana salad page 50.
Preservation: Banana chutney page 35.

11

	PRIME CONDITION	TIME FOR SEASONAL GLUT	STORAGE	METHODS OF PRESERVING
Bean, broad	The smaller pods will contain sweeter beans. Avoid any pods with blemishes	June–August	5–8 days in the refrigerator	Freezing Drying

Basic preparation and cooking page 35; Broad beans with ham in wine sauce page 36.
Preservation: freezing page 113.

	PRIME CONDITION	TIME FOR SEASONAL GLUT	STORAGE	METHODS OF PRESERVING
Bean, French and runner	The beans should be bright green in colour and crisp. Avoid over-grown and stringy beans	July–August	5–8 days in the refrigerator	Freezing Pickling Salting

Basic preparation and cooking page 35; Chilli pork with green beans page 37; Green beans with lemon cheese dressing page 36; Hot bean and corn rice ring page 36; Peppered beans page 37.
Preservation: freezing page 113; Mild mustard pickle page 36; salting page 117.

	PRIME CONDITION	TIME FOR SEASONAL GLUT	STORAGE	METHODS OF PRESERVING
Beetroot	Uncooked – avoid beetroot with damaged or wrinkled skin. Cooked – the skin should look fresh and moist	December–January	5–7 days in a cool place or refrigerator	Freezing Chutney Pickling

Basic preparation and cooking page 38; Beetroots with horseradish cream sauce page 38; Jellied beetroot and apple salad page 38.
Preservation: Beetroot chutney page 38; freezing page 113; Pickled beetroots page 38.

	PRIME CONDITION	TIME FOR SEASONAL GLUT	STORAGE	METHODS OF PRESERVING
Blackberry	Berries should be glossy and a dark colour. Avoid squashed or damaged fruit	August–October	1–3 days in a covered container in the refrigerator; do not wash before storage	Freezing Bottling Jam Jelly

Basic preparation and cooking page 39; Baked blackberry and apple loaf page 39; Hazel nut meringues with bramble sauce page 39; Melon with jellied blackberries page 76; Orange bramble mousse page 40; Spiced blackberry layer page 40.
Preservation: Blackberry and apple jam page 40; Blackberry jam page 40; bottling page 118; Bramble jelly page 40; freezing page 111.

	PRIME CONDITION	TIME FOR SEASONAL GLUT	STORAGE	METHODS OF PRESERVING
Blackcurrant	Select dark ripe berries. Avoid punnets of damaged or moist fruit	July–August	1–3 days in covered containers in the refrigerator; do not wash before storage	Freezing Bottling Jam Jelly

Basic preparation and cooking page 41; Blackcurrant fluff page 42; Blackcurrant galette page 42; Blackcurrant and raspberry strudels page 41; Chocolate blackcurrant gâteau page 41; Summer berry mousse page 42.
Preservation: Blackcurrant jam page 43; Blackcurrant jelly page 43; bottling page 118; freezing page 111.

	PRIME CONDITION	TIME FOR SEASONAL GLUT	STORAGE	METHODS OF PRESERVING
Broccoli	Select small tightly packed heads or curls. The stalks should be crisp when snapped	Purple: November–December Green or Calabrese: July–August	5–8 days in the refrigerator; wrap to prevent discoloration	Freezing

Basic preparation and cooking page 43; Broccoli amandine page 44; Broccoli cheese bake page 44; Cream of broccoli and lemon soup page 43.
Preservation: freezing page 114.

Brussels Sprout	Select even-sized sprouts, bright green in colour and without wilting leaves	November–March	3–4 days in the vegetable rack; 5–8 days in the refrigerator	Freezing

Basic preparation and cooking page 44; Brussels sprout and leek salad page 44; Lemon Brussels sprouts with mushrooms page 44; Spicy Brussels sprouts with rice page 45.
Preservation: freezing page 114.

Cabbage	Select firm, crisp heads without wilting or damaged outer leaves	Spring cabbage: April–May Spring greens: November–April Summer cabbage: June–October White cabbage: October–February Savoy cabbage: August–May Red cabbage: August–January	2–3 days in the vegetable rack; 5–6 days in the refrigerator	Freezing Pickling

Basic preparation and cooking page 45; Bean stuffed cabbage rolls page 45; Bubble and squeak bake page 46; Cabbage in nutmeg cream page 46; Cabbage stuffed with bacon page 46; Red cabbage with apple page 47.
Preservation: freezing page 114; Mild mustard pickle page 36; Pickled red cabbage page 47.

Carrot	Select fresh-looking carrots without bruises or blemishes	November–March	3–4 days in the vegetable rack; 5–8 days in the refrigerator	Freezing

Basic preparation and cooking page 47; Carrot and cheese soufflé page 48; Carrot croquettes page 49; Cheesy carrot ring page 48; Chicken, carrot and lemon pie page 49; Chilled carrot and orange soup page 47; Creamy swede soup page 101; Parsnip and carrot purée page 83; Rich oxtail and carrot hot pot page 48.
Preservation: freezing page 114.

	PRIME CONDITION	TIME FOR SEASONAL GLUT	STORAGE	METHODS OF PRESERVING
Cauliflower	Select white, tightly packed curds without yellow blemishes. Leaves should also look fresh	August–November	2–3 days in the vegetable rack; 5–8 days in the refrigerator	Freezing Pickling Chutney

Basic preparation and cooking page 49; Cauliflower and cheese bake page 53; Cauliflower, date and banana salad page 50; Cauliflower gratinata page 50; Cauliflower maltaise page 49.
Preservation: freezing page 114; Mild mustard pickle page 36.

Celery	Select thick stalks with fresh leaves. English celery is usually covered with soil – avoid any broken or blemished stalks	July–March	3–4 days in the vegetable rack; 5–8 days in the refrigerator. Wash if necessary before sorting	Freezing Pickling

Basic preparation and cooking page 50; Braised celery in soured cream page 51; Chunky beef with celery page 51; Creamy swede soup page 101; Hot blue cheese and celery mousse page 53; Smoked mackerel and celery cocktail page 51.
Preservation: freezing page 114; Mild mustard pickle page 36.

Cheese	Select fresh firm moist cheese. Avoid 'dried out' cheese – usually cracked at the edges or two tone in colour, being darker at the outside. Also avoid sweaty or soft cheese	All year	Hard and blue cheeses: 1–2 weeks wrapped in polythene or foil in a cool larder or refrigerator. Cream cheese: 5–7 days in a covered container in the refrigerator	Freezing

Basic preparation and cooking page 52: Apple and almond tart page 25; Asparagus Stilton pizza page 30; Broccoli cheese bake page 44; Carrot and cheese soufflé page 48; Cauliflower and cheese bake page 53; Cauliflower gratinata page 50; Cheese and bacon pudding page 52; Cheesy carrot ring page 48; Cheesy leek pancakes page 78; Courgette and cheese flan page 53; Creamy cheese lasagne page 52; Damson cheesecake page 60; Gooseberry cheesecake page 64; Green beans with lemon cheese dressing page 36; Hot blue cheese and celery mousse page 53; Sage Derby florentine page 99; Spanish onion salad page 80; Strawberry cheese creams page 100; Summer berry mousse page 42; Sweetcorn, cheese and chive soufflé page 103.
Preservation: freezing page 109.

Cherry	Select fruit that is firm and dry whether black, red or white	June–July	1–3 days in a covered container in the refrigerator	Freezing Bottling Jam

Basic preparation and cooking page 54; Cherry sorbet bombe page 54; Cherry stuffed loin of pork page 54.
Preservation: bottling page 118; Cherry jam page 55; freezing page 111.

Chestnut	Outer shells or casing should be shiny and not brittle	November–January	3–4 weeks in a cool dry place	Salting Bottling

Basic preparation and cooking page 55; Chestnut purée – sweetened page 55; Chestnut purée – unsweetened page 55; Tia Maria chestnut creams page 55.
Preservation: Chestnuts in syrup page 56; salting page 117.

	PRIME CONDITION	TIME FOR SEASONAL GLUT	STORAGE	METHODS OF PRESERVING
Chicken	Select a chicken that has a plump breast, smooth skin, soft flexible legs and is clean smelling	All year	Uncooked: 2–3 days; wash inside and out, dry and wrap in fresh polythene or foil Cooked: 2–3 days; cool quickly and store in covered container in the refrigerator	Freezing

Basic preparation and cooking page 56; Chicken, carrot and lemon pie page 49; Chicken en cocotte with apples and cream page 57; Chicken and cranberry curry page 57; Chicken and pear casserole page 86; Chilled chicken and pea mousse page 84; Fiesta peppered chicken page 88; Moroccan lemon chicken page 71; Mushroom and chicken savoury page 79; Pan-cooked chicken with cumin page 58.
Preservation: freezing pages 108–109.

	PRIME CONDITION	TIME FOR SEASONAL GLUT	STORAGE	METHODS OF PRESERVING
Courgette	Select smooth-skinned, even-sized courgettes about 7.5–10 cm (3–4 in) long	August–September	3–4 days in the vegetable rack; 5–8 days in the refrigerator	Freezing

Basic preparation and cooking page 58; Courgette and cheese flan page 53; Dressed leek and courgette salad page 70; Marinated courgette, corn and lemon salad page 58; Spicy beef stuffed courgettes page 58.
Preservation: freezing page 114.

	PRIME CONDITION	TIME FOR SEASONAL GLUT	STORAGE	METHODS OF PRESERVING
Cucumber	Select even-shaped, smooth-skinned cucumbers which are firm to the touch	July–August	4–6 days in a covered container in the refrigerator	Pickling

Basic preparation and cooking page 59; Cucumber and mint salad page 59; Cucumber with orange yogurt sauce page 59; Sweet and sour cucumber page 59.
Preservation: Mild mustard pickle page 36.

	PRIME CONDITION	TIME FOR SEASONAL GLUT	STORAGE	METHODS OF PRESERVING
Damson	Select dark fruits with a bloom on the skins. Avoid marked or blemished fruits	August–September	3–5 days in a covered container in the refrigerator	Freezing Bottling Jam Jelly Chutney

Basic preparation and cooking page 60; Damson cheesecake page 60; One-crust spiced damson pie page 60.
Preservation: bottling page 118; Damson jam page 61; freezing page 111.

	PRIME CONDITION	TIME FOR SEASONAL GLUT	STORAGE	METHODS OF PRESERVING
Egg	To test for freshness, place the egg in a bowl of cold water: it will lie on its side if very fresh, stand on its end if not so fresh, and float if very stale or bad	All year	Whole: 1–2 weeks small end down in refrigerator or at room temperature Yolks: 2–3 days covered in water in container in refrigerator Whites: 3–4 days in covered container in refrigerator Hard-boiled: 5–7 days uncovered in refrigerator	Freezing Pickling

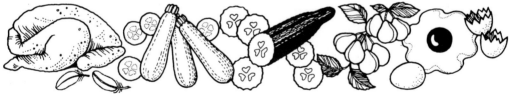

	PRIME CONDITION	TIME FOR SEASONAL GLUT	STORAGE	METHODS OF PRESERVING

Basic preparation and cooking page 61; *Recipes using whole eggs:* Almond orange mousse page 63; Broccoli cheese bake page 44; Carrot and cheese soufflé page 48; Cheese and bacon pudding page 52; Creamy plum tart page 91; Egg stuffed aubergines page 62; Greengage cinnamon upside down cake page 66; Ham stuffed artichokes page 28; Hazel nut rum gâteau plage 67; Hot blue cheese and celery mousse page 53; Mocha roulade page 62; Redcurrant choux puffs page 96; Redcurrant griestorte page 95; Spiced blackberry layer page 40; Strawberry hazel nut meringue flan page 100; Tortilla (potato omelette) page 62. *Recipes using egg whites:* Blackcurrant fluff page 42; Gooseberry flummery page 64; Orange bramble mousse page 40; Plum syllabub page 92; Prawn and asparagus mousse page 29; Redcurrant raspberry water ice page 95; Strawberry cream sorbet page 99. *Recipes using egg yolks:* Braised celery in soured cream page 51; Hazel nut tart page 68; Individual spinach quiches page 63; Spinach layer pie page 98.
Preservation: freezing page 109; Pickled eggs page 61.

	PRIME CONDITION	TIME FOR SEASONAL GLUT	STORAGE	METHODS OF PRESERVING
Gooseberry	Select the berries that have a slight yellow tinge. Avoid split or damaged fruit	July–August	1–3 days in a covered container in the refrigerator; do not wash before storage	Freezing Bottling Jam Jelly Chutney

Basic preparation and cooking page 64; Gooseberry cheesecake page 64; Gooseberry flummery page 64; Gooseberry sauce page 64.
Preservation: bottling page 118; freezing page 111.

	PRIME CONDITION	TIME FOR SEASONAL GLUT	STORAGE	METHODS OF PRESERVING
Grapefruit	Select fruit that is bright yellow in colour with an undamaged or unblemished skin. Avoid squashy skin – usually means dry fruit	January–March	3–5 days in the refrigerator	Freezing Marmalade

Basic preparation and cooking page 65; Grapefruit, apple and mint cocktail page 65; Honeyed spare ribs page 65.
Preservation: freezing page 111; Grapefruit marmalade page 65.

	PRIME CONDITION	TIME FOR SEASONAL GLUT	STORAGE	METHODS OF PRESERVING
Greengage	Select fruit that is firm to the touch with a yellow tinge. Avoid wrinkled skins and damaged or blemished fruit	August	3–5 days in a covered container in the refrigerator	Freezing Bottling Jam

Basic preparation and cooking page 66; Chilled greengages in red wine page 66; Greengage cinnamon upside down cake page 66; Greengage pancakes page 66.
Preservation: bottling page 118; freezing page 111; Greengage jam page 67.

	PRIME CONDITION	TIME FOR SEASONAL GLUT	STORAGE	METHODS OF PRESERVING
Hazel Nut	Select firm, unshrivelled husks or bright shiny shells	October–December	2–3 months in a cool dry place	Salting

Basic preparation and cooking page 67; Hazel nut meringues with bramble sauce page 39; Hazel nut rum gâteau page 67; Hazel nut tart page 68; Strawberry hazel nut meringue flan page 100.
Preservation: salting page 117.

	PRIME CONDITION	TIME FOR SEASONAL GLUT	STORAGE	METHODS OF PRESERVING
Herbs	Select fresh undamaged leaves	May–September (according to variety)	3–4 days in a jug of cold water	Freezing Drying Jelly

Basic preparation page 68; Apple and mint stuffed lamb page 69; Beetroots with horseradish cream sauce page 38; Cucumber and mint salad page 59; Grapefruit, apple and mint cocktail page 65; Lovage soup page 68; Marrow with herby tomato sauce page 74; Peas in parsley cream sauce page 84; Pineapple mint frappé page 89; Pork fillet with sage page 68; Spanish onion salad page 80; Sweetcorn, cheese and chive soufflé page 103.
Preservation: drying page 116; freezing page 109.

	PRIME CONDITION	TIME FOR SEASONAL GLUT	STORAGE	METHODS OF PRESERVING
Leek	Select even-sized straight leeks. The tops should be trimmed but are a guidance to freshness	October–January	2–3 days in the vegetable rack; 4–6 days, wrapped, in the refrigerator	Freezing

Basic preparation and cooking page 69; Brussels sprout and leek salad page 44; Cheesy leek pancakes page 78; Dressed leek and courgette salad page 70; Leek and bacon pinwheels page 70; Potato leek pie page 69.
Preservation: freezing page 114.

	PRIME CONDITION	TIME FOR SEASONAL GLUT	STORAGE	METHODS OF PRESERVING
Lemon	Smooth-skinned lemons will usually produce more juice and have thin skins	All year	5–7 days in a cool place or in the refrigerator	Marmalade Curd Chutney

Basic preparation and cooking page 70; Chicken, carrot and lemon pie page 49; Cream of broccoli and lemon soup page 43; Green beans with lemon cheese dressing page 36; Lamb with lemon and walnuts page 71; Lemon and apple flan page 72; Lemon Brussels sprouts with mushrooms page 44; Lemon sorbet page 72; Marinated courgette, corn and lemon salad page 58; Moroccan lemon chicken page 71; Mushroom salad in lemon dressing page 78; White fish with lemon crumble page 71.
Preservation: Lemon curd page 72; Lemon jelly marmalade page 71; Pear and lemon chutney page 87.

	PRIME CONDITION	TIME FOR SEASONAL GLUT	STORAGE	METHODS OF PRESERVING
Lettuce	Select lettuces that are bright green in colour. Avoid any with brown marks at the edge of the leaves	June–August	2–3 days, trimmed and washed, in a cool place; 4–6 days, trimmed and washed, in a covered container in the refrigerator; 4–6 days with root intact in the vegetable rack	

Basic preparation and cooking page 73; Individual tuna coleslaws page 73; Lettuce in cream sauce page 73.

	PRIME CONDITION	TIME FOR SEASONAL GLUT	STORAGE	METHODS OF PRESERVING
Marrow	Select smaller marrows about 1 kg (2 lb) in weight	August–October	5–8 days, whole in the vegetable rack; 5–8 days cut; 7–10 days whole in the refrigerator	Freezing Jam Chutney

Basic preparation and cooking page 74; Danish stuffed marrow rings page 75; Marrow in cider page 74; Marrow with herby tomato sauce page 74; Marrow and tomato au gratin page 74; Spiced marrow and beef supper page 75.
Preservation: freezing page 114; Marrow chutney page 75; Marrow and ginger jam page 75.

	PRIME CONDITION	TIME FOR SEASONAL GLUT	STORAGE	METHODS OF PRESERVING
Melon	Test for ripeness by gently pressing the top of the fruit – it should yield	April–June	1–3 days in a covered container in the refrigerator	Freezing

Basic preparation page 76; Honeydew ice-cream with melon balls page 77; Melon with jellied blackberries page 76; Melon and pear compote page 76; Spiced melon with dates page 76.
Preservation: freezing page 112.

Milk	Select milk that is in a sealed bottle or carton, stored in a cool cabinet. Avoid any milk which has been left to stand in a warm place	All year	1–2 days, covered, in a cool place; 2–3 days covered, in the refrigerator	Freezing

Basic preparation and cooking page 77; Artichokes and button onions in tomato sauce page 28; Bacon toad in the hole page 77; Cauliflower and cheese bake page 53; Cauliflower gratinata page 50; Cheesy leek pancakes page 78; Cream of broccoli and lemon soup page 43; Creamy cheese lasagne page 52; Gooseberry flummery page 64; Layered lamb and pea bake page 84; Lovage soup page 68; Mushroom and chicken savoury page 79; Orange bramble mousse page 40; Parsnip and almond loaf page 83; Potato leek pie page 69; Prawn and asparagus mousse page 29; Spinach soufflé page 99.
Preservation: freezing page 109.

Mushroom	Select mushrooms that are clean and white. Avoid those that are discoloured or limp	All year	Use on the day of purchase	Freezing Pickling Drying

Basic preparation and cooking page 78; Lemon Brussels sprouts with mushrooms page 44; Mushroom and chicken savoury page 79; Mushroom quiche page 79; Mushroom salad in lemon dressing page 78; Tomatoes baked in garlic butter page 104.
Preservation: drying page 116; freezing page 114; Pickled mushrooms page 79.

Onion	Select firm onions with a dry papery skin. Press onions at the neck to test for softness and decay	October–March	10–14 days in the vegetable rack	Freezing Pickling Drying

Basic preparation and cooking page 79; Artichokes and button onions in tomato sauce page 28; Beef stuffed onions page 80; Rich rabbit and onion casserole page 80; Spanish onion salad page 80.
Preservation: drying page 116; freezing page 114; Mild mustard pickle page 36; Pickled onions page 81.

Orange	Select fruit that is light rather than dark orange in colour. Buy under ripe with green tinge rather than over ripe	Seville: January–February	3–5 days in a cool place	Freezing Marmalade Chutney

Basic preparation page 81; Almond orange mousse page 63; Chilled carrot and orange soup page 47; Cucumber with orange yogurt sauce page 59; Glazed orange cheesecake page 82; Orange bramble mousse page 40; Orange

PRIME CONDITION	TIME FOR SEASONAL GLUT	STORAGE	METHODS OF PRESERVING

and pork duchesse page 81; Pears brûlée with orange cream page 87; Rhubarb and port compote page 97. *Preservation*: freezing page 112; Rhubarb and orange chutney page 98; Seville orange marmalade page 82.

Parsnip	Select clean, pale-coloured roots. Avoid those that are split or have brown blemishes	October– March	3–4 days in the vegetable rack; 5–8 days in the refrigerator	Freezing

Basic preparation and cooking page 83; Buttered parsnips with nutmeg page 83; Parsnip and almond loaf page 83; Parsnip and carrot purée page 83; Sautéed parsnip straws page 83. *Preservation*: freezing page 114.

Pea	Select bright green pods that are crisp when snapped. Avoid large pods that will contain large starchy peas	July–August	2–3 days in the vegetable rack; 4–6 days in the refrigerator	Freezing

Basic preparation and cooking page 84; Chilled chicken and pea mousse page 84; Layered lamb and pea bake page 84; Peas in parsley cream sauce page 84. *Preservation*: freezing page 114.

Peach	Select peach-coloured fruit rather than yellow for ripeness. Avoid split or blemished fruit	July–August	3–7 days in a covered container in the refrigerator	Freezing Bottling Jam

Basic preparation and cooking page 85; Nut meringue with peach compote page 85; Peach syllabub page 85. *Preservation*: bottling pages 120–121; freezing page 112; Peach jam page 85.

Pear	Select under rather than over ripe fruits and store for 1–2 days at room temperature. Avoid split or blemished fruit	Cooking: October– December Eating: August– November	3–7 days in a covered container in the refrigerator	Freezing Bottling Chutney Jam Drying

Basic preparation and cooking page 86; Chicken and pear casserole page 86; Melon and pear compote page 76; Pears brûlée with orange cream page 87; Pear mayonnaise page 87; Pear and walnut pie page 86. *Preservation*: bottling page 118; drying page 116; freezing page 112; Pear jam page 88; Pear and lemon chutney page 87.

Pepper	Select shiny even-shaped peppers. Avoid split or blemished peppers	Red: March Green: July– August	3–4 days in the vegetable rack; 5–8 days in the refrigerator	Freezing Drying Chutney

Basic preparation and cooking page 88; Fiesta peppered chicken page 88; Sautéed peppers in soured cream page 88. *Preservation*: drying page 116; freezing page 114; Spiced pepper chutney page 89.

	PRIME CONDITION	TIME FOR SEASONAL GLUT	STORAGE	METHODS OF PRESERVING
Pineapple	Select fruit that yield to slight pressure, with stiff leaves. Avoid bruised or blemished fruit	April–May	1–3 days in a covered container in the refrigerator	Freezing Bottling Jam

Basic preparation and cooking page 89; Pineapple bûché page 90; Pineapple in caramel syrup page 89; Pineapple mint frappé page 89.
Preservation: bottling page 118; freezing page 112; Pineapple jam page 90.

	PRIME CONDITION	TIME FOR SEASONAL GLUT	STORAGE	METHODS OF PRESERVING
Plum	Select fruit with a bloom on the skin. Buy firm, slightly under ripe fruit and store for 1–2 days	September	3–7 days in a covered container in the refrigerator	Freezing Bottling Jam Drying

Basic preparation and cooking page 90; Choux puffs with plum rum sauce page 91; Creamy plum tart page 91; Crunchy plum trifle page 91; Plum almond crisp page 90; Plum syllabub page 92.
Preservation: bottling page 118; drying page 116; freezing page 112; Plum jam page 92.

	PRIME CONDITION	TIME FOR SEASONAL GLUT	STORAGE	METHODS OF PRESERVING
Potato	Select clean even-sized, even-shaped potatoes free from eyes, splits and blemishes	Main crop: October–March Early: July–September	Main crop: 1–2 weeks in the vegetable rack; Early: 1–2 days in the vegetable rack	Freezing

Basic preparation and cooking page 92; French style potatoes page 93; Mushroom and chicken savoury page 79; Potato crusted chilli pie page 93; Potato leek pie page 69; Tomato and potato au gratin page 105; Tortilla page 62.
Preservation: freezing page 114.

	PRIME CONDITION	TIME FOR SEASONAL GLUT	STORAGE	METHODS OF PRESERVING
Raspberry	Select deep-coloured firm fruits. Pale-coloured fruits will not be so ripe or juicy	July–August	1–3 days in a covered container in the refrigerator; do not wash before storage	Freezing Bottling Jam Jelly

Basic preparation and cooking page 94; Blackcurrant and raspberry strudels page 41; Fresh raspberry caramel page 94; Raspberry shortcake gâteau page 94; Raspberry whirls page 94; Redcurrant raspberry water ice page 95.
Preservation: bottling page 118; freezing page 111; Raspberry jam page 95; Redcurrant and raspberry jam page 96.

	PRIME CONDITION	TIME FOR SEASONAL GLUT	STORAGE	METHODS OF PRESERVING
Redcurrant	Select firm dry fruit. Avoid damp or blemished fruit which will rot quickly	July–August	1–3 days in a covered container in the refrigerator; do not wash before storage	Freezing Bottling Jam Jelly

Basic preparation and cooking page 95; Redcurrant choux puffs page 96; Redcurrant griestorte page 95; Redcurrant raspberry water ice page 95.
Preservation: bottling page 118; freezing page 111; Redcurrant and raspberry jam page 96.

	PRIME CONDITION	TIME FOR SEASONAL GLUT	STORAGE	METHODS OF PRESERVING
Rhubarb	Select firm crisp stalks with clean fresh ends. Avoid split or blemished stalks or those with brown ends	March–June	1–3 days in a covered container in the refrigerator	Freezing Bottling Chutney Jam

Basic preparation and cooking page 96; Hot rhubarb meringue page 97; Rhubarb and ginger upside down pudding page 97; Rhubarb and orange chiffon pie page 97; Rhubarb and port compote page 97.
Preservation: bottling page 118; freezing page 112; Rhubarb ginger jam page 98; Rhubarb and orange chutney page 98.

	PRIME CONDITION	TIME FOR SEASONAL GLUT	STORAGE	METHODS OF PRESERVING
Spinach	Select crisp unwilted leaves	May and September–December	1–2 days in the refrigerator although best used immediately	Freezing

Basic preparation and cooking page 98; Bacon and spinach quiche page 34; Individual spinach quiches page 63; Sage Derby florentine page 99; Spinach layer pie page 98; Spinach soufflé page 99.
Preservation: freezing page 115.

	PRIME CONDITION	TIME FOR SEASONAL GLUT	STORAGE	METHODS OF PRESERVING
Strawberry	Select fruit that is bright red in colour and firm to the touch. Avoid over or under ripe fruit	June–July	1–2 days in a covered container in the refrigerator; do not wash before storage. Best used immediately	Freezing Jam

Basic preparation and cooking page 99; Caramelled strawberries page 99; Strawberry cheese creams page 100; Strawberry cream sorbet page 99; Strawberry hazel nut meringue flan page 100; Strawberry shortbread gâteau page 101.
Preservation: freezing page 111; Strawberry jam page 101.

	PRIME CONDITION	TIME FOR SEASONAL GLUT	STORAGE	METHODS OF PRESERVING
Swede	Select the smaller roots that will be less woody. Avoid split or damaged swede	October–March	3–4 days in the vegetable rack; 5–8 days in the refrigerator	

Basic preparation and cooking page 101; Cheesy topped swede casserole page 102; Creamy swede soup page 101; Swede and lentil purée page 102.

	PRIME CONDITION	TIME FOR SEASONAL GLUT	STORAGE	METHODS OF PRESERVING
Sweetcorn	Select cobs with stiff bright green leaves with a dark brown 'silk' at the top. The corn should be pale golden and extrude milky coloured liquid when squeezed	September–November	1–2 days in the vegetable rack; 2–3 days in the refrigerator, although best used immediately	Freezing Relish

Basic preparation and cooking page 102; Marinated courgette, corn and lemon salad page 58; Sweetcorn and bacon fritters page 103; Sweetcorn, cheese and chive soufflé page 103.
Preservation: freezing page 115; Sweetcorn relish page 103.

	PRIME CONDITION	TIME FOR SEASONAL GLUT	STORAGE	METHODS OF PRESERVING
Tomato	Select firm bright red/orange fruits. Buy under rather than over ripe fruit. Avoid squashy or damaged fruit	August–September	2–3 days in the vegetable rack; 5–7 days in the refrigerator	Freezing Bottling Pickling Chutney

Basic preparation and cooking page 104; Artichokes and button onions in tomato sauce page 28; Dressed tomato with avocado page 32; Marrow with herby tomato sauce page 74; Prawn stuffed tomatoes page 104; Tomatoes baked in garlic butter page 104; Tomato fish bake page 105; Tomato and potato au gratin page 105; Tomato quiche page 104; Tomato sauce page 106.
Preservation: bottled tomato purée page 123; bottled tomato juice page 123; bottling page 122; freezing page 115; Green tomato and apple chutney page 105; Mild mustard pickle page 36.

	PRIME CONDITION	TIME FOR SEASONAL GLUT	STORAGE	METHODS OF PRESERVING
Turnip	Select small even-sized turnips. Avoid any that are blemished or have soft patches	October–March	3–4 days in the vegetable rack; 5–8 days in the refrigerator	Freezing

Basic preparation and cooking page 106; Mustard turnips page 106; Turnips braised with bacon page 106.
Preservation: freezing page 115.

Zucchini,
  see Courgette

Recipe
File

cApple

To prepare

Peel the skin thinly using a potato peeler or small vegetable knife. Remove any bruises or damaged parts. Cut the apple into quarters, cut out the core and cut into thin slices. Alternatively, remove the core with an apple corer, leaving the fruit whole.

Basic cooking

To poach, place prepared apple slices in a saucepan with water to cover the bottom of the pan and 25–50 g (1–2 oz) sugar to taste. A strip of orange or lemon rind may be added for flavour. Cover the pan, bring to the boil and simmer gently for 10–15 minutes, stirring occasionally, until the apple is tender.

To purée, cook the apples as above without covering. Stir during cooking to prevent the apples sticking to the pan. Cook until the liquid is evaporated and the apples are tender, then sieve or beat until smooth.

To bake, cut through the skin of each apple round the middle and remove the cores. Stand in an ovenproof dish and pour 60 ml (4 tbsp) water around the apples. Fill the centre of each apple with demerara or soft brown sugar and place a knob of butter on top of each. Bake in the oven at 200°C (400°F) mark 6 for 30–45 minutes until the apples are tender.

Apple nut appetiser

Illustrated on the jacket

4 red-skinned dessert apples
10 ml (2 tsp) lemon juice
$\frac{1}{4}$ cucumber, diced
25 g (1 oz) walnuts, chopped
5 ml (1 tsp) chopped fresh mint
150 ml ($\frac{1}{4}$ pint) natural yogurt
1 curly endive
mint sprigs to garnish

Reserve one quarter of one apple for the garnish. Core and dice the remaining apples. Mix together in a bowl the diced apple, lemon juice, cucumber and nuts. Add the mint to the yogurt and stir into the apple mixture. Arrange the endive in the bottoms of four individual dishes. Spoon the apple mixture on top and chill before serving. Cut the reserved apple into slices and garnish each dish with sliced apple and mint sprigs.

Apple glazed bacon with herb stuffed apples

Illustrated on the jacket

1.8-kg (4-lb) joint of bacon, soaked for 2 hours
6 small cooking apples, cored
whole cloves
60 ml (4 tbsp) apple jelly, melted

For the stuffing
100 g (4 oz) dry breadcrumbs
100 g (4 oz) onion, skinned and chopped
2 stalks celery, trimmed and chopped
5 ml (1 level tsp) dried sage
30 ml (2 tbsp) chopped fresh parsley
salt and freshly ground black pepper
1 egg, beaten

Place the bacon joint in a large saucepan, cover with water and bring to the boil. Remove any scum from the water, cover and simmer gently for 1 hour. Drain, then place the bacon in a roasting tin. Cover with foil and bake in the oven at 180°C (350°F) mark 4 for 35 minutes.

For the stuffing, mix together in a bowl the stuffing ingredients with enough egg to bind. Score the apples around the centre and fill with the stuffing. Remove the skin from the bacon and score the fat with a knife. Stud with cloves and brush over the apple jelly. Place the stuffed apples around the bacon and continue cooking for 30 minutes. Serve the bacon sliced with the apples.

Fish fillets Normandy style

4 white fish fillets
seasoned flour
50 g (2 oz) butter
30 ml (2 tbsp) vegetable oil
2 eating apples, peeled, cored and sliced
juice of $\frac{1}{2}$ lemon
freshly ground pepper
chopped fresh parsley to garnish

Dip the fish in the flour. Melt 25 g (1 oz) butter with the oil in a large frying pan. Fry the fillets for 10 minutes until golden brown and crisp on both sides. Arrange the fillets, overlapping, on a warmed serving dish and keep warm.

Wipe the pan out with kitchen paper towel. Add the remaining butter with the apple, lemon juice and pepper. Fry gently for 5 minutes until the apple is tender. Spoon the apple mixture over the fillets and garnish with chopped parsley.

Apple gingerbread ring

Illustrated on the jacket

225 g (8 oz) plain flour
2.5 ml (½ level tsp) salt
7.5 ml (1½ level tsp) ground ginger
7.5 ml (1½ level tsp) baking powder
2.5 ml (½ level tsp) bicarbonate of soda
100 g (4 oz) brown sugar
75 g (3 oz) butter
25 g (1 oz) black treacle
100 g (4 oz) golden syrup
150 ml (¼ pint) milk
1 egg, beaten
3 eating apples, cored, peeled and halved
16 whole stoned dates
2 large pieces of preserved stem ginger

For the glaze
2.5 ml (½ level tsp) ground ginger
10 ml (2 level tsp) arrowroot
150 ml (¼ pint) sugar syrup
30 ml (2 tbsp) preserved stem ginger syrup

Grease and line a 19-cm (7½-in) ring mould or a round cake tin. Place a foil-wrapped 5-cm (2-in) diameter empty can in the centre. Sift the flour, salt, ground ginger, baking powder and bicarbonate of soda into a large mixing bowl. Put the sugar, butter, treacle and syrup in a saucepan and heat gently, until the butter melts. Pour the milk into a small pan and warm slightly, then beat in the egg. Add the treacle and milk mixtures to the dry ingredients. Mix thoroughly and pour into the cake tin. Bake in the oven at 180°C (350°F) mark 4 for about 35 minutes or until well risen.

For the glaze, blend together the ground ginger and arrowroot with a little of the sugar syrup. Bring the remaining sugar and ginger syrups to the boil in a saucepan and pour over the arrowroot. Stir well and return to the pan. Continue boiling and stirring for 2 minutes. Poach the apples in the glaze for 10–15 minutes or until just tender.

Remove the foil-covered can from the centre of the cake and turn out the cake. Arrange the apple halves around the edge with the dates and ginger. Pour the glaze over the cake.

Apple and almond tart

Illustrated in colour facing page 32

225 g (8 oz) rich shortcrust pastry (see page 42)
225 g (8 oz) curd cheese
50 g (2 oz) sugar
1 egg, separated
50 g (2 oz) ground almonds
1.25 ml (¼ tsp) almond essence
300 ml (½ pint) apple purée
grated rind and juice of 1 lemon
3 red-skinned dessert apples, cored and sliced
melted butter
apricot glaze

Roll out the dough and use to line a 25.5-cm (10-in) flan case. Bake blind in the oven at 190°C (375°F) mark 5 for 15 minutes.

Meanwhile, beat together the curd cheese, sugar and egg yolk until smooth. Stir in the ground almonds, almond essence, apple purée, lemon rind and juice. Whisk the egg white until stiff and fold into the apple mixture. Pour into the pastry case. Arrange the apple slices in two rings on top of the filling. Brush the apple with a little melted butter. Return to the oven at 180°C (350°F) mark 4 and continue cooking for 35 minutes, until set. Brush with apricot glaze and chill.
Serves 6–8

Apple jam

Illustrated on the jacket

1.4 kg (3 lb) sharp cooking apples
600 ml (1 pint) water
6 whole cloves
10 ml (2 level tsp) citric acid
sugar
red food colouring, if required

Wash and slice the apples without peeling or coring. Place in a pan with the water, cloves and acid. Cook until reduced to a pulp. Remove the cloves, then rub the pulp through a sieve and weigh. Allowing 350 g (12 oz) sugar to each 450 g (1 lb) pulp, add the sugar to the pulp and stir until dissolved. Bring to the boil and continue boiling, stirring occasionally, until setting point is reached. Add a few drops of red food colouring, if required. Pot and cover in the usual way.
Makes about 2.3 kg (5 lb) jam for each 1.4 kg (3 lb) sugar used

Spicy mincemeat

Illustrated on the jacket

1.4 kg (3 lb) cooking apples, peeled, cored and chopped
225 g (8 oz) currants
225 g (8 oz) sultanas
225 g (8 oz) seedless raisins
100 g (4 oz) chopped mixed peel
225 g (8 oz) shredded suet
grated rind and juice of 1 lemon
275 g (10 oz) demerara sugar
2.5 ml ($\frac{1}{2}$ level tsp) ground cinnamon
2.5 ml ($\frac{1}{2}$ level tsp) ground cloves
2.5 ml ($\frac{1}{2}$ level tsp) grated nutmeg
2.5 ml ($\frac{1}{2}$ level tsp) ground mace
2.5 ml ($\frac{1}{2}$ level tsp) ground allspice
2.5 ml ($\frac{1}{2}$ level tsp) salt
brandy

Mix together all the ingredients except the brandy. Leave to stand in a large mixing bowl, covered, for 3 days, stirring frequently.

Pack into jars, to about 2.5 cm (1 in) from the top. Place the jars in a shallow pan of water and bake for 1 hour in the oven at 150°C (300°F) mark 2. Remove, add 10 ml (2 tsp) brandy to each jar and seal immediately as for jam.

Makes about 1.4 kg (3 lb)

Apple chutney

Illustrated on the jacket

1.4 kg (3 lb) cooking apples, peeled, cored and diced
1.4 kg (3 lb) onions, skinned and chopped
450 g (1 lb) sultanas or seedless raisins
grated rind and juice of 2 lemons
700 g (1$\frac{1}{2}$ lb) demerara sugar
600 ml (1 pint) malt vinegar

Put the apples, onions, sultanas or raisins, lemon rind, sugar and vinegar in a pan. Strain in the lemon juice. Bring to the boil, reduce the heat and simmer, uncovered, until the mixture is of a thick consistency, with no free liquid. Pot and cover.

Variation: an electric blender can be used to produce a smoother texture if required. In this case, bring all the ingredients except the sultanas or raisins to the boil and simmer until really soft. Pour into the blender goblet, a little at a time, and blend until smooth. Return to the saucepan with the sultanas or raisins and cook for a further 15 minutes or until thick. Pot and cover.

Makes about 1.8 kg (4 lb)

Apple jelly

Illustrated on the jacket

2.7 kg (6 lb) windfall or other cooking apples
90 ml (6 tbsp) lemon juice
sugar

Wash the apples and remove any bruised or damaged portions. Cut into thick slices without peeling or coring. Put into a pan with the lemon juice and water to cover. Simmer until the apples are soft and the liquid is reduced by about one-third, then strain the pulp through a jelly bag.

Measure the juice and return it to the pan with 450 g (1 lb) sugar to each 600 ml (1 pint) of juice. Stir over a low heat to dissolve the sugar, then bring to the boil and boil rapidly until setting point is reached. Skim, pot and cover in the usual way.

To improve the colour of the jelly, a few blackberries, raspberries, redcurrants, cranberries or loganberries can be included with the apples.

cApricot

To prepare

Wash the fruit and remove the stalks. If under-ripe, using a small vegetable knife, cut around the apricot to release the stone while cooking. If ripe, ease the stone out of the apricot with the tip of the knife.

Basic cooking

To poach, place the prepared apricots in a saucepan with water to cover the bottom of the pan and 25–50 g (1–2 oz) sugar to taste. Cover the pan, bring to the boil and simmer gently for 15–20 minutes, until the fruit is tender.

Apricot oat pudding

100 g (4 oz) butter or block margarine
100 g (4 oz) soft brown sugar
2 eggs, beaten
75 g (3 oz) self raising flour
100 g (4 oz) rolled oats
pinch of ground cloves
150 ml ($\frac{1}{4}$ pint) milk
700 g ($1\frac{1}{2}$ lb) apricots, halved and stoned
apricot glaze

Cream together the butter or margarine and sugar until pale and fluffy. Add the eggs a little at a time, beating well after each addition. Fold in the flour, oats, cloves and milk to make a soft consistency. Place half the mixture in a greased ovenproof dish and cover with half the apricots. Spread over the remaining creamed mixture and top with the remaining apricot halves, cut sides down. Brush the top with apricot glaze. Bake in the oven at 180°C (350°F) mark 4 for 45 minutes, until risen and golden brown. Serve with cream or custard sauce.

Apricot jam

1.8 kg (4 lb) apricots, halved and stoned
400 ml ($\frac{3}{4}$ pint) water
45 ml (3 tbsp) lemon juice
1.8 kg (4 lb) sugar

Crack a few apricot stones and remove the kernels. Blanch these by dipping in boiling water. Put the apricots into a pan with the water, lemon juice and blanched kernels. Simmer until the fruit is soft and the contents of the pan well reduced. Add the sugar, stir until dissolved, then boil rapidly for about 15 minutes, or until setting point is reached. Pot and cover in the usual way.
Makes about 3 kg (6$\frac{1}{2}$ lb)

Apricot stuffed veal rolls

Veal escalopes filled with apricots and cream cheese with a crisp breadcrumb coating make a delicious main course for a midsummer dinner party.

225 g (8 oz) cream cheese
1 small onion, skinned and chopped
450 g (1 lb) apricots, skinned, stoned and chopped
salt and freshly ground black pepper
6 veal escalopes, 150 g (5 oz) each, beaten
25 g (1 oz) flour
2 eggs, beaten
30 ml (2 tbsp) milk
175 g (6 oz) fresh white breadcrumbs
100 g (4 oz) butter
watercress to garnish

Beat the cream cheese until smooth, then add the onion, apricots and seasoning and mix well. Divide the mixture into six portions and spread over each escalope. Roll up to enclose the filling and secure with wooden cocktail sticks. Roll in seasoned flour. Beat together the eggs and milk. Coat each veal roll with the egg mixture and breadcrumbs.

Melt the butter in a large frying pan. Add the veal rolls, cover the pan and fry for 20 minutes until golden brown. Turn once during the cooking time, taking care not to break the breadcrumb coating. Remove the veal rolls from the pan and drain on kitchen paper towel.

Serve garnished with watercress, with buttered new potatoes, courgettes with almonds and glazed carrots.
Serves 6

Artichoke, Globe

To prepare

Break off the toughest outer leaves. With a sharp knife, cut off the stem quite close to the base leaves. Trim the spiky leaf tips, and rub with a cut lemon to prevent discoloration. Wash the artichokes well under cold running water or soak them in a bowl of cold water, to which a little lemon juice has been added, for about 30 minutes.

The 'choke' must never be eaten as the little barbs can irritate the throat. It can be pulled out with the fingers, or scooped out with a spoon or knife.

To prepare artichoke hearts, remove the outside leaves and cut off the stem. Remove the remaining leaves above the heart. Carefully remove the choke. Immerse the artichoke heart in cold water with a little lemon juice until ready to cook.

Basic cooking

To boil, place the heads in a large saucepan of boiling salted water and simmer gently for 35–40 minutes, according to size. To test whether the artichoke is cooked, try pulling out one of the leaves. If it comes out easily, the artichoke is cooked. Turn the heads upside down in a colander to drain.

Ham-stuffed artichokes

4 globe artichokes, trimmed
60 ml (4 tbsp) lemon juice
150–300 ml ($\frac{1}{4}$–$\frac{1}{2}$ pint) thick mayonnaise
1 clove garlic, skinned and crushed
100 g (4 oz) sliced cooked ham, diced
2 hard-boiled eggs, roughly chopped
salt and freshly ground black pepper

Put the artichokes in a pan of boiling salted water and add half of the lemon juice. Cook for about 35–40 minutes until a leaf can be easily pulled away. Drain well.

When cold, carefully open the centre with your fingers and remove the choke with a teaspoon. Combine the mayonnaise, remaining lemon juice, ham and eggs. Adjust the seasoning. Use to stuff the centres of the artichokes.

Artichoke, Jerusalem

To prepare

Scrub the artichokes under cold running water. Peel away any discolored or knobbly parts and put the artichokes quickly into cold water with a little lemon juice or vinegar added. Older artichoke skins will be thicker and tougher and will have to be peeled away completely.

Alternatively, scrub artichokes, then boil or steam with their jackets on. These are easily stripped off while draining.

Basic cooking

To steam, place the prepared artichokes in a steamer and cook for 20–25 minutes.

To boil, cook in boiling salted water with a slice of lemon for 15–20 minutes. Drain well. Toss in melted butter and sprinkle with chopped fresh herbs or coat in béchamel, mornay or hollandaise sauce.

To poach, cover with cold milk, bring to the boil and simmer for 15–20 minutes. Mash with the milk, adding an egg yolk, butter or cream.

To sauté, blanch in boiling salted water for 5–10 minutes. Drain and then sauté in melted butter until golden brown.

To roast, blanch in boiling salted water for 5 minutes. Drain and place around the roasting joint or cook in hot fat in the oven at 200°C (400°F) mark 6 for 40–50 minutes.

Artichokes and button onions in tomato sauce

8–10 button onions or shallots
700 g (1$\frac{1}{2}$ lb) Jerusalem artichokes
300 ml ($\frac{1}{2}$ pint) milk
1 bay leaf
1.25 ml ($\frac{1}{4}$ level tsp) salt
25 g (1 oz) butter
30 ml (2 level tbsp) flour
salt and freshly ground white pepper
2 tomatoes, skinned, halved, seeded and chopped

Place the onions or shallots in a pan. Cover with cold water, bring to the boil and simmer for 5 minutes. Drain, cool slightly and skin. Cut the artichokes into walnut-size pieces. Place immediately in a bowl of cold water with a little lemon juice added.

Put the milk and 150 ml ($\frac{1}{4}$ pint) water in a pan and add the onions, bay leaf, salt and artichokes. Cover and simmer gently for 15–20 minutes until tender. Drain, reserving the cooking liquor. Discard the bay leaf.

Melt the butter in the pan, add the flour and cook for 1–2 minutes, stirring. Remove from the heat and gradually stir in 300 ml ($\frac{1}{2}$ pint) of the artichoke liquor and seasoning. Bring to the boil and cook for 1–2 minutes. Add the artichokes, onions and tomatoes and reheat.

Asparagus

To prepare
Rinse each stalk very gently to wash away any dirt. Scrape or shave the length of each stalk, starting just below the tip. Cut off the end if it is very tough and woody. Trim the stalks to roughly the same length. Place each stalk in a bowl of cold water while preparing the remainder. Tie the asparagus into neat bundles of six to eight stalks of an even thickness, heads uppermost. Secure each bundle under the tips and near the base.

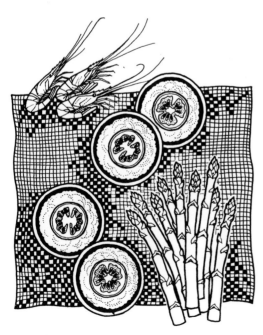

Prawn and asparagus mousse

Basic cooking
Cook asparagus with care.

To steam/boil, use a special asparagus pan or wedge the bundles upright in a deep saucepan. The pan should contain enough boiling salted water to come three-quarters of the way up the stalks. Cover the tips with a cap made of foil and simmer gently for about 10 minutes, until tender. This way the stalks are poached while the delicate tips are gently steamed. Drain the water carefully from the pan, remove the asparagus and serve.

Home-grown asparagus cooked within an hour of cutting takes even less cooking time – from 3–5 minutes. Even if you don't want to use it at once, absolutely fresh asparagus is best cooked immediately. Keep it cool and use in omelettes, as garnishes, or warm it and serve with melted butter.

Prawn and asparagus mousse

300 ml ($\frac{1}{2}$ pint) milk
1 slice of carrot and onion
1 bay leaf
6 peppercorns
1 blade mace
25 g (1 oz) butter or margarine
30 ml (2 level tbsp) flour
15 ml (1 level tbsp) powdered gelatine
450 g (1 lb) green asparagus, trimmed and cooked
2.5 ml ($\frac{1}{2}$ level tsp) salt
freshly ground black pepper
75 ml (5 tbsp) double cream
200-g (7-oz) can peeled prawns
2 egg whites
2 tomatoes to garnish

29

For the sauce, put the milk, carrot, onion, bay leaf, peppercorns and mace in a pan and bring nearly to the boil. Remove from the heat, cover the pan and leave to infuse for 10 minutes.

Strain the milk. Melt the butter or margarine in the cleaned-out pan, stir in the flour and cook for 1–2 minutes. Remove the pan from the heat and gradually stir in the milk. Return to the heat, bring to the boil, stirring, and cook for 1–2 minutes or until thickened.

Sprinkle the gelatine over 45 ml (3 tbsp) water in a cup and leave for a few minutes to soften. Beat into the hot sauce and stir to dissolve. Turn into a basin, cover tightly and allow to cool but not set.

Reserve a few pieces of asparagus for garnish. Purée the rest in an electric blender with the sauce. Season. Whip the cream and fold into the puréed mixture with the drained prawns. Stiffly whisk the egg whites and fold in. Turn into six individual dishes and refrigerate to set. Garnish.

Serves 6

Asparagus Stilton pizza

275-g (10-oz) packet bread mix
450 g (1 lb) asparagus, trimmed
25 g (1 oz) butter
1 medium onion, skinned and chopped
225 g (8 oz) bacon, rinded and chopped
salt and freshly ground black pepper
225 g (8 oz) Stilton cheese, crumbled

Make up the bread mix following the packet instructions. Cut any thick stalks of asparagus in half lengthways. Blanch the stalks in boiling salted water for 5–10 minutes. Drain well.

Roll out the dough into a 25.5-cm (10-in) circle and place on a greased baking sheet. Melt the butter in a pan and fry the onion, bacon and seasoning for 5 minutes. Spread over the dough base. Arrange the asparagus over the top, tips towards the centre. Sprinkle the cheese over the asparagus, making sure the ends of the stalks are covered. Bake in the oven at 230°C (450°F) mark 8 for 20 minutes until the cheese has melted and is golden brown.

Serves 6–8

Aubergine

To prepare

Cut off the stalk, 'calyx' and leaves around it. Slice the aubergine into about 0.5-cm ($\frac{1}{4}$-in) slices. Place the slices in a colander or sieve, sprinkle the cut surfaces with salt and leave for about 30 minutes. This will drain out the bitter juice – you will see beads of moisture forming. Rinse the slices thoroughly and pat them dry with kitchen paper towel.

Basic cooking

To fry, coat aubergine slices in flour and cook in melted butter for 5 minutes on each side until golden brown.

To grill, coat slices in flour, brush with melted butter and cook under a hot grill for 5–10 minutes until golden brown, turning once.

Bean and aubergine curry

225 g (8 oz) dried blackeye beans, soaked overnight
25 g (1 oz) butter
225 g (8 oz) onion, skinned and sliced
2.5 ml ($\frac{1}{2}$ level tsp) ground ginger
2.5 ml ($\frac{1}{2}$ level tsp) turmeric
2.5 ml ($\frac{1}{2}$ level tsp) ground coriander
30 ml (2 level tbsp) curry paste
15 ml (1 level tbsp) flour
300 ml ($\frac{1}{2}$ pint) beef stock or water
225 g (8 oz) aubergine, trimmed, sliced and salted

Drain the beans and cook in boiling water for about 50 minutes or until almost tender. Drain.

Melt the butter in a saucepan and fry the onion for 5 minutes until soft. Add the spices and curry paste. Cook gently, stirring, for 5 minutes. Stir in the flour, then gradually add

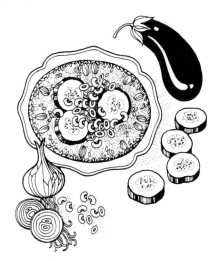

Bean and aubergine curry

the stock or water. Bring to the boil and add the beans and aubergine. Cover and simmer very gently for 15–20 minutes until the aubergine is tender. Adjust the seasoning and serve with boiled rice.

To freeze: cool quickly, transfer to a rigid container and freeze. To use, turn into a saucepan and heat gently from frozen, stirring, until boiling. Add more stock if necessary.

Aubergine au gratin

450 g (1 lb) aubergines, trimmed
salt and freshly ground pepper
butter
225 g (8 oz) tomatoes, skinned and sliced
25–40 g (1–1½ oz) Parmesan cheese, grated
150 ml (¼ pint) single cream
50 g (2 oz) fresh white breadcrumbs

Cut the aubergines into 1-cm (½-in) slices and salt the slices. Rinse, dry and sprinkle with seasoning. Grease a 1.7-litre (3-pint) ovenproof casserole with butter. Place a third of the aubergine slices on the bottom. Cover with half of the tomatoes. Sprinkle a thin layer of cheese over and dot with butter before repeating the layers. Finish with a layer of aubergine slices. Pour the cream over. Combine the breadcrumbs and the remaining cheese together and sprinkle evenly over the top. Cover and bake in the oven at 180°C (350°F) mark 4 for about 1¼ hours. If necessary, remove the lid and turn the temperature up to 200°C (400°F) mark 6 for 15 minutes to brown the topping.

Aubergines in yogurt dressing

2 large aubergines, trimmed, sliced and salted
salt and freshly ground pepper
40 g (1½ oz) flour
vegetable oil for frying

For the dressing
1 small onion, skinned and finely chopped
1 clove garlic, skinned and crushed
grated rind and juice of 1 lemon
15 ml (1 tbsp) chopped fresh herbs e.g. chives,
    mint, balm, basil
300 ml (½ pint) natural yogurt

Coat the aubergine slices in seasoned flour. Heat a little oil in a large frying pan and cook the aubergine slices, a few at a time, until golden brown on both sides. Drain on kitchen paper towel and keep warm.

Meanwhile, heat 15 ml (1 tbsp) oil in a small pan. Add the onion and garlic and cook for 10 minutes, until soft. Stir in the lemon rind and juice, herbs and yogurt and reheat gently without boiling. Spoon the dressing over the aubergines and serve immediately.

cAvocado

To prepare
Make sure the avocado is ripe by holding it in the palm of the hand and squeezing the flesh gently – it should feel soft all over. It is better to buy avocados in advance and allow them to ripen at room temperature for

2–3 days. Ripe avocados can be stored successfully for 3–4 days on the lower shelf of the refrigerator.

With a stainless steel knife, cut the avocado in half lengthways, around the stone. Hold the avocado in both hands and twist gently. Open the halves and remove the stone. If necessary, the skin can be removed with a potato peeler, or lightly score the skin once or twice and peel it back. Always brush exposed flesh immediately with lemon juice to prevent discoloration.

Dressed tomato with avocado

2 avocados, halved, stoned and peeled
juice of 1 lemon
60 ml (4 tbsp) vegetable oil
30 ml (2 tbsp) red wine vinegar
5 ml (1 level tsp) tomato paste
5 ml (1 level tsp) paprika pepper
salt and freshly ground black pepper
$\frac{1}{2}$ clove garlic, skinned and crushed
6 firm tomatoes, skinned and thinly sliced
1 small onion, skinned and thinly sliced into rings

Cut the avocado flesh into dice and spoon over the lemon juice. In a screwtop jar, combine the oil, vinegar, tomato paste, paprika, seasoning and garlic. Arrange the tomatoes and onion rings in overlapping circles around the edge of four small plates. Pile the diced avocado in the centre and spoon over the dressing.
Note: prepare within 1 hour of serving.

Veal sauté with avocados

25 g (1 oz) butter
1 medium onion, skinned and chopped
700 g (1$\frac{1}{2}$ lb) pie veal, cut into 2.5-cm (1-in) cubes
salt and freshly ground black pepper
40 g (1$\frac{1}{2}$ oz) flour
100 g (4 oz) button mushrooms, sliced
300 ml ($\frac{1}{2}$ pint) chicken stock
150 ml ($\frac{1}{4}$ pint) dry white wine
2 ripe medium avocados
30–45 ml (2–3 tbsp) soured cream

Melt the butter in a frying pan, add the onion and cook for 5 minutes until soft but not coloured. Coat the veal cubes in seasoned flour. Add to the onion and cook for 4–5 minutes to brown. Add the mushrooms and any remaining flour. Stir in the chicken stock and wine, season well and bring to the boil, stirring. Pour into a casserole, cover and cook in the oven at 180°C (350°F) mark 4 for 1–1$\frac{1}{2}$ hours until the veal is tender.

Peel, stone and slice the avocados and stir immediately into the veal with the soured cream. Serve.
Serves 4–6

Avocado shrimp creams

15 g ($\frac{1}{2}$ oz) powdered gelatine
30 ml (2 tbsp) water
2 ripe avocados, halved and stoned
30 ml (2 tbsp) lemon juice
100 g (4 oz) peeled shrimps
grated rind of 1 lemon
salt and freshly ground pepper
45 ml (3 tbsp) soured cream
30 ml (2 tbsp) mayonnaise
1 egg white

Place the gelatine and water in a small heat-proof bowl and stand over a pan of hot water to dissolve the gelatine. Cool. Scoop the avocado flesh from the skins and purée in an electric blender, or rub through a sieve with the lemon juice.

Reserve 25 g (1 oz) of the shrimps for garnish and chop the remainder. Stir the chopped shrimps into the avocado purée with the lemon rind, seasoning, soured cream, mayonnaise and dissolved gelatine. Whisk the egg white until stiff and carefully fold into the avocado mixture. Pour the mixture into six individual oiled moulds, smooth the tops and leave in a refrigerator to set.

To serve, stand the moulds in warm water for a few seconds, then unmould on to serving plates. Garnish with the reserved whole shrimps.
Serves 6

Apple and almond tart (page 25), Chicken and pear casserole (page 86), Plum syllabub (page 92).

Bacon

To prepare

Bacon joints: the length of soaking bacon joints is considerably reduced by mild cures. If soaking, do not allow more than 2–3 hours. Overnight soaking should be reserved for large joints; 8 hours is sufficient. Or a bacon joint of an average size may be placed in a saucepan of cold water to cover, brought to the boil and drained.

Bacon rashers: rind rashers thinly with kitchen scissors or a sharp knife. Remove any bone. Thick rashers or chops should be snipped at intervals along the fat edge to help them remain flat during cooking. If you suspect that chops or other thick bacon or gammon slices are salty, soak them or poach them in water for a few minutes.

Basic cooking

To boil, weigh the bacon joint, then calculate the cooking time, allowing 20–25 minutes per 450 g (1 lb) plus 20 minutes over. If you are cooking a joint 4.5 kg (10 lb) or over, allow 15–20 minutes per 450 g (1 lb) plus 15 minutes. Place the bacon in a large pan, skin side down, cover with cold water and bring slowly to the boil, skimming off any scum that forms. Time the cooking from this point. Cover and simmer until cooked. For extra flavour, add 2 skinned and quartered onions, 2 peeled and quartered carrots, 1 bay leaf and 4 peppercorns. When the bacon is cooked, ease away the rind and serve the joint hot. Or remove the rind and press browned breadcrumbs into the fat and serve cold.

To bake and glaze, weigh the joint, calculate the cooking time and boil as above for half the cooking time. Drain and wrap in kitchen foil. Place on a baking sheet and bake in the centre of the oven at 180°C (350°F) mark 4 until 30 minutes before cooking time is complete. Raise the oven temperature to 220°C (425°F) mark 7. Undo the foil, remove the rind from the bacon and score the fat in diamonds. Stud with cloves and sprinkle the surface with demerara sugar. Pat in. Return the joint to the oven until crisp and golden.

For spiced marmalade and honey glaze, blend together in a small basin 60 ml (4 level tbsp) fine shred marmalade, 75 ml (5 tbsp) clear honey and 4–5 drops Tabasco sauce.

Brush about one third of this glaze over the bacon fat 30 minutes before the end of cooking time. Return to the oven for 10 minutes before applying the second glaze. Don't use the glaze that has run into the pan as this will dull the shine. Repeat with the final third of the glaze.

To grill and fry bacon rashers, for frying, lay the bacon rashers in a cold pan, with the lean parts over the fat; for grilling, arrange them in the reverse way. Lean rashers are better brushed with fat or oil for grilling. Cook quickly to obtain a crisp effect, slowly if you prefer the rashers softer. Thread bacon rolls on a skewer and grill for 3–5 minutes until crisp, turning once.

To grill gammon, choose rashers that are not less than 0.5 cm ($\frac{1}{4}$ in) thick. Cut off the rind and snip the fat at intervals. Pre-heat the grill. Put the rashers on to a lightly greased grill grid, brush with melted butter or oil and cook under a medium heat for about 5 minutes. Turn them, brush the second side with butter or oil and cook for a further 5–10 minutes.

Midweek bacon stew

Illustrated in colour opposite

100 g (4 oz) dried butter beans, soaked overnight
700-g (1½-lb) bacon slipper joint
225 g (8 oz) turnips, peeled and diced
225 g (8 oz) parsnips, peeled and diced
25 g (1 oz) lard
30 ml (2 level tbsp) flour
7.5 ml (1½ level tsp) dry mustard
600 ml (1 pint) chicken stock
freshly ground pepper
chopped fresh parsley to garnish

Drain the beans. Remove any rind from the bacon and cut the meat into 2.5-cm (1-in) cubes. Place in a pan of cold water, bring to the boil and simmer for 5 minutes. Drain well.

Fry the vegetables gently in the hot fat in a flameproof casserole for 5 minutes. Stir in the flour and mustard and cook for 1 minute, then gradually stir in the stock. Stir until boiling. Add the beans, meat and pepper. Cover and simmer gently for about 1½ hours. Serve garnished with parsley.

To freeze: complete cooking before freezing.

33

Midweek bacon stew (above), Cheese and bacon pudding mixture (page 52), Chicken en cocotte with apples and cream (page 57).

Reheat slowly from frozen (adding more stock if needed) over a very gentle heat, stirring occasionally, until boiling.
Serves 6

Bacon and spinach quiche

225 g (8 oz) shortcrust pastry (see page 63)
350 g (12 oz) streaky bacon, rinded
1 medium onion, skinned and sliced
15 ml (1 tbsp) vegetable oil
2 eggs, beaten
150 ml (¼ pint) natural yogurt
150 ml (¼ pint) milk
salt and freshly ground black pepper
226-g (8-oz) packet frozen chopped spinach, thawed

Roll out the dough and use to line a 24-cm (9½-in) loose-bottomed flan ring. Bake blind in the oven at 200°C (400°F) mark 6 for about 15 minutes until dry but not brown.

Dice 100 g (4 oz) of the bacon. Lightly fry the diced bacon and onion in the oil for about 10 minutes until golden. Mix the eggs with the yogurt, milk and seasoning. Stir in the onion and bacon mixture. Mix in the well drained spinach. Pour into the flan case and bake in the oven at 190°C (375°F) mark 5 for about 30 minutes, or until just set.

Form the rest of the bacon into little rolls. Place in a baking dish and bake next to the flan for about 20 minutes. Use to garnish the flan.

To freeze: pack and freeze the baked ungarnished flan. To use, thaw at room temperature for about 6 hours. Refresh at 190°C (375°F) mark 5 for about 20 minutes. Garnish as above.

Variation: replace the spinach and onion with 350 g (12 oz) sliced leeks. Fry with the bacon as above.
Serves 6

Cumberland bacon

900-g (2-lb) boneless smoked bacon joint
15 ml (1 tbsp) vegetable oil
15 g (½ oz) butter
175 g (6 oz) onion, skinned and sliced
15 ml (1 level tbsp) French mustard
15 ml (1 level tbsp) flour
grated rind of 1 orange
60 ml (4 tbsp) orange juice
300 ml (½ pint) light stock
45 ml (3 level tbsp) redcurrant jelly
5 ml (1 tsp) wine vinegar
450 g (1 lb) potatoes, peeled and cut into 2.5-cm (1-in) chunks
198-g (7-oz) can sweetcorn kernels, drained
1 medium green pepper, seeded and sliced
freshly ground black pepper

Remove the rind and excess fat from the bacon and cut into 1.5-cm (¾-in) cubes. Place in a pan of cold water and bring to the boil. Drain well.

Heat the oil and butter in a flameproof casserole and cook the onion for 5 minutes until soft. Stir in the mustard and flour and cook for 1 minute. Add the orange rind and juice, stock, redcurrant jelly and vinegar. Bring to the boil, stirring. Blend in the bacon, potatoes, sweetcorn, green pepper and seasoning. Cover and cook in the oven at 180°C (350°F) mark 4 for about 1¼ hours until the bacon is tender.

To freeze: pack and freeze after 1 hour of cooking. To use, thaw at cool room temperature overnight. Reheat, covered, in the oven at 180°C (350°F) mark 4 for 1 hour.
Serves 6

Bacon and spinach quiche

Banana

To prepare

Peel bananas when you are ready to use them. If they must be peeled and sliced in advance, brush with lemon juice to prevent discoloration.

Basic cooking

To fry, melt 25 g (1 oz) butter in a frying pan. Cut the bananas into thick slices or cut in half lengthways. Add to the pan and fry gently for 3–4 minutes until golden brown but not mushy. Sprinkle with brown sugar and serve with fresh or soured cream. Or omit the sugar and serve with Chicken Maryland.

Baked banana and fig pudding

426-g (15-oz) can figs
2 bananas
50 g (2 oz) seedless raisins
75 g (3 oz) butter
75 g (3 oz) caster sugar
2 eggs, beaten
100 g (4 oz) self raising flour

Measure 150 ml ($\frac{1}{4}$ pint) of the fig syrup and place the drained figs and the measured syrup in a 1.7-litre (3-pint) capacity ovenproof dish. Cut the bananas on a slant into fairly large pieces and stir into the figs together with the raisins.

Cream the butter with the sugar until light and fluffy. Add the eggs one at a time and beat thoroughly. Fold in the sifted flour and mix to a soft consistency. Spread over the fruit mixture and bake in the oven at 180°C (350°F) mark 4 for 55 minutes–1 hour.

Banana chutney

900 g (2 lb) cooking apples, peeled, cored and chopped
225 g (8 oz) onions, skinned and chopped
225 g (8 oz) seedless raisins
225 g (8 oz) stoned dates, chopped
1.8 kg (4 lb) bananas, sliced
10 ml (2 level tsp) salt
350 g (12 oz) demerara sugar
30 ml (2 level tbsp) ground ginger
1.25–2.5 ml ($\frac{1}{4}$–$\frac{1}{2}$ level tsp) cayenne pepper
600 ml (1 pint) white vinegar

Put the apples, onions, raisins, dates and bananas in a preserving pan. Sprinkle with the salt, sugar and spices. Pour in the vinegar and bring to the boil. Simmer gently, uncovered, for about 1 hour, stirring occasionally, until soft and pulpy. Pot and cover in the usual way.

Makes about 3.4 kg (7$\frac{1}{2}$ lb)

Bean

BROAD BEANS
To prepare

If the pods are tender and beans still small, simply trim the pods and cook whole. For larger beans, remove the beans from the pod.

Basic cooking

To boil, cook in boiling salted water for 15–20 minutes and drain well. Slip large beans out of their skins. Toss the whole pods or beans in melted butter and serve sprinkled with chopped fresh parsley or summer savory. Alternatively, stir cooked beans into a creamy white sauce. Very large old beans should be turned into soup or purée.

To purée, cook in boiling salted water as above. Remove the outer skins and purée in a blender or rub through a sieve with 25–50 g (1–2 oz) butter and a little chopped fresh summer savory.

FRENCH AND RUNNER BEANS
To prepare

Young beans need only topping and tailing, but if they are a little coarse, remove the stringy sides.

Basic cooking

To steam, place prepared beans in a steamer and cook for 15–20 minutes.

To boil, cook in boiling salted water for 10–15 minutes. Drain well. Toss in melted butter or reheat in a clean pan with a little cream. French beans are really tasty when reheated in bacon fat and served scattered with snippets of crisply fried bacon.

Broad beans with ham in wine sauce

This is a good accompaniment to beef or lamb.

45 ml (3 tbsp) vegetable oil
1 medium onion, skinned and chopped
1 clove garlic, skinned and crushed
50 g (2 oz) cooked ham, chopped
900 g (2 lb) broad beans, shelled
100 g (4 oz) new carrots, scraped and sliced
2.5 ml ($\frac{1}{2}$ level tsp) paprika
salt and freshly ground pepper
300 ml ($\frac{1}{2}$ pint) chicken stock
150 ml ($\frac{1}{4}$ pint) white wine
15 ml (1 level tbsp) cornflour

Heat the oil in a large pan, add the onion and garlic and cook for about 10 minutes until soft and golden brown. Add the ham, beans, carrots, paprika, seasoning, stock and wine. Bring to the boil, cover and cook for 15–20 minutes, until the vegetables are tender. Mix the cornflour to a smooth cream with a little cold water and add to the pan. Bring back to the boil and cook for 1–2 minutes, stirring.

Hot bean and corn rice ring

350 g (12 oz) runner beans, trimmed and chopped
350 g (12 oz) sweetcorn kernels
100 g (4 oz) long-grain rice
50 g (2 oz) butter
4 tomatoes, skinned, seeded and diced
salt and freshly ground pepper
small bunch of watercress

Cook the beans, corn kernels and rice together in boiling salted water for 15 minutes, until the rice and vegetables are tender. Drain well, add the butter and stir until melted. Stir the tomatoes into the corn mixture with seasoning and reheat gently for 5–10 minutes. Turn the mixture into a well-greased 1.1-litre–(2-pint) ring mould and press down firmly with the back of a spoon. Invert on to a warmed serving plate and remove the mould. Fill the centre with watercress and serve.

Green beans with lemon cheese dressing

450 g (1 lb) runner or French beans, trimmed
75 g (3 oz) Danish blue cheese, crumbled
90 ml (6 tbsp) vegetable oil
45 ml (3 tbsp) wine vinegar
30 ml (2 tbsp) lemon juice
5 ml (1 tsp) salt
freshly ground black pepper
2.5 ml ($\frac{1}{2}$ level tsp) paprika

Cook the beans in boiling salted water for 10–15 minutes. Drain and place in cold water to cool. Beat the cheese with the oil, vinegar, lemon juice, seasoning and paprika. Drain the cooled beans well, pour over the cheese dressing and toss. Place in a serving dish and chill for 30 minutes.

Mild mustard pickle

450 g (1 lb) runner or French beans, trimmed and sliced
450 g (1 lb) cucumber, chopped
450 g (1 lb) green tomatoes, chopped
about 250 g (9 oz) salt
450 g (1 lb) cauliflower, divided into florets
450 g (1 lb) celery, trimmed and chopped
450 g (1 lb) cabbage, cored and finely shredded
450 g (1 lb) onions, skinned and chopped
225 g (8 oz) sugar
75 g (3 oz) dry mustard
50 g (2 oz) flour
15 g ($\frac{1}{2}$ oz) turmeric

For the aromatic vinegar
15 g ($\frac{1}{2}$ oz) whole allspice berries
15 g ($\frac{1}{2}$ oz) whole coriander seeds
8 g ($\frac{1}{4}$ oz) cardamom seeds
12 whole cloves
$\frac{1}{2}$ stick cinnamon
6 bay leaves
1.1 litres (2 pints) distilled malt vinegar

Layer the prepared beans, cucumber and tomatoes in a large bowl and sprinkle each layer with salt, allowing 15 ml (1 level tbsp) to each 450 g (1 lb) of vegetables. Cover and leave overnight. Drain well and rinse off any undissolved salt.

Place the prepared cauliflower, celery, cabbage and onions in another large bowl. Cover with a brine solution of 50 g (2 oz) salt dissolved in 600 ml (1 pint) water to each 450 g (1 lb) vegetables. Cover and leave overnight. Drain well.

Put all the ingredients for the aromatic vinegar in a large pan and bring to the boil. Remove from the heat and leave to infuse for about 1 hour. Strain, discard the spices and return to the pan. Blend the sugar, mustard, flour and turmeric to a smooth paste with a little water. Stir into the vinegar with the vegetables. Bring to the boil and simmer gently for 25–30 minutes. Cool slightly, then pot and cover in the normal way.

Makes about 4 kg (9 lb)

Peppered beans

700 g (1½ lb) runner or French beans, trimmed
150 ml (¼ pint) chicken stock
30 ml (2 tbsp) vegetable oil
1 clove garlic, skinned
15 ml (1 level tbsp) paprika
1 red pepper, seeded and sliced
salt and freshly ground pepper

Leave the French beans whole; cut the runner beans into thin strips. Cook in the stock for 10–15 minutes, until tender but still crisp. Drain well. Heat the oil in a separate pan, add the garlic and paprika and cook for 1 minute, stirring. Add the sliced pepper to the pan and cook over a gentle heat for 10–15 minutes, until the pepper is tender. Remove the garlic from the pan, stir in the drained beans and seasoning and reheat thoroughly.

Chilli pork with green beans

Illustrated in colour facing page 48

25 g (1 oz) butter
1 medium onion, skinned and chopped
salt and freshly ground black pepper
40 g (1½ oz) flour
700 g (1½ lb) boned shoulder of pork, diced
5 ml (1 level tsp) chilli seasoning
30 ml (2 level tbsp) tomato paste
400 ml (¾ pint) chicken stock
450 g (1 lb) runner or French beans, trimmed and sliced

Melt the butter in a large saucepan and fry the onion gently for 5 minutes. Season the flour and use to coat the pork. Add to the onion in the pan and cook for 5 minutes, until browned. Stir in the chilli seasoning, tomato paste and stock. Bring to the boil, stirring. Cover and simmer gently for 45 minutes. Stir in the beans and continue cooking for 10–15 minutes until the beans are tender.

Mild mustard pickle

Beetroot

To prepare

During preparation or cooking, handle carefully and never damage the skin as this causes the beetroot to 'bleed', losing colour and flavour. Leave the root whole and twist off the stems to within 2.5 cm (1 in) of the top of the root (cutting with a knife will cause bleeding). Wash thoroughly in cold water.

Basic cooking

To boil, place the beetroots in a pan of salted water, bring to the boil and simmer gently for 1–3 hours, according to size. To test if cooked, remove the beetroot from the pan: the skin should slide or rub off. Do not test by piercing the beetroot or it will bleed, causing loss of flavour and colour. To serve hot, coat in melted butter and sprinkle with chopped fresh dill or parsley. To serve cold, add to vinegar dressing.

To bake, scrub the beetroots, without trimming, wrap in foil or place in a greased ovenproof dish and cook in the oven at 180°C (350°F) mark 4 for 2–3 hours, according to size. To serve, either scoop out the flesh or peel back the skin and cut into slices or dice. Serve with butter and plenty of seasoning.

Jellied beetroot and apple salad

600-ml (1-pint) red jelly tablet
300 ml ($\frac{1}{2}$ pint) boiling water
150 ml ($\frac{1}{4}$ pint) vinegar
30 ml (2 tbsp) lemon juice
50 g (2 oz) walnut halves
450 g (1 lb) beetroots, cooked, peeled and sliced or diced
2 eating apples, peeled, cored and sliced
1 bunch of watercress, washed

Break up the jelly tablet and place in a basin. Dissolve it in the boiling water. Mix together the vinegar and lemon juice, make up to 300 ml ($\frac{1}{2}$ pint) with cold water and add to the hot jelly liquid.

Rinse a 1.1-litre (2-pint) ring mould with cold water. Place the walnut halves in the bottom of the ring mould and add the beetroot and apple in layers. Pour on the liquid jelly and leave to set in the refrigerator. Unmould on to a flat plate and garnish with watercress in the centre of the ring.

Beetroots with horseradish cream sauce

700 g (1$\frac{1}{2}$ lb) beetroots, cooked and peeled
150 ml ($\frac{1}{4}$ pint) dry white wine
150 ml ($\frac{1}{4}$ pint) soured cream
30 ml (2 level tbsp) horseradish cream
salt and freshly ground black pepper

Cut the beetroots into 0.5-cm ($\frac{1}{4}$-in) thick slices and place in a shallow frying pan with the wine. Beat the soured cream and reserve 30 ml (2 tbsp) for garnish. Add the remaining cream and the horseradish cream to the beetroot. Season well and stir gently. Simmer the beetroot for 20 minutes. Place in a warmed serving dish and drizzle over the remaining soured cream to garnish.

Beetroot chutney

900 g (2 lb) raw beetroot, peeled and shredded or grated
450 g (1 lb) onions, skinned and chopped
700 g (1$\frac{1}{2}$ lb) cooking apples, peeled, cored and chopped
450 g (1 lb) seedless raisins
1.1 litres (2 pints) malt vinegar
900 g (2 lb) sugar
30 ml (2 level tbsp) ground ginger

Place all the ingredients in a preserving pan and bring to the boil. Simmer over a moderate heat, uncovered, for about 1 hour until soft and pulpy. Pot and cover in the usual way.
Makes about 2.7 kg (6 lb)

Pickled beetroots

Wash the beetroots carefully, taking care not to damage the skins. Bake in foil in the oven at 180°C (350°F) mark 4, or cook in boiling salted water – 25 g (1 oz) salt for each 600 ml (1 pint) of water – until tender. This will take 1–3 hours, depending on the size of the beetroots. Cool, peel and slice thinly or dice. Pack into jars and cover with cold spiced vinegar, adding 5 ml (1 level tsp) salt to each 600 ml (1 pint) of vinegar if the beetroots were baked. Cover the jars. This should be eaten fairly soon.

Blackberry

To prepare
Remove the hulls from the fruit and wash in salted water to remove any insects. Wash in clean water and drain well.

Basic cooking
To poach, place the prepared blackberries in a saucepan with water to cover the bottom of the pan and 25–50 g (1–2 oz) sugar to taste. Cover, bring to the boil and simmer gently for 10–15 minutes, until tender.

Baked blackberry and apple loaf

For the pastry
225 g (8 oz) self raising flour
pinch of salt
100 g (4 oz) shredded suet

For the filling
225 g (8 oz) cooking apples, peeled, cored and sliced
225 g (8 oz) blackberries
50 g (2 oz) caster sugar
15 ml (1 level tbsp) cornflour
egg white
crushed sugar lumps

For the pastry, sift the flour and salt into a bowl and stir in the suet. Add enough cold water to bind to a firm dough. Roll out and use three-quarters of the dough to line a non-stick 1.1-litre (2-pint) loaf tin.

For the filling, mix the apples with the blackberries, sugar and cornflour. Pack the fruit into the dough-lined tin and cover with the remaining dough, sealing the edges well. Place on a baking sheet. Bake in the oven at 180°C (350°F) mark 4 for about 1 hour until golden and firm. Towards the end of the cooking time, brush the top with egg white and sprinkle with the crushed sugar lumps. Turn out and serve with pouring custard.

To freeze: freeze unbaked after over-wrapping. To use, unwrap and bake from frozen for about 1½ hours at the temperature given above.
Serves 6

Hazel nut meringues with bramble sauce

4 egg whites
225 g (8 oz) caster sugar
50 g (2 oz) hazel nuts, ground or grated

For the sauce
450 g (1 lb) cooking apples, peeled, cored and chopped
450 g (1 lb) blackberries
50 g (2 oz) granulated sugar
30 ml (2 tbsp) water
150 ml (¼ pint) double cream
150 ml (¼ pint) single cream

Stiffly whisk the egg whites. Whisk in the sugar, a spoonful at a time, until really thick and white. Fold in the hazel nuts. Turn the meringue mixture into a large forcing bag fitted with a large vegetable star nozzle. Pipe 10 small baskets on baking sheets lined with non-stick paper and bake in the coolest part of the oven at 130°C (250°F) mark ½ for about 2 hours until well dried out. Cool on a wire rack.

Put the apples, blackberries, sugar and water in a saucepan. Simmer until tender. Rub through a sieve, or purée in an electric blender until smooth and then sieve to remove the seeds. Allow to go cold. Whip the creams together until 'floppy' and fold through the purée. Spoon into the meringue baskets and serve.
Makes 10

Baked blackberry and apple loaf

Spiced blackberry layer

450 g (1 lb) blackberries
60 ml (4 level tbsp) golden syrup
175 g (6 oz) soft tub margarine
175 g (6 oz) caster sugar
3 eggs, beaten
175 g (6 oz) self raising flour
2.5 ml ($\frac{1}{2}$ level tsp) ground mixed spice
15–30 ml (1–2 tbsp) milk

Place the blackberries in a 25.5 × 23-cm
(10 × 9-in) greased ovenproof dish and spoon
over the golden syrup. Cream together the
margarine and sugar until light and fluffy.
Beat in the eggs a little at a time. Fold in the
flour and mixed spice. Add just enough milk
to mix to a soft dropping consistency. Spread
over the top of the blackberries. Cook in the
oven at 180°C (350°F) mark 4 for 45 minutes,
until risen and golden brown. Serve hot with
whipped cream.
Serves 6

Orange bramble mousse

225 g (8 oz) blackberries
300 ml ($\frac{1}{2}$ pint) milk
15 ml (1 level tbsp) custard powder
30 ml (2 level tbsp) sugar
15 ml (1 level tbsp) powdered gelatine
45 ml (3 tbsp) frozen concentrated orange juice
15 ml (1 tbsp) kirsch, optional
3 egg whites
toasted flaked almonds to decorate

Simmer the fruit with a little water for
10–15 minutes until tender, then purée in a
blender and sieve, or rub through a sieve.
Make up the custard with the milk, custard
powder and sugar. Cool. Dissolve the gelatine
in the thawed orange juice in the usual way –
the juice should not be diluted; make up any
left over for a breakfast drink.

Whisk together the custard, gelatine,
blackberry purée and kirsch, if used. Stiffly
whisk the egg whites. When the blackberry
mixture is on the point of setting, beat in
30 ml (2 level tbsp) of the whisked egg white,
then fold in the rest. (The initial quantity of
egg white lightens the mixture, allowing the
rest to fold in easily.) Spoon into individual
glasses. Chill. Decorate with nuts.

To freeze: pack without nuts in freezer-proof
serving dishes. To use, thaw, loosely covered,
at room temperature for 3 hours.
Serves 4–6

Blackberry jam

2.7 kg (6 lb) blackberries, not over-ripe
60 ml (4 tbsp) lemon juice or 5 ml (1 level tsp) citric
  or tartaric acid
150 ml ($\frac{1}{4}$ pint) water
2.7 kg (6 lb) sugar

Put the blackberries in a pan with the lemon
juice, or acid, and water. Simmer very gently
until the berries are cooked and the contents
of the pan well reduced. Add the sugar, stir
to dissolve and bring to the boil, stirring
continuously. Boil rapidly for about 10
minutes or until setting point is reached.
Pot and cover in the usual way.
Makes about 4.5 kg (10 lb)

Blackberry and apple jam

1.8 kg (4 lb) blackberries
300 ml ($\frac{1}{2}$ pint) water
700 g (1$\frac{1}{2}$ lb) peeled, cored and sliced sour apples,
  prepared weight
2.7 kg (6 lb) sugar

Put the blackberries in a pan with 150 ml
($\frac{1}{4}$ pint) of the water and simmer slowly until
soft. Put the apples in another pan with the
remaining 150 ml ($\frac{1}{4}$ pint) of water and
simmer slowly until soft. Pulp with a spoon
or potato masher.

Combine the apples and blackberries. Add
the sugar and stir until dissolved. Bring to
the boil and boil rapidly until setting point is
reached, stirring frequently. Pot and cover in
the usual way.
Makes about 4.5 kg (10 lb)

Bramble jelly

1.8 kg (4 lb) blackberries, slightly under-ripe
60 ml (4 tbsp) lemon juice or 5 ml (1 level tsp) citric
  or tartaric acid
400 ml ($\frac{3}{4}$ pint) water
sugar

Put the blackberries in a pan with the lemon
juice, or acid, and water. Simmer gently for
about 1 hour, or until really soft and pulped.
Strain through a jelly bag.

Measure the juice and return to the pan with 450 g (1 lb) sugar to each 600 ml (1 pint) of juice. Bring to the boil, stirring until the sugar has dissolved, then boil rapidly until setting point is reached. Skim, pot and cover in the usual way.

Blackcurrant

To prepare
Remove the berries from the stalks and wash carefully in cold water. Drain well.

Basic cooking
To poach, place the prepared blackcurrants in a saucepan with water to cover the bottom of the pan and 50–100 g (2–4 oz) sugar to taste. Cover, bring to the boil and simmer gently for 5–10 minutes until tender.

Chocolate blackcurrant gâteau

Illustrated in colour facing page 64

50 g (2 oz) plain chocolate
2 eggs
100 g (4 oz) soft tub margarine
100 g (4 oz) caster sugar
100 g (4 oz) self raising flour
225 g (8 oz) blackcurrants, trimmed
50 g (2 oz) granulated sugar
15 ml (1 level tbsp) arrowroot
150 ml ($\frac{1}{4}$ pint) whipping cream, whipped
icing sugar, sifted

Melt the chocolate in a heatproof basin with 30 ml (2 tbsp) water over hot, not boiling, water. Cool. Place the still liquid chocolate in an electric blender. Add the eggs, margarine, caster sugar and flour and whirl for a few seconds until well blended.

Alternatively, cream the margarine and sugar together until pale and fluffy. Beat in the eggs and chocolate and fold in the flour.

Pour into a greased bottom-lined 21.5-cm (8$\frac{1}{2}$-in) sandwich tin. Bake in the oven at 190°C (375°F) mark 5 for about 30 minutes. Turn out and cool on wire rack.

Meanwhile, cook the blackcurrants with the granulated sugar and 150 ml ($\frac{1}{4}$ pint) water for 5–10 minutes until soft. Blend the arrowroot with a little water, stir into the currants and boil until clear. Cool.

Split the chocolate cake in half. Fold the cold blackcurrant mixture through the whipped cream and use to sandwich the cakes. Position the top layer and dust with icing sugar. Eat the day of making.

To freeze: pack cake and currants separately. Finish with cream after thawing.
Serves 8–10

Blackcurrant and raspberry strudels

For the dough
225 g (8 oz) plain flour
2.5 ml ($\frac{1}{2}$ level tsp) salt
1 egg, beaten
30 ml (2 tbsp) corn oil
75 ml (5 tbsp) lukewarm water

For the filling
450 g (1 lb) blackcurrants
225 g (8 oz) raspberries, hulled
75 g (3 oz) ground almonds
100 g (4 oz) caster sugar
1 egg, beaten
30 ml (2 tbsp) single cream
75 g (3 oz) melted butter
icing sugar, sifted

Sift the flour and salt into a bowl. Make a well in the centre and stir in the egg and oil. Add the water gradually and mix to a soft dough. Knead the dough until it leaves the sides of the bowl, then knead on a floured surface for about 15 minutes, until elastic and no longer sticky. Form into a ball, cover with oiled polythene and leave in a warm place for 1 hour.

For the filling, mix together the blackcurrants, raspberries, ground almonds, sugar, egg and cream. Divide the dough in half. Cover one half and roll out the other half on

41

a floured teatowel to an oblong 30.5 × 18 cm (12 × 7 in). Using the back of your hands, gently stretch the dough from the centre towards the outer edges until wafer thin, 38 × 25.5 cm (15 × 10 in). Neaten the edges. Brush with a little butter and cut into three 12.5-cm (5-in) wide strips. Divide half the blackcurrant mixture between the three strips and spread to within 1 cm ($\frac{1}{2}$ in) of the long edges. Roll up each strip lengthways, and place on a greased baking sheet. Brush with butter. Repeat with the second half of dough.

Bake in the oven at 190°C (375°F) mark 5 for 25–30 minutes. Cut each strudel in half and serve while still warm, dusted with icing sugar.

Makes 12

Summer berry mousse

For the topping
50 g (2 oz) caster sugar
225 g (8 oz) blackcurrants, trimmed
10 ml (2 level tsp) powdered gelatine
100 g (4 oz) raspberries

For the mousse
grated rind and juice of 1 orange
grated rind and juice of 1 lemon
75 g (3 oz) caster sugar
150 ml ($\frac{1}{4}$ pint) soured cream
350 g (12 oz) cottage cheese
2 eggs, separated
20 ml (1$\frac{1}{2}$ level tbsp) powdered gelatine
150 ml ($\frac{1}{4}$ pint) double cream

For the topping, dissolve the caster sugar in 150 ml ($\frac{1}{4}$ pint) water. Add the blackcurrants and simmer gently for 5–10 minutes until tender. Dissolve the gelatine in 30 ml (2 tbsp) water, then stir into the blackcurrants while still warm. Cool and add the raspberries. Pour into a 1.7-litre (3-pint) ring mould and leave to set.

For the mousse, place the orange and lemon rinds and juice, caster sugar, soured cream, cottage cheese and egg yolks in a blender and blend until smooth. Turn the mixture into a bowl. Dissolve gelatine in 45 ml (3 tbsp) water. Cool and stir into the cheese mixture. Whip the cream lightly. Whisk the egg whites stiffly. Fold both into the cheese mixture. Pour into the ring mould and leave to set.

Serves 6–8

Blackcurrant galette

For the pastry
200 g (8 oz) plain flour
100 g (4 oz) butter
50 g (2 oz) lard
30 ml (2 level tbsp) caster sugar

For the filling
50 g (2 oz) fine semolina
50 g (2 oz) caster sugar
550 g (1$\frac{1}{4}$ lb) blackcurrants, trimmed
1 small egg, beaten

For the pastry, sift the flour into a bowl and rub in the fats until the mixture resembles fine breadcrumbs. Stir in the sugar and mix to a firm dough with cold water. Roll out and use to line a 23-cm (9-in) flan dish. Reserve any dough trimmings.

For the filling, stir the semolina and caster sugar together. Arrange the blackcurrants and semolina mixture in layers in the flan case. Roll out the dough trimmings, cut into strips and use to lattice the top of the flan. Brush with beaten egg and bake in the oven at 220°C (425°F) mark 7 for 30–40 minutes or until the pastry is golden.

Blackcurrant fluff

450 g (1 lb) blackcurrants, trimmed
100 g (4 oz) caster sugar
15 ml (1 level tbsp) powdered gelatine
45 ml (3 tbsp) water
45 ml (3 tbsp) Cassis
150 ml ($\frac{1}{4}$ pint) double cream
3 egg whites
whipped cream, optional, and chopped nuts or
grated chocolate to decorate

Cook the fruit gently with the sugar for 5–10 minutes until pulpy. Sieve to remove the pips. Dissolve the gelatine in the water in a heatproof bowl over a pan of hot water. Stir into the fruit purée with the Cassis. Cool until beginning to set.

Whip the cream until 'floppy'. Fold into the half-set mixture. Whisk the egg whites until stiff and fold into the fruit mixture. Spoon into individual glasses and decorate with whipped cream and nuts or chocolate. Chill lightly before serving.

To freeze: when prepared, place in freezer-proof dishes without decoration. When set,

wrap, label and freeze. To use, thaw at room temperature for about 3 hours, then decorate.
Serves 6

Blackcurrant jelly

1.8 kg (4 lb) blackcurrants
1.1–1.7 litres (2–3 pints) water
sugar

Put the blackcurrants (still on stalks) into a pan with the water and simmer gently for about 1 hour, or until really soft and pulped. Strain through a jelly bag.

Measure the juice, then return it to the pan with 450 g (1 lb) sugar to each 600 ml (1 pint) of juice. Stir until the sugar has dissolved, then boil briskly until setting point is reached. Skim, pot and cover in the usual way.

Blackcurrant jam

Tart and full of vitamin C, this jam will be welcome on wintry mornings.

1.8 kg (4 lb) blackcurrants, trimmed
1.7 litres (3 pints) water
2.7 kg (6 lb) sugar

Put the blackcurrants into a pan with the water. Simmer gently until the fruit is soft and the contents of the pan well reduced. As the skin of blackcurrants tends to be rather tough, cook really well, stirring from time to time to prevent sticking. When the fruit is soft, add the sugar and stir until dissolved, then boil rapidly until setting point is reached. Pot and cover in the usual way.
Makes about 4.5 kg (10 lb)

Broccoli

To prepare
Trim heading varieties and break into florets or cook whole. For sprouting varieties, simply trim the base of the stalk and, if the shoots are very large, cut into two or three pieces lengthways. Tie in small bundles of four or five pieces.

Basic cooking
To steam/boil, stand bundles of broccoli upright in a pan of boiling salted water with the stalks in the water and the delicate heads above. The stalks are then 'boiled' while the heads are 'steamed'. Cook for 10–15 minutes. Drain. (To cook whole see Cauliflower basic cooking page 49.)

To steam, place in a steamer and cook for 20 minutes.

To serve broccoli, toss gently in melted butter and sprinkle with toasted almonds, or coat with hollandaise or cheese sauce (see page 52).

Broccoli makes an excellent starter or salad if blanched, chilled and served with mayonnaise or French dressing. Add fresh herbs to the dressing for a special touch.

Cream of broccoli and lemon soup

1 lemon
450 g (1 lb) broccoli, trimmed
600 ml (1 pint) chicken stock
1 small onion, skinned and chopped
5 ml (1 level tsp) salt
freshly ground black pepper
5 ml (1 level tsp) sugar
300 ml ($\frac{1}{2}$ pint) milk
15 ml (1 level tbsp) cornflour
30–45 ml (2–3 tbsp) double cream

Cut three slices of lemon for the garnish. Put the broccoli, stock, onion, seasoning, sugar, the grated rind of the remaining lemon and 45 ml (3 tbsp) of lemon juice in a large saucepan. Cover, bring to the boil and simmer for about 1 hour until very tender.

Purée the broccoli mixture in an electric blender or rub through a sieve. Return to the pan with the milk. Blend the cornflour to a smooth paste with a little water. Stir into the soup and bring to the boil to thicken. Stir in the cream. Pour into a warmed serving dish and garnish with the sliced lemon.
Serves 4–6

Broccoli cheese bake

450 g (1 lb) broccoli, trimmed
25 g (1 oz) butter
25 g (1 oz) flour
150 ml ($\frac{1}{4}$ pint) milk
100 g (4 oz) Cheddar cheese, grated
4 eggs, separated
5 ml (1 level tsp) dry mustard
salt and freshly ground pepper

Cook the broccoli in boiling salted water for 10–15 minutes until tender. Drain well, roughly chop and place in the bottom of a shallow ovenproof dish.

Melt the butter in a pan, add the flour and cook for 2 minutes. Gradually stir in the milk and bring to the boil, stirring. Beat in the cheese, egg yolks, dry mustard and seasoning. Whisk the egg whites until stiff and fold into the sauce. Pour over the broccoli and bake in the oven at 200°C (400°F) mark 6 for 30–35 minutes until risen and golden brown. Serve immediately.

Broccoli amandine

Wine enhances the flavour of the broccoli, and the almonds add the finishing touch.

25 g (1 oz) butter
1 medium onion, skinned and chopped
450 g (1 lb) broccoli, trimmed
150 ml ($\frac{1}{4}$ pint) dry red wine
salt and freshly ground pepper
50 g (2 oz) flaked almonds, toasted

Melt the butter in a pan, add the onion and fry for 5 minutes until soft. Add the broccoli, wine and seasoning. Bring to the boil and simmer gently for 10–15 minutes until the broccoli is tender but still crisp. Place in a warmed serving dish and sprinkle with the toasted almonds.

Brussels sprout

To prepare
Remove any damaged or wilted outer leaves and slice off the stalk. Cut a small cross in the stalk end – this will ensure even cooking of the thick stalk end and the leaves. Wash thoroughly and drain well. Cook immediately after preparing to prevent loss of flavour.

Basic cooking
To steam, place the prepared Brussels sprouts in a steamer and cook for 15–20 minutes.
To boil, cook in boiling salted water for 10–15 minutes. Drain well and press, if large, to remove all excess water.

Toss in melted butter, butter-fried crumbs or coat in cheese sauce (see page 52).

Brussels sprout and leek salad

350 g (12 oz) Brussels sprouts, trimmed and thinly sliced
175 g (6 oz) leeks, thinly sliced
5 ml (1 level tsp) celery seeds
45 ml (3 tbsp) vegetable oil
45 ml (3 tbsp) white vinegar
salt and freshly ground black pepper

Put the sprouts in a large mixing bowl with the leeks. Place the remaining ingredients in a screwtop jar and shake well for 1–2 minutes. Pour the dressing over the sprouts and leeks and toss well. Spoon the vegetables into a serving dish with the dressing and chill before serving.

Lemon Brussels sprouts with mushrooms

700 g (1$\frac{1}{2}$ lb) Brussels sprouts, trimmed
50 g (2 oz) butter
1 small onion, skinned and finely chopped
100 g (4 oz) button mushrooms, sliced
5–10 ml (1–2 tsp) lemon juice
salt and freshly ground pepper

Cook the Brussels sprouts in boiling salted water for 10–15 minutes until just tender.

Meanwhile, melt the butter in a pan, add the onion and cook for 10 minutes until soft and golden brown. Add the mushrooms to the onion and cook for a further 10 minutes until soft. Stir the drained sprouts into the onion and mushroom mixture. Add the lemon juice and seasoning and continue cooking for about 5 minutes, until heated through.

Spicy Brussels sprouts with rice

Illustrated in colour facing page 49

30 ml (2 tbsp) vegetable oil
2.5 ml (½ level tsp) ground coriander
2.5 ml (½ level tsp) dry mustard
2.5 ml (½ level tsp) turmeric
pinch of cayenne pepper
700 g (1½ lb) Brussels sprouts, trimmed
1 medium onion, skinned and chopped
1 cooking apple, peeled, cored and chopped
120 ml (4 fl oz) water
300 ml (½ pint) natural yogurt

For the rice
100 g (4 oz) long-grain rice
50 g (2 oz) sultanas
2.5 ml (½ level tsp) turmeric
salt

Heat the oil in a large saucepan, add the spices and cook for 2 minutes, stirring. Add the Brussels sprouts, onion and apple. Cook for 5 minutes, then pour in the water, bring to the boil and cover. Simmer gently for 10 minutes.

Meanwhile, cook the rice with the sultanas and turmeric in salted water for 20 minutes until tender. Drain well and stir into the Brussels sprouts with the yogurt. Serve in a warmed vegetable dish.

Cabbage

To prepare

Remove any damaged and wilted leaves and cut the cabbage in half. Cut each half into three to four pieces and remove the core or centre stalks. Wash thoroughly and shred finely or cut into smaller wedges.

Basic cooking

To steam, place shredded cabbage in a steamer and cook for 10–15 minutes.
To boil, cook shredded cabbage in boiling salted water for 5–10 minutes. Cook cabbage wedges in boiling salted water for about 15 minutes. Drain well.
To braise, pour boiling water over shredded cabbage to wilt it. Drain and cook in a covered pan with 25–50 g (1–2 oz) butter for 15–20 minutes.

Toss shredded cabbage or cabbage wedges in melted butter, if liked, and sprinkle with grated nutmeg or freshly ground black pepper. For a change, toss in a little single cream and sprinkle with nutmeg.

Bean stuffed cabbage rolls

175 g (6 oz) dried foule or haricot beans, soaked overnight
175 g (6 oz) garlic sausage, finely chopped
226-g (8-oz) can tomatoes, drained
75 g (3 oz) butter
1 medium onion, skinned and chopped
15 ml (1 level tbsp) tomato paste
salt and freshly ground pepper
8 large cabbage leaves, e.g. Savoy
30 ml (2 tbsp) chopped fresh parsley

Drain the beans and cook in boiling, salted water for about 1¼ hours until very tender. Drain. Mix the garlic sausage and tomatoes into the beans. Melt 25 g (1 oz) of the butter in a saucepan and fry the onion for 5 minutes until soft. Add to the bean mixture with the tomato paste and seasoning.

Trim out any tough centre stalk from the cabbage leaves. Blanch in boiling salted water for about 4 minutes. Drain. Divide the bean stuffing between the leaves, roll up securely and place in a buttered oval ovenproof dish. Cover tightly with foil and cook in the oven at 180°C (350°F) mark 4 for 30–35 minutes.

Beat the remaining butter with a wooden spoon to soften, then mix in the parsley. Serve the cabbage rolls topped with dabs of parsley butter.

NOT SUITABLE FOR FREEZING

Bubble and squeak bake

450 g (1 lb) potatoes, peeled
knob of butter
milk
salt and freshly ground pepper
450 g (1 lb) cabbage, cored and shredded
225 g (8 oz) onions, skinned and chopped
225 g (8 oz) carrots, peeled and grated
175 g (6 oz) mature Cheddar cheese, grated

Cook the potatoes in boiling salted water for 15–20 minutes until tender. Drain and cream them with a knob of butter and a little milk. Season well.

Cook the cabbage in a little boiling salted water for 5–10 minutes. Drain well. Cook the onions and carrots in boiling salted water for

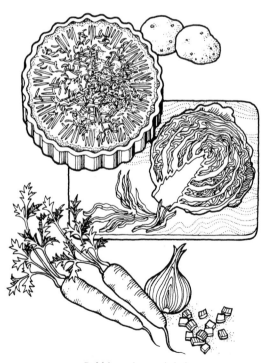

Bubble and squeak bake

5 minutes and drain. Blend the cabbage and potato together. Turn half the cabbage mixture into a buttered shallow 1-litre (1¾-pint) ovenproof dish. Cover with the onion and carrot mixture and top with 100 g (4 oz) of the grated cheese. Top with the remaining cabbage mixture. Smooth the surface with a fork and sprinkle the remaining cheese over the top. Bake in the oven at 200°C (400°F) mark 6 for about 25 minutes until golden brown. Serve in wedges.
Serves 4–6

Cabbage in nutmeg cream

700 g (1½ lb) green cabbage, cored and shredded
salt and freshly ground pepper
1.25 ml (¼ level tsp) grated nutmeg
150 ml (¼ pint) soured cream

Cook the cabbage in a little boiling salted water for 5–10 minutes until just tender. Drain well. Return the cabbage to the pan with the seasoning and nutmeg. Cook over a low heat for 2–3 minutes. Add the soured cream and heat gently, stirring.

Cabbage stuffed with bacon

Illustrated in colour facing page 49

1.4 kg (3 lb) green cabbage, trimmed
salt and freshly ground black pepper
225 g (8 oz) gammon slipper or trimmed bacon chops
15 ml (1 tbsp) vegetable oil
440-g (15½-oz) can whole chestnuts, drained
300 ml (½ pint) chicken stock
10 ml (2 level tsp) cornflour

Put the cabbage in a large, deep pan, cover with boiling salted water and simmer for 15 minutes. Drain the cabbage. Break off and reserve four or five of the outside leaves. Scoop the inside from the cabbage and discard the hard core, leaving just a shell. Shred 225 g (8 oz) of the cabbage finely. Keep the rest for another dish.

Cut the gammon or bacon into thin strips and fry gently in hot oil for about 10 minutes, stirring. Add the shredded cabbage and cook gently for a further 5 minutes. Add the chestnuts and seasoning to taste, then pile the filling into the cabbage shell. Place in an ovenproof casserole and pour over the stock.

Cover tightly and cook in the oven at 180°C (350°F) mark 4 for 1¼ hours.

Strain off the juices into a saucepan. Blend the cornflour to a smooth paste with a little water and stir into the juices. Bring to the boil and pour over the cabbage. Serve surrounded with the reserved leaves.

NOT SUITABLE FOR FREEZING
Serves 4–6

Red cabbage with apple

25 g (1 oz) margarine
1 medium onion, skinned and chopped
700 g (1½ lb) red cabbage, cored and finely shredded
225 g (8 oz) cooking or eating apples, peeled, cored and chopped
15 ml (1 level tbsp) demerara sugar
10 ml (2 tsp) lemon juice
15 ml (1 tbsp) red wine vinegar
2.5 ml (½ level tsp) salt
freshly ground pepper

Melt the margarine in a flameproof casserole. Fry the onion for 5 minutes until soft. Remove the pan from the heat, add the remaining ingredients and stir well. Cover and cook in the oven at 200°C (400°F) mark 6 for about 2 hours until the cabbage is tender.
Serves 6

Pickled red cabbage

900 g (2 lb) firm red cabbage, cored and finely shredded
salt
1.1 litres (2 pints) cold spiced vinegar

Place the cabbage in a bowl, layering with salt. Cover and leave overnight. Next day, drain the cabbage thoroughly and rinse off any surplus salt. Pack loosely into jars. Cover with the cold, spiced vinegar and cover the jars.

Use within 2–3 months, as the cabbage tends to lose its crispness.

Carrot

To prepare
For new carrots, remove the stalks and scrub thoroughly – leave whole. For larger maincrop carrots, cut a slice from the stalk and root end, then scrape or peel thinly. Slice thinly, dice or cut into quarters lengthways or into lengthways strips 0.5–1 cm (¼–½ in) wide. Remove the core if coarse and woody. Very old maincrop carrots are best puréed or made into soup.

Basic cooking
To steam, place sliced or new carrots in a steamer and cook for 20–25 minutes.
To boil, cook in boiling salted water for 6–8 minutes (new, sliced or diced) and 10–12 minutes (whole or quartered). Drain thoroughly, toss in melted butter and sprinkle with chopped fresh herbs or coat in parsley or white sauce (see page 77), if liked.
To purée, cook diced old carrots in boiling salted water for 15–20 minutes, until really tender. Cool. Purée in an electric blender or rub through a sieve with 25–50 g (1–2 oz) butter per each 450 g (1 lb) carrots.

Chilled carrot and orange soup

15 g (½ oz) butter
1 small onion, skinned and chopped
900 g (2 lb) carrots, peeled and sliced
1.1 litres (2 pints) chicken stock
30 ml (2 tbsp) chopped fresh parsley
10 ml (2 level tsp) salt
white pepper
1 bay leaf
juice of 1 orange
30 ml (2 tbsp) double cream

Melt the butter in a large saucepan and fry the onion for 5 minutes. Add the carrots and fry for 2 minutes. Stir in the stock, parsley, seasoning and bay leaf. Cover, bring to the boil and simmer gently for about 1 hour until the carrots are very tender.

Remove the bay leaf and purée the soup in an electric blender or rub through a sieve.

Pour the soup into a large bowl and chill in the refrigerator. Stir in the orange juice and 15 ml (1 tbsp) of the cream. Pour into a serving dish. Pour the remaining cream into the centre of the soup and swirl with a spoon.
Serves 6

Carrot and cheese soufflé

100 g (4 oz) butter or margarine
12 slices French-type bread, 0.5 cm ($\frac{1}{4}$ in) thick
45 ml (3 level tbsp) flour
200 ml (7 fl oz) milk
3 eggs, separated
100 g (4 oz) cooked carrot, mashed roughly
50 g (2 oz) Cheddar cheese, grated
salt and freshly ground pepper

Melt half the butter or margarine and brush over the bread slices. Arrange the slices, overlapping, around the sides of a 1.7-litre (3-pint) soufflé dish, or divide between three 600-ml (1-pint) dishes. Melt the remaining fat in a saucepan and stir in the flour. Cook for 2 minutes, then gradually stir in the milk and cook until thickened. Remove from the heat. Beat the egg yolks into the thickened sauce, then add the carrot, cheese and seasoning. Whisk the egg whites until stiff and fold into the mixture. Turn into the prepared soufflé dish or dishes. Bake in the oven at 190°C (375°F) mark 5 for about 50 minutes for the large soufflé, 30 minutes for the small ones, until well risen and golden brown. Serve immediately.
Serves 3–4

Cheesy carrot ring

1.1 kg (2$\frac{1}{2}$ lb) carrots, peeled
25 g (1 oz) butter
150 ml ($\frac{1}{4}$ pint) chicken stock
15 ml (1 level tbsp) caster sugar
2.5 ml ($\frac{1}{2}$ level tsp) salt
freshly ground pepper
50 g (2 oz) Canadian Cheddar cheese, grated
1 large egg, beaten
175 g (6 oz) shelled peas, freshly cooked

Cut the carrots into short lengths. Place in a large saucepan with the butter, stock, sugar, salt and pepper. Cover and cook until the carrots are tender and the liquid has been absorbed. Mash the carrots well until of an even texture. Add the cheese and egg and stir until well blended. Adjust the seasoning.

Turn the mixture into an oiled 900-ml (1$\frac{1}{2}$-pint) aluminium ring mould. Place on a baking sheet and cook in the oven at 180°C (350°F) mark 4 for 45 minutes. Ease around the edges with a palette knife. Invert on to a warmed serving plate, unmould and fill the centre with freshly cooked peas.

Rich oxtail and carrot hot pot

2 oxtails, jointed
5 ml (1 level tsp) salt
freshly ground pepper
50 g (2 oz) flour
40 g (1$\frac{1}{2}$ oz) beef dripping
450 g (1 lb) carrots, peeled
2 large onions, skinned and sliced
3 stalks celery, trimmed and chopped
300 ml ($\frac{1}{2}$ pint) beef stock
300 ml ($\frac{1}{2}$ pint) brown ale
10 ml (2 level tsp) soft brown sugar
1 bay leaf
45 ml (3 level tbsp) tomato paste
30 ml (2 tbsp) chopped fresh parsley

Coat the oxtail pieces in seasoned flour. Melt the dripping in a large saucepan and fry the oxtail pieces for 10 minutes until golden brown, then transfer to a large casserole.

Cut the carrots into quarters, lengthways. In the remaining fat, fry the carrots with the onions and celery for 5 minutes. Remove from the pan with a slotted spoon and add to the casserole. Blend the remaining seasoned flour with the fat in the pan and gradually stir in the stock and ale. Bring to the boil, add the sugar, bay leaf and tomato paste and pour over the oxtail and vegetables. Cover and cook in the oven at 170°C (325°F) mark 3 for 2$\frac{1}{2}$–3 hours, until the oxtail is tender. Serve sprinkled with chopped parsley.

Chilled chicken and pea mousse (page 84), Chilli pork with green beans (page 37), Marinated courgette, corn and lemon salad (page 58).

Carrot croquettes

Serve as a vegetable accompaniment to grilled meat.

900 g (2 lb) carrots, peeled and sliced
50 g (2 oz) butter
100 g (4 oz) rolled oats
5 ml (1 level tsp) salt
freshly ground black pepper
1.25 ml (¼ level tsp) grated nutmeg
flour for coating
2 eggs, beaten
225 g (8 oz) fresh white breadcrumbs
oil for deep frying

Cook the carrots in a large pan of boiling salted water for about 20–25 minutes until very soft. Drain well and mash with the butter. Cool slightly, then stir in the oats, seasoning and nutmeg to make a firm mixture. Place spoonfuls of the carrot mixture on to a floured surface and roll each into the shape of a small log. Dip each roll in beaten egg and coat in the breadcrumbs. Chill in the refrigerator for 30 minutes.

Heat the oil to 180°C (350°F) and fry the croquettes, a few at a time, for 10 minutes until golden brown. Drain on kitchen paper towel and place in a warmed serving dish. Serve as soon as all croquettes are fried.
Makes 16–20

Chicken, carrot and lemon pie

700 g (1½ lb) cooked chicken meat
50 g (2 oz) butter
1 large onion, skinned and chopped
700 g (1½ lb) carrots, peeled and diced
100 g (4 oz) button mushrooms
40 g (1½ oz) flour
150 ml (¼ pint) chicken stock
grated rind and juice of 1 large lemon
salt and freshly ground pepper
150 ml (¼ pint) single cream
175 g (6 oz) shortcrust pastry (see page 63)
beaten egg to glaze

Cut the chicken into 1-cm (½-in) pieces. Melt the butter in a large saucepan and fry the onion and carrots for 10 minutes. Add the mushrooms and fry for a further 5 minutes. Remove the vegetables from the pan with a slotted spoon and add to the chicken. Blend the flour into the butter remaining in the pan and gradually stir in the stock, lemon rind and juice. Bring to the boil, stirring. Season and add the chicken and vegetables. Gradually stir in the cream, then pour into a 1.1-litre (2-pint) pie dish.

Roll out the dough and use to cover the pie. Flute the edges. Brush the top with beaten egg and bake in the oven at 190°C (375°F) mark 5 for 30–40 minutes until the pastry is golden brown.

Cauliflower

To prepare
Cut away the outside green leaves, leaving only the tiny ones. Level the base of the stem and cut a cross in it. Cut away any bruised or damaged parts of the head. Wash the cauliflower carefully and place in a bowl of cold salted water to remove any dirt, grit or grubs.

Basic cooking
To steam/boil, place the whole cauliflower head, stem down, in a large pan containing 2.5–5 cm (1–2 in) boiling salted water. Cook for 10–15 minutes according to size – the tender florets are then steamed rather than boiled. Drain well and divide into florets, if wished. Cooking time can be shortened by cooking separated florets in boiling salted water for 5–10 minutes. Drain.

To steam, place the florets in a steamer and cook for 15 minutes. If liked, serve with melted butter, béchamel or mornay sauce.

Cauliflower maltaise

1 large cauliflower, trimmed
25 g (1 oz) butter or margarine
30 ml (2 level tbsp) flour
300 ml (½ pint) chicken stock
45 ml (3 tbsp) orange juice
salt and freshly ground pepper
paprika

Cabbage stuffed with bacon (page 46), Spicy Brussels sprouts with rice (page 45), Cauliflower, date and banana salad (page 50).

Cut the cauliflower into large florets. Cook in boiling salted water for about 5–10 minutes until tender but still firm. Meanwhile, melt the butter or margarine in a saucepan, add the flour and cook for 1 minute. Stir in the stock, orange juice and seasoning. Bring to the boil and cook until thickened.

Drain the cauliflower and place in a warmed serving dish. Pour over the sauce, sprinkle with paprika and serve.
Serves 6

Cauliflower, date and banana salad

Illustrated in colour facing page 49

350 g (12 oz) cauliflower florets
2 bananas
50 g (2 oz) stoned dates
75 g (3 oz) curly endive

For the mayonnaise
1 egg yolk
1.25 ml ($\frac{1}{4}$ level tsp) salt
freshly ground pepper
1.25 ml ($\frac{1}{4}$ level tsp) dry mustard
150 ml ($\frac{1}{4}$ pint) vegetable oil
5 ml (1 level tsp) caster sugar
15 ml (1 tbsp) distilled vinegar
1 lemon

For the lemon mayonnaise, in a small but deep basin very thoroughly whisk the egg yolk, seasoning and mustard together. Gradually beat in the oil, a little at a time, until all is incorporated, then add the sugar, vinegar, grated rind from half the lemon and 15 ml (1 tbsp) of the juice.

Blanch the cauliflower florets in boiling water for 3 minutes. Drain and plunge at once into cold water. Pat dry with kitchen paper towel. Cut the bananas into 0.5-cm ($\frac{1}{4}$-in) slices. Toss in the juice from half the lemon for the mayonnaise. Add two-thirds of the banana slices to the cauliflower and mash the rest. Add the mashed banana to the mayonnaise. Lightly combine the cauliflower, mayonnaise and dates.

Cover the bottom of four small side plates with the endive. Divide the cauliflower mayonnaise into four and spoon into the centre of the endive. Chill for about 30 minutes before serving.

Cauliflower gratinata

50 g (2 oz) butter
1 medium onion, skinned and chopped
60 ml (4 level tbsp) flour
5 ml (1 level tsp) dry mustard
568 ml (1 pint) milk
salt and freshly ground pepper
175 g (6 oz) mature cheese, grated
175 g (6 oz) cut macaroni, cooked
4 large tomatoes, sliced
550 g (1$\frac{1}{4}$ lb) cauliflower florets, trimmed and lightly cooked

Melt the butter and fry the onion for 5 minutes. Stir in the flour and mustard and cook for 1 minute. Gradually stir in the milk and cook gently until thickened. Season and stir in 100 g (4 oz) of the cheese.

Combine half the sauce with the macaroni. Place in a 1.7-litre (3-pint) buttered oven-proof serving dish. Arrange the tomato slices around the edge of the dish and pile the cauliflower in the centre. Spoon over the rest of the sauce. Top with the remaining cheese and bake in the oven at 220°C (425°F) mark 7 for 20 minutes. Serve at once.

Celery

To prepare
For the maincrop variety, trim off the root and the top leaves, but do not throw them away – use them for flavouring stock or soup. Separate the stalks and leave to soak in cold salted water for 10–15 minutes to crisp up the celery and loosen the dirt. Scrub thoroughly and rinse well. The self-blanching variety needs very little cleaning but proceed as above. If stored in a polythene bag or con-

tainer in the bottom of the refrigerator, celery will stay crisp enough to eat for 4–5 days and fresh enough for cooking for 7–8 days.

Basic cooking

To braise, cook 2.5-cm (1-in) lengths of celery in butter for 5 minutes. Add sufficient stock to cover and simmer gently for 15–20 minutes until tender.

Braised celery in soured cream

2 heads of celery, trimmed and cut into 5-cm (2-in)
    lengths
1 medium onion, skinned and chopped
salt and freshly ground pepper
2 egg yolks
150 ml ($\frac{1}{4}$ pint) soured cream
1.25 ml ($\frac{1}{4}$ level tsp) freshly grated nutmeg

Put the celery in a saucepan with the onion, seasoning and 300 ml ($\frac{1}{2}$ pint) water. Cover and simmer gently for 15–20 minutes until tender. Drain and return to the saucepan. Beat together the egg yolks, soured cream and nutmeg, pour over the celery and stir. Heat gently for 1 minute without boiling.

Chunky beef with celery

Illustrated in colour facing page 80

25 g (1 oz) lard or dripping
4 chunky pieces top rib beef, 125 g (4 oz) each
225 g (8 oz) celery, trimmed and cut into 5-cm
    (2-in) lengths
1 medium onion, skinned and sliced
50 g (2 oz) dried red kidney beans, soaked
    overnight
400 ml ($\frac{3}{4}$ pint) herb or beef stock
30 ml (2 tbsp) sherry
salt and freshly ground pepper
30 ml (2 level tbsp) cornflour

Heat the lard or dripping in a flameproof casserole and fry the pieces of beef for 10 minutes until brown. Remove from the fat. Add the vegetables to the casserole and cook for 5–8 minutes until brown. Mix in the drained beans. Sit the meat on top of the vegetables. Pour the stock and sherry over and season well. Bring to the boil. Cover and cook in the oven at 180°C (350°F) mark 4 for about 2 hours.

Strain off the liquid into a saucepan and thicken with the cornflour mixed to a smooth paste with a little water. Bubble for a few minutes. Adjust the seasoning. Serve the stew in a shallow dish with some of the sauce spooned over. Serve the vegetables and remaining sauce separately.

To freeze: cool, pack and freeze after cooking. To use, thaw overnight at cool room temperature. Reheat and complete as above.

Smoked mackerel and celery cocktail

350 g (12 oz) smoked mackerel
175 g (6 oz) celery, trimmed and finely chopped
100 g (4 oz) cucumber, peeled and finely chopped
100 g (4 oz) red-skinned eating apple, cored and
    finely chopped
150 ml ($\frac{1}{4}$ pint) soured cream
30 ml (2 tbsp) lemon juice
paprika
1 lettuce
1 lemon

Skin and flake the fish, discarding the bones. Combine the celery, cucumber, apple and mackerel in a basin. Stir in the soured cream and lemon juice. Season to taste with paprika.

Dry the lettuce well. Shred finely and place a little in the bottoms of six stemmed glasses. Spoon the mackerel mixture over. Cut the lemon into six wedges. Garnish each cocktail with a lemon wedge and sprinkle with paprika.
Serves 6

51

Cheese

To prepare

To prepare cheese that is to become hard and dry for grating, leave exposed to the air in a dry, cool place. It is best to hang it in a muslin bag, as then the air can circulate completely. If the cheese is left on a plate or board to dry, stand it on its rind; cheese that has no rind should be turned occasionally, otherwise the underside will remain soft and will very likely mould.

Cheese that has formed mould on the surface is not necessarily spoiled – the mould should be scraped or sliced off and the cheese either used up quickly or dried for grating. Hard cheese can be grated for cooking (use a fine grater), but a soft cheese should be shredded rather than grated. Very soft cheeses can be sliced or chopped and added to sauces, without grating or shredding.

Cheddar, Lancashire, Leicester and Wensleydale are the British cheeses best for cooking. Among the well-known continental cooking cheeses are Gruyère, Mozzarella and Parmesan.

Basic cooking

When cooking cheese remember that too fierce a heat can make it stringy. The cheese needs to melt rather than cook. Do not boil sauces after the cheese has been added.

For cheese sauce, melt 20 g ($\frac{3}{4}$ oz) butter, add 30 ml (2 level tbsp) flour and stir with a wooden spoon until smooth. Cook over a gentle heat for 2–3 minutes, stirring until the mixture (called a roux) begins to bubble. Remove from the heat and gradually add 300 ml ($\frac{1}{2}$ pint) milk, stirring after each addition to prevent lumps forming. Bring the sauce to the boil, stirring continuously, and when it has thickened, cook for a further 1–2 minutes. Add salt and pepper to taste. Remove from the heat and stir in 100 g (4 oz) grated cheese and a pinch of dry mustard.

For cheese pastry, sift together 100 g (4 oz) plain flour and a pinch of salt in a large mixing bowl. Rub in 25 g (1 oz) butter and 25 g (1 oz) lard until the mixture resembles fine breadcrumbs. Stir in 50 g (2 oz) finely grated cheese and bind together with a little egg. Knead lightly to form a soft dough. Roll out as for shortcrust pastry and use as required. Bake in the oven at 200°C (400°F) mark 6.

52

Cheese and bacon pudding

Illustrated in colour facing page 33

225 g (8 oz) Cheddar cheese, grated
225 g (8 oz) Red Leicester cheese, grated
350 g (12 oz) lean bacon, finely chopped
1 medium onion, skinned and chopped
1 clove garlic, skinned and crushed
225 g (8 oz) fresh brown breadcrumbs
5 ml (1 level tsp) dried mixed herbs
5 ml (1 level tsp) dry mustard
salt and freshly ground pepper
3 eggs, beaten

Grease a 1.1-litre (2-pint) pudding basin. In a large bowl mix together the cheeses, bacon, onion, garlic, breadcrumbs, herbs, mustard and seasoning. Bind together with the eggs and spoon into the pudding basin. Cover with a piece of greased foil and secure with string. Steam for 2–2$\frac{1}{4}$ hours. Turn out and serve with grilled tomatoes and buttered peas.
Serves 6

Creamy cheese lasagne

900 ml (1$\frac{1}{2}$ pints) milk
2 slices onion
2 slices carrot
1 bay leaf
3 peppercorns
50 g (2 oz) butter or margarine
50 g (2 oz) flour
150 ml ($\frac{1}{4}$ pint) soured cream
100 g (4 oz) cooked ham, finely diced
225 g (8 oz) cheese, grated (mixture of Cheddar, Edam and blue cheese)
salt and freshly ground black pepper
175 g (6 oz) lasagne verde

Heat the milk with the onion, carrot, bay leaf and peppercorns to boiling point and leave to infuse off the heat for 5 minutes. Strain and discard the flavourings. Melt the fat in a pan, stir in the flour and cook for 1 minute. Gradually stir in the flavoured milk. Bring to the boil and cook for 1 minute.

Remove the pan from the heat and stir in the soured cream, ham, three-quarters of the cheese and seasoning. Arrange the uncooked pasta and cheese sauce in layers – starting with pasta and ending with a good covering of sauce – in a lightly greased 1.4-litre (2$\frac{1}{2}$-pint) shallow ovenproof dish. Sprinkle with the remaining cheese. Cook in the oven at

200°C (400°F) mark 6 for about 1 hour, or until golden brown and the pasta just tender. Cover if necessary.

To freeze: pack and freeze before cooking. To use, thaw overnight at cool room temperature. Cook as above.

Note: any combinations of cheese can be used, but add salt sparingly if using much blue cheese.

Cauliflower and cheese bake

1 large cauliflower, trimmed
40 g (1½ oz) butter
225 g (8 oz) back bacon, rinded and chopped
1 medium onion, skinned and chopped
5 ml (1 level tsp) dried oregano
40 g (1½ oz) flour
400 ml (¾ pint) milk
salt and freshly ground pepper
175 g (6 oz) Cheddar cheese, grated
2.5 ml (½ level tsp) dry mustard
225 g (8 oz) tomatoes, skinned and sliced

Divide the cauliflower into florets and cook in boiling salted water for 5 minutes. Drain and place in an ovenproof dish. Melt 15 g (½ oz) of the butter in a frying pan and fry the bacon and onion for 10 minutes until golden brown. Sprinkle over the cauliflower with half the oregano.

Melt the remaining butter in a saucepan, add the flour and cook for 2 minutes. Gradually stir in the milk and bring to the boil, stirring. Season and add 100 g (4 oz) of the cheese and the mustard. Stir until melted. Pour over the cauliflower. Arrange the sliced tomatoes over the top and sprinkle with the remaining oregano and seasoning, and then the rest of the cheese. Bake in the oven at 190°C (375°F) mark 5 for 15–20 minutes until golden brown.

Hot blue cheese and celery mousse

225 g (8 oz) celery, trimmed and thinly sliced
30 ml (2 tbsp) single cream or top of milk
75 g (3 oz) Danish blue cheese
3 egg yolks
freshly ground black pepper
4 egg whites
browned breadcrumbs or grated Parmesan cheese to garnish

Cook the celery in the minimum of water in a covered pan for about 30 minutes until really soft. Remove the lid and boil to evaporate the water completely. Purée the celery with the cream and cheese in an electric blender until smooth. Cool slightly, then beat in the egg yolks and black pepper.

Stiffly whisk the egg whites and fold into the celery mixture. Turn into a lightly greased 1.4-litre (2½-pint) soufflé dish. Cook in the oven at 180°C (350°F) mark 4 for about 30 minutes until well risen and golden brown. Serve at once dusted with browned breadcrumbs or grated Parmesan.
Serves 4–6

Courgette and cheese flan

For the pastry
175 g (6 oz) plain flour
15 ml (1 level tbsp) grated Parmesan cheese
2.5 ml (½ level tsp) dry mustard
1.25 ml (¼ level tsp) paprika
75 g (3 oz) butter

For the filling
450 g (1 lb) small courgettes, trimmed and sliced
75 g (3 oz) butter
1 clove garlic, skinned and crushed
grated rind of ½ lemon
10 ml (2 tsp) lemon juice
salt and freshly ground pepper
45 ml (3 level tbsp) flour
150 ml (¼ pint) milk
150 ml (¼ pint) soured cream
1 egg, separated
175 g (6 oz) mature Cheddar cheese, grated
chopped chives to garnish

Sift the flour, Parmesan, mustard and paprika into a bowl. Rub in the butter. Add enough cold water to mix to a soft dough. Roll out and use to line a 23-cm (9-in) fluted flan dish. Bake blind in the oven at 200°C (400°F) mark 6 for about 25 minutes.

Blanch the courgettes in boiling water for 1 minute. Drain. Melt 50 g (2 oz) of the butter in a pan and add the courgettes, garlic, lemon rind and juice and seasoning. Fry slowly for about 5 minutes until the courgettes are soft. Lift out the courgettes. Add the remaining butter to the juices. Stir in the flour. Cook for 1 minute. Gradually stir in the milk and cook for 2–3 minutes. Remove from the heat. Beat in the soured cream and beaten egg yolk.

Whisk the egg white stiffly. Fold into the sauce with the cheese. Check the seasoning. Spread the sauce over the bottom of the flan case. Top with the courgettes. Reheat in the oven for 10–15 minutes. Garnish with chives. *Serves 4–6*

Cherry

To prepare
Remove the stalks and wash the fruit carefully. Remove the stones with a cherry stoner or cook whole.

Basic cooking
To poach, place 450 g (1 lb) of prepared cherries in a pan with water to cover the bottom of the pan and 25–50 g (1–2 oz) sugar to taste. Cover, bring to the boil and simmer gently for 5–10 minutes until tender.

Cherry stuffed loin of pork

1.1-kg (2½-lb) loin of pork, boned
225 g (8 oz) cherries, stoned and chopped
50 g (2 oz) fresh white breadcrumbs
5 ml (1 tsp) chopped fresh rosemary
salt and freshly ground black pepper
1 egg, beaten
15 g (½ oz) lard

For the sauce
225 g (8 oz) cherries, stoned and chopped
300 ml (½ pint) chicken stock
15 g (½ oz) butter
25 g (1 oz) skinned and finely chopped onion
15 g (½ oz) flour

Make a horizontal cut in the flesh of the pork to form a pocket. In a bowl mix together the cherries, breadcrumbs, rosemary and seasoning. Bind together with the egg and fill the pocket in the pork. Sew up securely with string. Score the skin and rub with salt. Melt the lard in a roasting pan and add the pork. Cook in the oven at 180°C (350°F) mark 4 for 1¾–2 hours, until the pork is tender and the skin golden and crispy.

For the sauce, simmer the cherries in the stock for 5–10 minutes. Cool and pureé in an electric blender or rub through a sieve. Melt the butter in a saucepan and cook the onion for 5–8 minutes until golden brown. Stir in the flour and cook for 2 minutes. Add the puréed cherries, bring to the boil and cook for 2 minutes until the sauce thickens.

To serve, remove the string from the pork and slice into four. Place on a warmed serving dish and pour over half the sauce. Serve the remaining sauce separately.

Cherry sorbet bombe

450 g (1 lb) cherries, stoned
400 ml (¾ pint) water
6 unblanched whole almonds
175 g (6 oz) sugar
juice of 1 lemon
60 ml (4 tbsp) Kirsch
1-litre (35-fl oz) carton vanilla ice-cream

Cherry sorbet bombe

Collect any cherry juice and make up to 400 ml ($\frac{3}{4}$ pint) with water. Roughly crush the cherry stones and almonds in an electric blender. In a saucepan gently heat the cherry juice mixture with the sugar until the sugar dissolves. Add the crushed stones and almonds. Boil for 5 minutes. Leave to cool, then strain the syrup.

Purée the cherries in an electric blender. Combine with the syrup. Chill, then stir in the lemon juice and Kirsch.

Line a 1.4-litre (2$\frac{1}{2}$-pint) or a 16-cm (6$\frac{1}{2}$-in) diameter pudding basin or a bombe mould with the ice cream, to come to within 1 cm ($\frac{1}{2}$ in) of the top. Press a 1-litre (1$\frac{3}{4}$-pint) basin inside to keep the shape. Freeze until firm.

Remove the smaller basin by pouring a little boiling water into it and twisting gently. Pour the cherry syrup into the centre. Freeze again until firm. Unmould and decorate with fresh cherries.
Serves 8–10

Cherry jam

This jam gives only a light set.

2.3 kg (5 lb) red cherries, stoned
75 ml (5 tbsp) lemon juice or 7.5 ml (1$\frac{1}{2}$ level tsp) citric or tartaric acid
1.6 kg (3$\frac{1}{2}$ lb) sugar

Crack some cherry stones and remove the kernels. Put the cherries, kernels and lemon juice or acid in a pan and simmer gently until really soft, stirring from time to time to prevent sticking. Add the sugar and stir until dissolved, then boil rapidly until setting point is reached. Pot and cover in the usual way.
Makes about 2.7 kg (6 lb)

Chestnut

To prepare
To peel, snip the brown outer skins with a pair of scissors or sharp knife and immerse the chestnuts in a pan of boiling water for 3–5 minutes. Lift out a few at a time and peel off both the brown outer and inner skins.

Basic cooking
To boil, place 450 g (1 lb) prepared chestnuts in a saucepan and cover with water. Cover, bring to the boil and simmer for 35–40 minutes until tender.
To roast, leave the brown skins on. With the tip of a sharp knife, slash a cross on the flat side of the chestnuts. Place the chestnuts, cut sides up, on a baking sheet. Roast in the oven at 200°C (400°F) mark 6 for 20–25 minutes until tender.

Chestnut purée – unsweetened

450 g (1 lb) chestnuts, peeled
300–400 ml ($\frac{1}{2}$–$\frac{3}{4}$ pint) chicken stock
salt and freshly ground white pepper

Place the chestnuts in a saucepan with enough stock to cover and season. Cover and simmer gently for 35–40 minutes until tender. Rub through a sieve or purée in an electric blender.
Makes about 400 g (14 oz) purée

Chestnut purée – sweetened

450 g (1 lb) chestnuts, peeled
300–400 ml ($\frac{1}{2}$–$\frac{3}{4}$ pint) milk
75–100 g (3–4 oz) caster sugar
2.5 ml ($\frac{1}{2}$ tsp) vanilla essence

Place the chestnuts in a saucepan with enough milk to cover and add the sugar and vanilla essence. Cover and simmer gently for 35–40 minutes until tender. Rub through a sieve or purée in an electric blender.
Makes about 400 g (14 oz) purée

Tia Maria chestnut creams

300 ml ($\frac{1}{2}$ pint) double cream, whipped
450 g (1 lb) unsweetened chestnut purée
75 g (3 oz) caster sugar
30 ml (2 tbsp) Tia Maria

Reserve 45 ml (3 level tbsp) of cream for the decoration. Mix together the remaining

cream, chestnut purée, sugar and Tia Maria. Spoon into six individual glasses. Pipe the reserved cream on the top to decorate. Chill for 2 hours or overnight.
Serves 6

Chestnuts in syrup

225 g (8 oz) sugar
225 g (8 oz) glucose or dextrose
175 ml (6 fl oz) water
350 g (12 oz) whole peeled chestnuts, prepared weight
6–8 drops vanilla essence

Put the sugar, glucose or dextrose and water in a pan large enough to hold the chestnuts and heat gently together until the sugars are dissolved. Bring to the boil. Remove from the heat, add the chestnuts and bring to the boil again. Remove from the heat, cover and leave overnight in a warm place.

Next day, re-boil the chestnuts and syrup, uncovered. Remove from the heat, cover and leave overnight in a warm place.

On the third day, add 6–8 drops of vanilla essence and repeat the boiling process as above. Warm some 450 g (1 lb) bottling jars in the oven, fill with the chestnuts and cover with the syrup. Dispel all air bubbles by jarring each bottle on the palm of the hand. Make sure the bottles are full to the brim, then seal.

Chicken

To prepare
To draw, firstly cut off the feet and the easiest way of doing this is to sever the leg at the joint; bend the foot back, insert the knife in the joint and cut through.

To cut off the head, first cut through the skin of the neck about 5 cm (2 in) from the body. Slip back the skin and cut off the neck close to the trunk. (The neck is kept for stock, but the head is discarded.)

Slit the skin of the neck a little way down the back of the bird – far enough to let you get your fingers inside and to loosen the wind-pipe and gullet, which simplifies drawing. Cut round the vent at the tail end with scissors or a sharp knife, taking care not to puncture the entrails. Make the hole large enough to get your fingers inside the body. Take hold of the gizzard (the large, oval, muscular organ containing food and grit) and draw out all the entrails, including the lungs, windpipe and gullet. Reserve the giblets (heart, gizzard and liver) and any fat. Discard the rest of the entrails, burning them if possible. Wipe out the inside of the bird with a clean, damp cloth.
Giblets Cut out the gall-bladder from the liver, keeping it intact, and discard it. Discard also the flesh on which it rested, as this may have a bitter flavour. Carefully cut through the flesh of the gizzard up to but not through the crop, peel off the flesh and discard the crop.

Wash the liver, gizzard and heart. Put them all in a saucepan, cover with water and stew gently for 45 minutes–1 hour, to make a stock that can be used for gravy or soup.
To truss, with chicken breast uppermost, push a skewer through the legs of the chicken, having bent the legs into position against the breast and pressed them well forward. With the chicken breast downwards, pull the neck flap of skin over to secure stuffing if used. Keep the wings splayed out at this stage.

Twist the wings and fold the tips over the neck flap of skin before securing with a skewer – through the fleshier part of one wing, across the bird's cavity and out through the other wing.

With the chicken breast uppermost, tie the legs and tail (parson's nose) neatly together with string.

If using a frozen chicken, allow it to thaw out completely, then remove the bag of giblets before cooking.

Basic cooking
To roast, wash the inside of the bird and stuff it at the neck before folding the neck skin over. To add flavour you can put an onion, a thick lemon wedge or a knob of butter in the

body of the bird. Put in a shallow roasting tin. Brush the chicken with melted butter or oil and sprinkle with salt and pepper. Roast in the oven at 200°C (400°F) mark 6, basting from time to time and allowing 20 minutes per 450 g (1 lb) plus 20 minutes. Put a piece of paper over the breast if the flesh shows signs of becoming too brown. Alternatively, wrap the chicken in foil before roasting; allow the same cooking time, but open the foil for the final 15–20 minutes, to allow the bird to brown.

To fry, cut a small bird in halves or quarters, a larger one into neat joints (or buy ready-cut pieces). Season with salt and pepper and coat all over with flour. Fry in hot fat, turning the pieces so that they brown on all sides, then reduce the heat; allow 15 minutes on each side.

Alternatively, season the joints and dip them in egg and breadcrumbs before frying.

To boil, prepare the bird and tie the legs together. Fold the wings under the body. Rub the bird over with lemon juice to preserve the colour, put it in a large pan and just cover with cold water. Add a little salt, an onion stuck with 3–4 cloves, a carrot and bouquet garni. Bring to the boil, cover and simmer for 3–4 hours if the bird is a boiling fowl; for a younger chicken, 45 minutes is enough. Drain the bird and keep it hot while making a parsley, egg or white sauce with 300 ml ($\frac{1}{2}$ pint) milk. Serve the chicken coated with the sauce.

Chicken and cranberry curry

50 g (2 oz) lard
1 large onion, skinned and chopped
1 clove garlic, skinned and chopped
15 ml (1 level tbsp) flour
25 ml (1$\frac{1}{2}$ level tbsp) curry powder
30 ml (2 level tbsp) tomato paste
juice of 1 lemon
226-g (8-oz) can whole berry cranberry sauce
300 ml ($\frac{1}{2}$ pint) water
2.5 ml ($\frac{1}{2}$ level tsp) salt
3 whole cloves
1 bay leaf
350 g (12 oz) cooked chicken meat, cut into 2.5-cm (1-in) pieces
175–225 g (6–8 oz) long grain rice, cooked
25 g (1 oz) flaked almonds, toasted

Heat the lard in a large frying pan and fry the onion slowly until golden brown. Add the garlic, then remove from the heat and stir in the flour, curry powder, tomato paste, lemon juice and cranberry sauce. Gradually stir in the water and return to the heat. Bring to the boil, stirring. Add the salt, cloves and bay leaf, cover the pan and simmer for 30 minutes, stirring occasionally.

Add the chicken to the sauce and heat through while the rice is cooking. Discard the cloves and bay leaf. Serve the curry in the centre of a border of rice, with a garnish of toasted flaked almonds.

Chicken en cocotte with apples and cream

Illustrated in colour facing page 33

1.4-kg (3-lb) roasting chicken
50 g (2 oz) butter
1 medium onion, skinned and chopped
2 stalks celery, trimmed and sliced
350 g (12 oz) cooking apples, peeled, cored and cut into thick wedges
45 ml (3 level tbsp) flour
150 ml ($\frac{1}{4}$ pint) dry cider
300 ml ($\frac{1}{2}$ pint) chicken stock
salt and freshly ground pepper
150 ml ($\frac{1}{4}$ pint) double cream

Wipe the chicken. Melt the butter in a large frying pan and brown the chicken on all sides. Transfer to a large casserole dish. Fry the onion and celery in the fat remaining in the pan for 5 minutes until the onion is soft. Add the apples. Stir in the flour and cook for 1 minute. Add the cider and stock and season well. Pour the sauce over the chicken, cover and cook in the oven at 190°C (375°F) mark 5 for 1$\frac{1}{4}$ hours until the chicken is tender.

Skim off any surface fat. Carve the chicken, place on a warmed serving dish and keep warm. Stir the cream into the casserole juices and heat gently without boiling. Adjust the seasoning to taste and pour over the chicken.

Pan-cooked chicken with cumin

1.6-kg (3½-lb) roasting chicken
30–45 ml (2–3 tbsp) cooking oil
1 large onion, skinned and chopped
2 cloves garlic, skinned and crushed
3 large tomatoes, skinned and quartered
175 g (6 oz) cooked ham or boiled bacon, diced
300 ml (½ pint) chicken stock
1 green pepper, seeded and sliced
1 bay leaf
5 ml (1 level tsp) salt
2.5 ml (½ level tsp) ground cumin
freshly ground pepper
175 g (6 oz) long-grain rice
chopped fresh parsley to garnish

Joint the chicken into small pieces. In a large frying pan heat the oil. Place the chicken in the pan skin-side down and fry slowly on all sides for 10 minutes until evenly brown. Remove to one side. Reheat the pan juices and fry the onion for 5 minutes until soft. Replace the chicken in the pan with the garlic and tomatoes. Cover and cook over a gentle heat for 25 minutes.

Uncover and add the remaining ingredients. Bring to the boil, then cover, reduce the heat and simmer for 20 minutes, until the rice is tender. Add a further 150 ml (¼ pint) stock if necessary to stop the rice sticking. Remove the bay leaf. Serve sprinkled with chopped parsley.
Serves 4–6

Courgette

To prepare
Top and tail, then wash or wipe with a damp cloth. The larger vegetables may need salting to draw out some of the moisture before cooking – sprinkle the sliced courgettes with a little salt and leave to drain in a colander for 30 minutes. Rinse well and pat dry.

Basic cooking
To steam, steam whole courgettes for 5–8 minutes until tender but still crisp. Toss in butter, seasoning and chopped fresh herbs.
To fry, slice the courgettes thickly and cook gently in melted butter in a covered pan for 5–10 minutes until just cooked.

Marinated courgette, corn and lemon salad

Illustrated in colour facing page 48

450 g (1 lb) courgettes, trimmed
vegetable oil for frying
175 g (6 oz) sweetcorn kernels, cooked

For the dressing
45 ml (3 tbsp) white wine vinegar
2 canned anchovies, finely chopped
½ clove garlic, skinned and crushed
30 ml (2 tbsp) chopped fresh parsley
grated rind and juice of 1 lemon
salt and freshly ground pepper

Cut the courgettes into 1-cm (½-in) slices. Heat the oil in a frying pan and cook the courgette slices, a few at a time, for 5–10 minutes, until golden brown on both sides. Turn into a serving dish with the sweetcorn and cool.

Place the dressing ingredients in a screwtop jar and shake to combine. Pour over the courgettes and sweetcorn and leave to marinate for 2–3 hours or overnight.

Spicy beef stuffed courgettes

4 courgettes, 175 g (6 oz) each, trimmed
15 g (½ oz) butter
350 g (12 oz) minced beef
50 g (2 oz) onion, skinned and chopped
15 ml (1 tbsp) vegetable oil
30 ml (2 level tbsp) flour
10 ml (2 level tsp) mild curry powder
300 ml (½ pint) beef stock
30 ml (2 level tbsp) rice
15 ml (1 level tbsp) tomato paste
salt and freshly ground pepper
198-g (7-oz) can sweetcorn kernels, drained
50 g (2 oz) Cheddar cheese, grated

Wrap the courgettes in buttered foil and cook in the oven at 180°C (350°F) mark 4 for about 1 hour until tender.

Meanwhile, fry the minced beef and onion in hot oil for about 10 minutes until brown.

Stir in the flour and curry powder and cook for 1 minute. Blend in the stock, rice, tomato paste and seasoning. Cover and simmer for 20 minutes.

Halve the courgettes, lengthways, scoop out the flesh and chop roughly. Stir it into the beef mixture with the corn. Place the courgette shells in a shallow ovenproof dish and fill with the beef mixture. Sprinkle with the grated cheese. Cook in the oven at 190°C (375°F) mark 5 for 25 minutes.

NOT SUITABLE FOR FREEZING

Cucumber

To prepare
When using small young tender cucumbers in salads, leave the skin on and cut into thin slices, chunks or dice. Larger cucumbers and ridge cucumbers should be peeled thinly. If cucumbers are bitter, peel and slice or dice and place in a colander. Sprinkle with salt and leave for 30 minutes–1 hour. Drain off the juice, rinse thoroughly and pat dry.

Basic cooking
To steam, place the prepared cucumber in a steamer and cook for 5–10 minutes. Drain well.
To boil, cook in boiling salted water for 5–10 minutes. Drain well. Toss steamed or boiled cucumber in a little melted butter or coat in hollandaise or white sauce (see page 77).
To sauté, cook in melted butter for 5–10 minutes. Stir in a squeeze of lemon juice and serve sprinkled with chopped fresh herbs.

Sweet and sour cucumber

1 large cucumber, peeled and diced
salt and freshly ground black pepper
40 g (1½ oz) onion, skinned and chopped
2 pickled gherkins, chopped
40 g (1½ oz) sultanas
200 ml (7 fl oz) soured cream
30 ml (2 tbsp) lemon juice
3.75 ml (¾ level tsp) caster sugar
dash of Tabasco sauce
watercress to garnish

Put the cucumber in a shallow dish and sprinkle with salt. Leave for 30 minutes. Rinse off the salt under cold water, drain well and dry with kitchen paper towel.

Mix together the onion, gherkins and sultanas in a large bowl. Stir in the soured cream, lemon juice, sugar, Tabasco and pepper and mix well. Fold in the diced cucumber. Spoon into a serving dish and chill for 1 hour. Garnish with sprigs of watercress.

Cucumber with orange yogurt sauce

2 cucumbers, peeled and diced
salt and freshly ground black pepper
25 g (1 oz) butter
1 large orange
5 ml (1 tsp) lemon juice
60 ml (4 level tbsp) natural yogurt

Spread the cucumbers out on a plate, sprinkle with salt and leave for 30 minutes. Rinse the cucumber and drain well. Melt the butter in a large saucepan, add the cucumber and season. Cook gently for 5 minutes. Cut two slices from the orange and reserve for the garnish. Grate the rind from the remaining orange and add to the cucumber with the juice from the orange and the lemon juice. Simmer gently for 10 minutes. Stir in the yogurt and heat through for 5 minutes. Spoon into a warmed serving dish and garnish with the slices of orange.

Cucumber and mint salad

Illustrated in colour facing page 80

150 ml (¼ pint) natural yogurt
30 ml (2 tbsp) chopped fresh mint
30 ml (2 tbsp) chopped fresh parsley
15 ml (1 tbsp) white wine vinegar
15 ml (1 tbsp) vegetable oil
30 ml (2 tbsp) milk
salt and freshly ground pepper
1 large cucumber, peeled and diced
1 clove garlic, skinned and crushed
few sprigs of mint to garnish

59

Stir the yogurt, mint, parsley, vinegar, oil, milk and seasoning together in a large bowl. Add the cucumber and garlic and stir well until evenly coated. Pile the cucumber mixture into a serving dish and garnish with mint sprigs.

Damson

To prepare
Remove the stalks and wash the fruit thoroughly. The skin will split during cooking and the stone slide out on its own, so no preparation is required.

Basic cooking
To poach, place the damsons in a saucepan with water to cover the bottom of the pan and 50–100 g (2–4 oz) sugar to taste. Cook for about 15 minutes or until soft. Damsons are much smaller than plums and produce lots of stones and skin for their weight so it is better to purée the fruit by rubbing through a sieve.

Damson cheesecake

75 g (3 oz) butter
150 g (5 oz) digestive biscuits, finely crushed
225 g (8 oz) caster sugar
700 g (1½ lb) damsons
25 ml (5 level tsp) powdered gelatine
350 g (12 oz) cream cheese
300 ml (½ pint) double cream
1.25 ml (¼ level tsp) arrowroot

Melt the butter in a large saucepan and add the biscuits and 50 g (2 oz) of the caster sugar. Stir well to coat the biscuit crumbs with butter. Line the bottom of a 20.5-cm (8-in) spring-release cake tin with the crumbs and chill.

Place the damsons in a pan with the remaining sugar and 60 ml (4 tbsp) water. Cover and simmer gently for 20 minutes until soft. Remove the stones and blend in an electric blender or rub through a sieve, to make 600 ml (1 pint) purée. Dissolve the gelatine in 30 ml (2 tbsp) water and stir into 400 ml (¾ pint) of the damson purée. Cool but do not set.

Beat the cream cheese until soft and gradually stir in the jellied purée. Lightly whip the cream and fold into the damson mixture. Pour into the cake tin and chill until firm.

Heat the remaining damson purée in a small saucepan. Blend the arrowroot with a little water and stir into the purée. Bring to the boil, stirring, and cook for 1 minute. Cool. Unmould the cheesecake and spread the thickened purée over the top.
Serves 6–8

One-crust spiced damson pie

700 g (1½ lb) damsons, halved and stoned
50 g (2 oz) preserved stem ginger, chopped
75–100 g (3–4 oz) granulated sugar
15 ml (1 level tbsp) cornflour
200 g (7 oz) plain flour
2.5 ml (½ level tsp) ground ginger
pinch of salt
125 g (4 oz) butter
milk to glaze
caster sugar

Place the damsons in the bottom of a 900-ml (1½-pint) pie dish. Combine together the stem ginger, sugar and cornflour and sprinkle over the damsons. Sift the flour, ground ginger and salt into a mixing bowl. Rub in the butter until the mixture resembles fine breadcrumbs. Add enough water to form a soft dough and knead lightly.

Turn the dough out on to a floured surface, and roll out and use to cover the pie dish. Seal well and knock up and decorate the edges. Brush with milk. Place on a baking sheet and bake in the oven at 220°C (425°F) mark 7 for 15 minutes, then reduce the heat to 180°C (350°F) mark 4 and bake for a further 25–30 minutes, until the crust is pale golden. Remove from the oven and dredge with caster sugar. Serve warm with pouring or whipped cream.
Serves 4–6

Damson jam

2.3 kg (5 lb) damsons
900 ml (1½ pints) water
2.7 kg (6 lb) sugar

Put the damsons in a pan with the water and simmer for about 30 minutes until the fruit is really soft and reduced in weight to 2 kg (4½ lb). Add the sugar and stir until dissolved. Boil rapidly until setting point is reached, removing the stones of the damsons as they rise to the surface. Pot and cover in the usual way.

Makes about 4.5 kg (10 lb)

Egg

To prepare
Break the eggs one at a time into a small basin or cup and use as required.

To separate an egg, give the egg a sharp knock against the side of a basin or cup and break the shell in half – tapping it lightly two or three times is liable to crush the shell instead of breaking it cleanly and may cause the yolk to mix into the white. Having broken the shell, pass the yolk back and forth from one half of the shell to the other, letting the white drop into the basin. Put the yolk into another basin.

Basic cooking

To boil, eggs should be simmered rather than boiled. Put them into boiling water, using a spoon, lower the heat and cook for 3 minutes for a light set and up to 4½ minutes for a firmer set. Alternatively, put the eggs in cold water and bring slowly to the boil – they will then be lightly set. The water in each case should be just sufficient to cover the eggs.

To hard-boil, put the eggs into boiling water, bring back to the boil and boil gently for 10–12 minutes. Hard-boiled eggs should be placed at once under cold running water, the shells tapped against the edge of a basin or work surface and left until they are cold; this prevents a discolored rim forming round the outside of the yolk and enables the shell to be easily removed. Crack the shell all round by tapping on a firm surface, then peel it off.

To poach, half-fill a frying pan with water, adding a pinch of salt or a few drops of vinegar to help the eggs keep their shape and give added flavour. Grease the required number of plain pastry cutters. Bring the water to the boil, put in the cutters and break an egg into each; or just slip the eggs into the water without rings. Cook gently until lightly set and lift out with a slotted spoon or fish slice. Drain the eggs before serving.

To fry, melt a little oil or butter in a frying pan. Break each egg separately into a cup and drop carefully into the fat. Cook gently and use a spoon to baste with the fat, so that the eggs cook evenly on top and underneath. When they are just set, remove them from the pan with a fish slice or palette knife.

To bake, place the required number of individual ovenproof dishes or cocottes on a baking sheet, with a knob of butter in each dish. Put them in the oven at 180°C (350°F) mark 4 for 1–2 minutes, until the butter has melted. Break an egg into each dish, sprinkle with a little salt and pepper and return to the oven. Bake until the eggs are just set – about 5–8 minutes. Garnish if you wish and serve.

To scramble, melt a knob of butter in a small saucepan. Whisk 2 eggs with 30 ml (2 tbsp) milk or water and some salt and pepper. Pour into the saucepan and stir slowly over a gentle heat until the mixture begins to thicken. Remove from the heat and stir until creamy. Pile on to hot buttered toast.

Pickled eggs

For every 6 hard-boiled fresh farm eggs, allow:

600 ml (1 pint) white wine or cider vinegar
6 cloves garlic, skinned
25 g (1 oz) pickling spice
small piece of orange rind
piece of mace blade

Put all the ingredients, except the eggs, in a heavy pan and bring to the boil. Cover tightly and simmer for 10 minutes. Cool, then strain some of the spiced vinegar into a wide-mouthed glass jar with a screw lid or tight cork. Put in the eggs, shelled but whole, and top up with more spiced vinegar. Leave for at least 6 weeks before using. More hard-boiled eggs can be added as convenient, but they must always be covered by the liquid.

Tortilla (potato omelette)

300 ml (½ pint) vegetable oil
450 g (1 lb) potatoes, peeled and sliced
1 small onion, skinned and chopped
4 eggs
salt and freshly ground pepper

Heat the oil and fry the potato slices until golden brown. Remove from the pan and drain well. Pour off the oil, leaving only 15 ml (1 tbsp). Fry the onion gently until soft but not coloured. Return the potatoes to the pan. Beat the eggs and seasoning together and pour over the potatoes. Cook over a gentle heat until the eggs are set and golden brown underneath. Place a large flat plate over the pan, invert the omelette and return it to the pan to cook the other side.
Serves 3–4

Egg stuffed aubergines

2 large aubergines, about 350 g (12 oz) each, trimmed
60 ml (4 tbsp) corn oil
50 g (2 oz) onion, skinned and chopped
30 ml (2 level tbsp) tomato paste
salt and freshly ground black pepper
4 eggs
chopped fresh parsley to garnish

Halve the aubergines lengthways and score the cut surfaces well. Sprinkle with salt and leave for about 30 minutes to draw out the bitter juices. Rinse under cold water and dry the aubergine halves with kitchen paper towel. Fry gently in hot oil (adding more oil if necessary), turning once, for about 10 minutes until just tender. Remove from the pan. Add the onion and fry for about 10 minutes until golden brown.

Meanwhile, scoop out the aubergine flesh, leaving the skin's intact. Chop the flesh roughly and stir into the onion in the pan with the tomato paste and seasoning. Simmer gently for about 5 minutes.

Pack the aubergine shells into a shallow ovenproof dish. Break the eggs into a cup one at a time and pour one carefully into each aubergine shell. Spoon the pan ingredients into each end of the aubergines. Cook in the oven at 180°C (350°F) mark 4 for about 20 minutes, or until eggs are just set. Sprinkle with parsley for serving.

Note: when the eggs are too large for the shells, allow the white to overflow and set in the bottom of the dish.

NOT SUITABLE FOR FREEZING

Mocha roulade

15 ml (1 level tbsp) instant coffee
15 ml (1 tbsp) water
100 g (4 oz) plain chocolate
4 large eggs, separated
100 g (4 oz) caster sugar
300 ml (½ pint) double cream, whipped
225 g (8 oz) white grapes, halved and pipped

Blend the coffee to a smooth paste with the water in a small heatproof bowl. Break up the chocolate, put into the bowl and melt over a pan of hot water. Cool slightly.

Cut a 30.5-cm (12-in) square of non-stick paper and fold up 2.5 cm (1 in) all round. Snip into the corners, then secure the edges with paper clips to form a free standing paper case. Place on a baking sheet. Whisk the yolks and sugar together until thick. Stir in the cool coffee chocolate and fold in the stiffly whisked egg whites. Spread into the paper case. Bake in the oven at 180°C (350°F) mark 4 for about 15 minutes, or until firm. Cover with a damp teatowel and leave overnight.

Remove the teatowel and flip the roulade over on to a sheet of sugared greaseproof paper. Spread with half the whipped cream and the grapes (reserve some for decoration). Roll up with the help of the paper. Decorate with whirls of the remaining cream and the reserved grapes.

To freeze: open freeze without decoration. Pack and return to freezer. To use, unwrap,

Mocha roulade

Dissolve the gelatine in the water in another heatproof bowl over a pan of hot water. Stir into the almond mixture. Whip the cream until thick and fold in. Whisk the egg whites until stiff but not dry and fold evenly through the mixture. Turn into a 1.1-litre (2-pint) serving dish. Chill until set. Decorate with orange slices.

To freeze: when ready, wrap in a freezer-proof dish without decoration and label. Freeze. To use, thaw at room temperature for about 4 hours. Decorate.
Serves 6

Individual spinach quiches

For the pastry
225 g (8 oz) flour
salt
50 g (2 oz) lard
50 g (2 oz) butter or block margarine

For the filling
225 g (8 oz) spinach, trimmed and chopped
salt and freshly ground pepper
15 g ($\frac{1}{2}$ oz) butter
300 ml ($\frac{1}{2}$ pint) single cream
4 egg yolks
100 g (4 oz) cream cheese

For the pastry, sift the flour and salt together into a bowl. Rub in the fats until the mixture resembles fine breadcrumbs. Add enough cold water to mix to a firm dough. Knead gently, then roll out and use to line six 10-cm (4-in) individual flan cases.

For the filling, cook the spinach in a saucepan with a little water, seasoning and butter for 5–10 minutes, until tender. Drain well, cool and chop finely. Divide the spinach between the pastry cases. Beat together the cream, egg yolks and cheese until smooth. Season and divide between the pastry cases. Bake in the oven at 200°C (400°F) mark 6 for 10 minutes. Reduce the oven temperature to 180°C (350°F) mark 4 and continue cooking for 20–25 minutes, until the filling is set.
Serves 6

put on a serving plate and leave at cool room temperature for about 4 hours. Complete as above.
Serves 6–8

Almond orange mousse

3 eggs, separated
75 g (3 oz) caster sugar
finely grated rind of 1 orange
30 ml (2 tbsp) orange juice
50 g (2 oz) ground almonds
10 ml (2 level tsp) powdered gelatine
30 ml (2 tbsp) water
150 ml ($\frac{1}{4}$ pint) double cream
2 oranges, thinly sliced, to decorate

Place the egg yolks, sugar, orange rind and juice in a heatproof bowl over a pan of hot water, and whisk until the whisk leaves a trail across the mixture. Remove the bowl from the heat and fold in the ground almonds.

Gooseberry

To prepare

Wash the fruit carefully. Using a pair of sharp scissors, snip away the stalk end and the tail at the opposite end – 'top and tail'.

Basic cooking

To poach, place 450 g (1 lb) of prepared gooseberries in a saucepan with water to cover the bottom of the pan and 50–75 g (2–3 oz) sugar to taste. Cover the pan, bring to the boil and simmer gently for 10–15 minutes until tender.

Gooseberry sauce

350 g (12 oz) gooseberries, topped and tailed
45 ml (3 tbsp) water
15 g ($\frac{1}{2}$ oz) butter
15 g ($\frac{1}{2}$ oz) flour
150 ml ($\frac{1}{4}$ pint) chicken stock
15 ml (1 tbsp) chopped fresh chives
salt and freshly ground pepper
5 ml (1 level tsp) caster sugar

Place the gooseberries in a saucepan with the water, cover and simmer for 10–15 minutes until soft and pulpy. Rub the gooseberries through a sieve or blend in an electric blender. Melt the butter in another saucepan and add the flour. Cook for 2–3 minutes until the flour begins to colour slightly. Gradually stir in the chicken stock. Bring to the boil to thicken, stirring constantly. Add the chives, seasoning and caster sugar. Blend in the gooseberry purée and mix well.

Serve gooseberry sauce with roast or grilled lamb or pork. It also complements oily fish.

Gooseberry flummery

350 g (12 oz) gooseberries, topped and tailed
115 g ($4\frac{1}{4}$ oz) caster sugar
grated rind and juice of 1 orange
300 ml ($\frac{1}{2}$ pint) milk
50 g (2 oz) semolina
45 ml (3 tbsp) lemon juice
2 egg whites
whipped cream and chopped almonds or crystallised rose petals to decorate

Place the gooseberries, 75 g (3 oz) of the caster sugar and the orange rind and juice in a saucepan. Cook gently until soft. Purée in an electric blender or rub through a sieve. Allow to cool.

Place the milk in a clean pan and sprinkle in the semolina. When beginning to thicken, add the lemon juice and simmer for about 10 minutes, stirring continuously. Add the remaining caster sugar and whisk well. Fold the gooseberry purée through the semolina mixture, whisking in well until light and fluffy. Allow to cool.

Stiffly whisk the egg whites and fold evenly into the semolina mixture. Turn into six stemmed glasses and chill. Decorate with lightly whipped cream and chopped toasted almonds or crystallised rose petals. Eat the same day.

Gooseberry cheesecake

Illustrated in colour opposite

150 g (5 oz) digestive biscuits, finely crushed
5 ml (1 level tsp) ground cinnamon
75 g ($2\frac{1}{2}$ oz) butter, melted
700 g ($1\frac{1}{2}$ lb) gooseberries, topped and tailed
175 g (6 oz) caster sugar
25 ml (5 level tsp) powdered gelatine
30 ml (2 tbsp) water
350 g (12 oz) cream cheese
300 ml ($\frac{1}{2}$ pint) double cream, half whipped
1.25 ml ($\frac{1}{4}$ level tsp) arrowroot

Stir the biscuits and cinnamon into the butter and press into a bottom-lined 20.5-cm (8-in) spring-release cake tin. Chill.

Place 450 g (1 lb) gooseberries in a pan with 100 g (4 oz) sugar and cook gently until the juice runs. Cover and simmer to a pulp. Sieve to remove the pips – there should be 600 ml (1 pint) purée. Sprinkle the gelatine over the water. When it has softened, stir it into 400 ml ($\frac{3}{4}$ pint) purée. Allow to cool but not set.

Beat the cream cheese until smooth and gradually beat in the jellied purée. Fold in the cream. Turn the mixture into the tin. Chill until firm.

In a pan, cook the remaining gooseberries with the 50 g (2 oz) sugar for 10 minutes. Blend the arrowroot with the gooseberries. Bring to the boil and cook for 1 minute. Cool; spread over the cheesecake. Leave to set.

To freeze: when prepared, open freeze in tin. Remove carefully, wrap and label. Return to freezer. To use, thaw unwrapped at room temperature for about 6 hours.
Serves 8

Gooseberry cheesecake (above), Chocolate blackcurrant gâteau (page 41), Strawberry cheese creams (page 100).

Grapefruit

To prepare

If the grapefruit is slightly misshapen gently knead it into shape with both hands – this will also help to release the juices. Cut the grapefruit in half, around the middle of the fruit between the stalk end and the round end. Alternatively, cut around the same line with alternating slanting cuts to give a water-lily shape. Remove any visible pips and cut the fruit into individual segments for ease of eating. This is done by inserting a grapefruit knife (a knife with a serrated edge and a curved blade) between the fruit and the skin and cutting around the fruit completely to free it from the skin. Insert the knife between the membrane and the fruit on both sides of the segment so the fruit can be easily lifted from the skin.

Basic cooking

Grapefruit halves are often eaten for breakfast or as a starter. Sprinkle with a little caster sugar if very tart and top with a cherry. **To bake or grill,** prepare the grapefruit as above and sprinkle each half with 15 ml (1 level tbsp) soft brown sugar and 15 ml (1 tbsp) sweet sherry. Bake in the oven at 180°C (350°F) mark 4 for 10–15 minutes or cook under a hot grill for 3–5 minutes until the sugar bubbles. Top with a cherry before serving immediately.

Grapefruit, apple and mint cocktail

Illustrated in colour opposite

10 ml (2 level tsp) powdered gelatine
15 ml (1 tbsp) water
175 ml (6 fl oz) dry cider
1 large red-skinned eating apple, cored and diced
2 medium grapefruit, halved and segments removed
15 ml (1 tbsp) chopped fresh mint
4 lettuce leaves
mint sprigs to garnish

In a small heatproof bowl over a pan of hot water, dissolve the gelatine in the measured water. Off the heat, stir in a little of the cider, then combine with the remaining cider. Stir in the apple, grapefruit and chopped mint. Chill until on the point of setting.

Finely shred the lettuce and arrange in the bottom of six sundae glasses. Divide the jellied fruit between the glasses. Garnish each with a tiny sprig of mint.
Serves 6

Honeyed spare ribs

1.4 kg (3 lb) spare ribs of pork
90 ml (6 tbsp) thin honey
60 ml (4 tbsp) lemon juice
150 ml ($\frac{1}{4}$ pint) dry cider
60 ml (4 tbsp) soy sauce
8 black peppercorns
2.5 ml ($\frac{1}{2}$ level tsp) salt
2 small grapefruit
15 ml (1 level tbsp) arrowroot
45 ml (3 tbsp) water
chopped fresh parsley to garnish

Divide the pork into individual ribs and trim off the excess fat. Arrange in a roasting tin in a single layer. Heat the honey, lemon juice, cider, soy sauce and seasoning in a saucepan and stir until well blended. Take off the heat, leave until cool, then pour over the ribs. Cover and marinate overnight in the refrigerator.

Cook the meat with the marinade, covered, in the oven at 190°C (375°F) mark 5 for 2 hours, basting frequently. Peel the grapefruit, removing all traces of white pith, and segment.

Arrange the spare ribs on a warmed serving platter and keep warm. Strain the marinade into a small pan and add the arrowroot blended to a smooth paste with the water. Bring to the boil, stirring. Add the grapefruit to the sauce, correct the seasoning and spoon over the spare ribs. Garnish with chopped parsley.

To freeze: cook the ribs for $1\frac{1}{2}$ hours only. Cool, pack and freeze. To use, reheat from frozen, covered, in the oven at 190°C (375°F) mark 5 for 1–$1\frac{1}{4}$ hours. Continue as above.

Grapefruit marmalade

3 grapefruit, about 1.2 kg ($2\frac{3}{4}$ lb)
3–4 lemons, about 350 g (12 oz)
2.6–3.4 litres ($4\frac{1}{2}$–6 pints) water
2.7 kg (6 lb) sugar

Wash and halve the fruit. Remove all pips and tie them in a muslin bag. Squeeze the juice from the fruit and cut up the peel. Put

*Moroccan lemon chicken (page 71), Glazed orange cheesecake (page 82),
Lemon jelly marmalade (page 71), Grapefruit, apple and mint cocktail (above).*

the cut-up peel, juice, water and bag of pips into a pan. Boil gently for about 2 hours until the peel is tender and the contents of the pan reduced by about half.

Remove the bag of pips, squeezing well, and add the sugar to the pan. Stir until dissolved, then boil briskly until setting point is reached. Allow to cool for about 15 minutes, then stir gently to distribute the peel before potting and covering in the usual way.

Makes about 4.5 kg (10 lb)

Greengage

To prepare
Remove the stalks and wash the fruit. Cut each gage around the middle: the gage will separate if very ripe and the stone can be removed. If under-ripe the stone may not be removable until after cooking.

Basic cooking
To poach, place the prepared fruit in a saucepan with water to cover the bottom of the pan and 25–50 g (1–2 oz) sugar to taste. Cover, bring to the boil and simmer gently for 10–15 minutes. Remove any stones that come to the surface of the juice.

Greengage cinnamon upside down cake

350 g (12 oz) greengages, halved and stoned
175 g (6 oz) soft tub margarine
175 g (6 oz) soft brown sugar
3 eggs, beaten
175 g (6 oz) self raising flour
5 ml (1 level tsp) ground cinnamon

Grease and line a 19-cm (7½-in) cake tin. Arrange half of the greengage halves over the bottom of the tin, cut sides down. Chop the remaining greengages. Cream together the margarine and sugar in a large bowl until light and fluffy. Beat in the eggs, a little at a time. Fold in the flour, cinnamon and chopped greengages. Spoon into the tin and carefully spread over the halved greengages. Smooth the top. Bake in the oven at 180°C (350°F) mark 4 for 1½–1¾ hours. Cover the top of the cake with foil after 1 hour to prevent it over browning. Turn out on to a serving dish and serve hot or cold with custard sauce or cream.
Serves 6

Chilled greengages in red wine

150 ml (¼ pint) red wine
30 ml (2 tbsp) port
50 g (2 oz) sugar
finely pared rind and juice of 1 orange
450 g (1 lb) greengages, halved and stoned

Place the wine, port, sugar and orange juice in a large saucepan. Bring to the boil, stirring to dissolve the sugar. Add the greengages and simmer for 10–15 minutes until the greengages are tender. Remove the greengages from the pan with a draining spoon and place in a serving dish. Return the liquid to the boil and continue to boil until it is reduced by half.

Meanwhile, cut a quarter of the orange rind into very thin strips. Boil in water for 25–30 minutes until the rind is tender. Drain. Pour the wine syrup over the greengages and decorate with the orange rind. Chill for 2 hours or overnight. Serve with cream.

Greengage pancakes

4 pancakes, 18-cm (7-in) diameter
450 g (1 lb) greengages, halved and stoned
50 g (2 oz) caster sugar
150 ml (¼ pint) dry white wine
5 ml (1 level tsp) arrowroot
knob of butter

Make the pancakes as usual and keep hot.

Put the greengages in a saucepan with the sugar and wine. Bring to the boil, cover and simmer very gently until the fruit is tender. Remove the fruit with a draining spoon and use to fill the four pancakes. Fold into quarters and arrange in an ovenproof dish.

Blend the arrowroot with a little of the cooking juice, then add to the remaining juice with the butter. Stir over a gentle heat until thickened and clear. Pour over the pancakes. Cover with foil or a lid and heat in the oven at 200°C (400°F) mark 6 for 10 minutes. Serve hot with whipped cream.

Greengage jam

2.7 kg (6 lb) greengages, halved and stoned
600 ml (1 pint) water
2.7 kg (6 lb) sugar

Crack some of the greengage stones, remove the kernels and blanch these by dipping in boiling water. Put the greengages, blanched kernels and the water into a pan and simmer for about 30 minutes until the fruit is really soft and reduced. Add the sugar, stir until dissolved, then boil rapidly until setting point is reached – about 15 minutes. Pot and cover in the usual way.
Note: if you wish, you can leave the stones in

Greengage pancakes

the fruit, removing them as they come to the surface when the jam boils.
Makes about 4.5 kg (10 lb)

ʃHazel nut

To prepare
Remove any leafy husks and shell the nuts using nut crackers. Use as required or store in an airtight jar covered with salt.

Basic cooking
To toast, place the shelled hazel nuts in a grill pan. Toast under a medium grill until the skins begin to dry and the hazel nuts brown. Cool and rub off the skins.

Hazel nut rum gâteau

175 g (6 oz) soft tub margarine
175 g (6 oz) caster sugar
3 eggs, beaten
few drops of vanilla essence
225 g (8 oz) hazel nuts, finely ground
175 g (6 oz) self raising flour
30 ml (2 tbsp) milk
25 g (1 oz) granulated sugar
60 ml (4 tbsp) water
30 ml (2 tbsp) rum
300 ml (½ pint) double cream, whipped
chocolate curls to decorate

Grease and line two 20.5-cm (8-in) sandwich tins. Cream together the margarine and caster sugar until light and fluffy. Beat in the eggs, a little at a time with a few drops of vanilla essence. Fold in the hazel nuts, flour and milk to form a soft dropping consistency. Divide the mixture between the two tins and bake in the oven at 180°C (350°F) mark 4 for 30 minutes, until risen and golden brown. Remove the cakes from the tins and leave them to cool.

Place the granulated sugar and water in a small saucepan. Bring to the boil and stir to dissolve the sugar. Boil rapidly for 5 minutes, then remove from the heat and cool. Stir in the rum and spoon the syrup over the two cakes.

Spread half of the whipped cream over one cake and place the other cake on top. Spread a layer of cream over the top and pipe the remaining cream around the edge of the cake. Fill the centre of the cream ring with chocolate curls.
Serves 8

Hazel nut tart

For the pastry
200 g (7 oz) plain flour
100 g (4 oz) butter
50 g (2 oz) caster sugar
1 egg yolk

For the filling
225 g (8 oz) hazel nuts, chopped
40 g (1½ oz) chopped mixed peel
75 g (3 oz) caster sugar
pinch of ground cinnamon
3 egg yolks
150 ml (¼ pint) single cream
150 ml (¼ pint) double cream

For the pastry, place the flour in a bowl and rub in the butter until the mixture resembles fine breadcrumbs. Stir in the sugar. Add the egg yolk and enough cold water to mix to a soft dough. Cover and leave to relax in the refrigerator or a cool place for 30 minutes.

Roll out the dough and use to line a 25.5-cm (10-in) fluted flan ring. Leave to relax for 20 minutes, then bake blind in the oven at 190°C (375°F) mark 5 for 25 minutes.

For the filling, mix together the hazel nuts, peel, caster sugar and cinnamon. Beat the egg yolks into the creams and stir into the hazel nut mixture. Fill the pastry case with the hazel nut filling. Return to the oven and bake for 20–25 minutes until set. Serve cold. *Serves 6–8*

⌐Herbs

To prepare

Remove any damaged leaves and wash under cold running water. Pat dry with kitchen paper towel. Use whole, chopped on a chopping board with a sharp knife, or snipped with sharp scissors.

Lovage soup

225 g (8 oz) onions, skinned and thinly sliced
25 g (1 oz) butter
45 ml (3 tbsp) chopped fresh lovage
30 ml (2 level tbsp) flour
600 ml (1 pint) chicken stock
300 ml (½ pint) milk
salt and freshly ground pepper
croûtons and fresh lovage leaves to garnish

Fry the onions in the melted butter for 5 minutes until soft. Add the chopped lovage and cook gently for 1 minute, then stir in the flour. Cook for 1–2 minutes, stirring continuously. Gradually stir in the stock and bring to the boil. Cover and simmer for 20 minutes. Add the milk and purée in an electric blender or rub through a sieve. Reheat to serving temperature and adjust the seasoning. Garnish with croûtons and fresh lovage leaves.

To freeze: cool, pack and freeze. To use, reheat from frozen.
Serves 4–5

Pork fillet with sage

2 pork fillets, 350 g (12 oz) each
200 ml (7 fl oz) dry white wine
60 ml (4 tbsp) soured cream
salt and freshly ground pepper
chopped fresh parsley to garnish

For the stuffing
225 g (8 oz) streaky bacon, rinded and minced
100 g (4 oz) fresh white breadcrumbs
75 g (3 oz) skinned and finely chopped onion
25 g (1 oz) butter, diced
30 ml (2 tbsp) chopped fresh sage
30 ml (2 tbsp) chopped fresh parsley
salt and freshly ground pepper
1 egg, beaten

Cut two-thirds through the fillets, along the length. Open out and cover with non-stick paper. Bat out to an even thickness. Remove the paper.

Mix the stuffing ingredients and bind with the beaten egg. Spread the stuffing evenly over the fillets. Roll up from the long edge and tie with string at intervals along the length. Place in a roasting tin, join underneath, pour over the wine and season. Cover loosely with foil and cook in the oven at 190°C (375°F) mark 5 for 45 minutes. Remove the foil and cook for a further 20–30 minutes until lightly browned. Remove the string from the fillets and slice thickly.

Place in a warmed dish. Stir the soured cream into the pan juices and pour over. Garnish with parsley. Serve with sautéed button mushrooms.

Serves 6

Apple and mint stuffed lamb

1 medium leg of lamb, about 1.4 kg (3 lb) boned
25 g (1 oz) dripping

For the stuffing
50 g (2 oz) fresh white breadcrumbs
25 g (1 oz) shredded suet
salt and freshly ground black pepper
1 small onion, skinned and finely grated
1 large cooking apple, peeled, cored and finely grated
75 g (3 oz) chopped fresh mint
1 egg, beaten

In a bowl, mix the stuffing ingredients together and bind with the beaten egg. Stuff into the cavity of the lamb and sew up the lamb with a trussing needle and string. Melt the dripping in a roasting tin and place the meat in the centre. Cover with foil and roast in the oven at 200°C (400°F) mark 6 for 1½ hours. Remove the foil and continue

Pork fillet with sage

cooking for 30 minutes so the lamb will crisp and brown well.

Leek

To prepare
Leeks hold a surprising amount of dirt and grit between their layers. Trim the root end and top, leaving about 5–7.5 cm (2–3 in) of green top. Cut a slit through to the centre lengthways, or slice. Wash thoroughly under cold running water to remove all the grit. To use whole, trim and cut a short way down the outer leaves. Put them, leaf downwards, tightly packed, into a deep container full of cold water. Leave for at least 30 minutes.

Basic cooking
To boil, cook pieces or slices in boiling salted water or stock for 10–15 minutes. Drain well. If liked, reheat in melted butter and serve sprinkled with chopped fresh herbs.
To braise, blanch in boiling salted water for

5 minutes. Drain well. Fry a selection of root vegetables in butter, add the whole leeks, a bouquet garni and enough stock to cover. Bring to the boil and simmer the leeks gently for about 1 hour.
To steam, place sliced leeks in a steamer and cook for 5–7 minutes. Serve with butter and freshly ground black pepper.

Potato leek pie

700 g (1½ lb) potatoes, peeled
75 g (3 oz) butter
900 g (2 lb) leeks, trimmed and thinly sliced
salt and freshly ground pepper
150 ml (¼ pint) chicken stock
45 ml (3 level tbsp) flour
400 ml (¾ pint) milk
75 g (3 oz) Double Gloucester cheese, grated

Cut the potatoes into 0.5-cm ($\frac{1}{4}$-in) slices and blanch in boiling water for 4–5 minutes. Drain well. Melt half the butter and cook the leeks for 10 minutes. Arrange the potatoes and leeks in layers in a 2.3-litre (4-pint) ovenproof dish, seasoning between each layer. Pour the stock over the vegetables.

Melt the remaining butter in a pan, stir in the flour and cook for 2 minutes. Gradually stir in the milk and cook for 2 minutes. Stir in the cheese and seasoning and pour the sauce over the vegetables. Cook in the oven at 190°C (375°F) mark 5 for 1 hour.

Dressed leek and courgette salad

350 g (12 oz) courgettes, trimmed
275 g (10 oz) leeks, trimmed and diced

For the dressing
30 ml (2 tbsp) corn oil
15 ml (1 tbsp) white vinegar
1.25 ml ($\frac{1}{4}$ level tsp) dried oregano or marjoram
1.25 ml ($\frac{1}{4}$ level tsp) dried mixed herbs
1.25 ml ($\frac{1}{4}$ level tsp) onion salt
2.5 ml ($\frac{1}{2}$ tsp) chopped fresh chives
salt and freshly ground pepper

In a screwtop jar combine the oil, vinegar, herbs, onion salt, chives and seasoning. Leave to infuse for 30 minutes.

Cut the courgettes into 0.5-cm ($\frac{1}{4}$-in) slices. Blanch in boiling salted water for 2 minutes until tender but still crisp. Drain and pat dry with kitchen paper towel. Blanch the leeks in boiling salted water for about 2 minutes.

Drain well and add to the courgettes. Shake the dressing until creamy and pour over the vegetables while still warm. Toss lightly, then chill.

Leek and bacon pinwheels

25 g (1 oz) butter
175 g (6 oz) leeks, trimmed and sliced
350 g (12 oz) streaky bacon rashers, rinded and chopped
15 ml (1 level tbsp) flour
150 ml ($\frac{1}{4}$ pint) milk
4 large parsley sprigs, chopped
freshly ground black pepper

For the pastry
175 g (6 oz) self raising flour
pinch of salt
75 g (3 oz) shredded suet

Melt the butter in a large frying pan. Add the leeks and bacon and cook for about 10 minutes until the bacon is crisp. Stir in the flour and cook for 1 minute. Stir in the milk and parsley and bring to the boil. Season to taste. Allow to cool slightly.

Sift the flour and salt together. Add the suet and mix to a soft but manageable dough with water. Roll out to a 30.5-cm (12-in) square. Spread the leek mixture over the dough. Roll up like a Swiss roll. Cut the roll into 12 pieces. Place the slices in a 1.1-litre (2-pint) buttered ovenproof dish. Cover with kitchen foil and bake in the oven at 200°C (400°F) mark 6 for 1 hour. Turn out and serve with parsley sauce.

Lemon

To prepare
Lemons are usually used for garnish and decoration on both sweet and savoury dishes. Cut into thin slices or wedges by cutting into segments lengthways. Always remove the pips before using to garnish. For sliced lemons, the edge of each slice can be fluted by drawing a crenelling knife down the length of the lemon before slicing.

To make butterflies, cut thin slices of lemon and cut them in half. Cut each piece into quarters without cutting completely through the centre and open out.
To make twists, cut thin slices of lemon and cut into the centre of each slice. Open the lemon slice and twist the two ends in opposite directions. Place on the food to be garnished so as to hold the twist.

White fish with lemon crumble

4 white fish steaks
salt and freshly ground black pepper
30 ml (2 tbsp) vegetable oil
50 g (2 oz) butter
50 g (2 oz) fresh white breadcrumbs
grated rind and juice of 1 lemon
60 ml (4 tbsp) chopped fresh parsley
lemon wedges to garnish

Season the fish steaks and brush with oil. Cook under a hot grill for 10–15 minutes, turning once. Meanwhile, melt the butter in a small saucepan and fry the breadcrumbs until golden brown. Remove from the heat and stir in the lemon rind, lemon juice and parsley. Place the fish steaks on a warmed serving dish and sprinkle over the crumb mixture. Garnish with lemon wedges.

Lamb with lemon and walnuts

2 breasts of lamb
300 ml ($\frac{1}{2}$ pint) beef stock
15 ml (1 level tbsp) flour
juice of $\frac{1}{2}$ lemon
10 ml (2 level tsp) caster sugar
salt and freshly ground black pepper
dash of gravy browning
lemon slices to garnish

For the stuffing
50 g (2 oz) onions, skinned and thinly sliced
50 g (2 oz) mushrooms, thinly sliced
15 ml (1 tbsp) vegetable oil
175 g (6 oz) fresh white breadcrumbs
50 g (2 oz) walnut pieces, chopped
finely grated rind and juice of 1 lemon
30 ml (2 tbsp) chopped fresh parsley
salt and freshly ground black pepper
1 egg, beaten

Bone the lamb and trim off the skin and excess fat. Flatten out.

For the stuffing, cook the onions and mushrooms in the oil for 5 minutes, until soft. Stir in the breadcrumbs, walnuts, lemon rind and juice, parsley and seasoning. Bind with the beaten egg. Spread over the lamb and roll up each piece separately. Tie loosely. Place in a small roasting tin and pour around 150 ml ($\frac{1}{4}$ pint) of the stock. Cook in the oven at 180°C (350°F) mark 4 for about 1 hour, basting occasionally.

Slice the meat thickly and keep warm on a warmed serving plate. Pour the skimmed juices into a small pan. Blend the flour to a smooth paste with a little cooled stock and stir into the cooking juices with the rest of the stock, lemon juice, sugar and seasoning. Bubble for 5 minutes, stirring. Add a dash of gravy browning. Spoon the sauce over the meat and garnish with lemon slices.

NOT SUITABLE FOR FREEZING

Moroccan lemon chicken

Illusrated in colour facing page 65

1 lemon
60 ml (4 level tbsp) thick honey
pinch of turmeric
2.5 ml ($\frac{1}{2}$ level tsp) ground white pepper
2.5 ml ($\frac{1}{2}$ level tsp) mild curry powder
pinch of ground allspice
5 ml (1 level tsp) salt
300 ml ($\frac{1}{2}$ pint) water
30 ml (2 tbsp) vegetable oil
8 chicken drumsticks
200 ml (7 fl oz) chicken stock

Halve the lemon lengthways and cut into thin slices, discarding the pips. Mix 30 ml (2 tbsp) of the honey with the turmeric, pepper, curry powder, allspice and salt. Add the lemon slices, cover and marinate overnight. The next day, simmer the lemon with the marinade and the water in a tightly covered pan for 1 hour, or until really tender.

Heat the oil in a frying pan. Add the remaining honey and the drumsticks and fry over a moderate heat, turning frequently, for 15–20 minutes, until a rich dark brown. Stir in the lemon mixture and stock. Bring to the boil, cover and simmer for 15–20 minutes. Adjust the seasoning, adding more honey if necessary. Serve with potatoes boiled in their jackets and leaf spinach.

NOT SUITABLE FOR FREEZING

Lemon jelly marmalade

Illustrated in colour facing page 65

6 thin-skinned, juicy lemons, thinly sliced
1.7 litres (3 pints) water
sugar

Put the lemons in a pan with the water and any pips. Bring to the boil and simmer for about 1$\frac{1}{2}$ hours. Strain through a jelly bag.

Lemon jelly marmalade

Measure the juice and return to the pan with 450 g (1 lb) of sugar to each 600 ml (1 pint) of juice. Stir to dissolve the sugar over a low heat, then bring to the boil and boil rapidly until setting point is reached. Skim, pot and cover in the usual way.

Lemon and apple flan

For the pastry
150 g (5 oz) plain flour
pinch of salt
75 g (2½ oz) butter or block margarine
25 g (1 oz) caster sugar
finely grated rind of 1 lemon
30 ml (2 tbsp) lemon juice

For the filling
2 eggs, beaten
100 g (4 oz) caster sugar
grated rind of 1 lemon
275 (10 oz) cooking apple, peeled, cored and grated
45 ml (3 tbsp) lemon juice

For the pastry, sift the flour and salt into a bowl and rub in the fat. Stir in the sugar and lemon rind and bind to a light dough with about 30 ml (2 tbsp) lemon juice. Roll out

the dough and use to line an 18-cm (7-in) deep fluted flan ring. Bake blind in the oven at 190°C (375°F) mark 5 for 10–15 minutes.

For the filling, beat the eggs and sugar together. Add the lemon rind, apple and lemon juice and mix well. Pour into the flan case and bake in the oven at 190°C (375°F) mark 5 for 30–35 minutes or until set and lightly browned. Serve warm with custard or chilled with whipped cream.

To freeze: chill, wrap and freeze. To use, thaw, loosely covered, at room temperature for about 4 hours, or reheat from frozen in the oven at 200°C (400°F) mark 6 for about 25 minutes to serve hot.

Lemon sorbet

175 g (6 oz) sugar
600 ml (1 pint) water
grated rind and juice of 4 lemons
2 egg whites, stiffly whisked
mint sprigs to decorate

Put the sugar and water in a saucepan and heat gently until the sugar dissolves. Bring to the boil and boil for 10 minutes. Remove the saucepan from the heat, add the lemon rind and juice and leave until cold. Pour into a polythene container or freezing tray and freeze until half frozen and slushy.

Turn into a bowl and fold in the stiffly whisked egg whites. Return to the polythene container and freeze until firm.

Serve spoonfuls of sorbet in glass dishes, decorated with mint sprigs.

Lemon curd

grated rind and juice of 4 lemons
4 large eggs, beaten
100 g (4 oz) butter
450 g (1 lb) sugar

Put all the ingredients into the top of a double boiler or in a heatproof basin standing in a pan of simmering water. Heat, stirring continuously, until the sugar has dissolved and the curd thickens – and do make sure that it is really thick. Pour into small, sterilised jars and cover as for jam.

Note: make this in small quantities only, as

above, as it will keep for only about 1 month. Store in a cool place. (Freezer-stored it will keep for up to 3 months.)

Variation

Use 175 ml (6 fl oz) PLJ lemon juice in-stead of the fresh lemon juice as above. The grated rind of a fresh lemon may be added with the other ingredients to give an extra tang, but this is optional. Cook and store as above.

Makes about 900 g (2 lb)

Lettuce

To prepare

To retain its flavour and texture, lettuce should be treated carefully. Trim the base of the stalk and discard any damaged, dis-colored or wilting outside leaves. Separate the remaining leaves and wash in a bowl of cold water. Dry the leaves thoroughly, prefer-ably in a salad basket, or shake them in a clean towel. This is particularly important if the lettuce is to be coated in a dressing, as dressing will only cling to dry leaves. If the lettuce is a little wilted, transfer to a polythene bag or container and chill in the bottom of the refrigerator for about 30 minutes. If the leaves need to be shredded for a recipe, tear them coarsely; do not cut them with a knife as this damages the leaves.

Basic cooking

The crisper leaves give the best results when cooked. A good way to cook them is in the Chinese stir-fried style.

To stir-fry, heat 15–30 ml (1–2 tbsp) vege-table oil or 25–50 g (1–2 oz) butter in a large saucepan. Add whole leaves and sauté over a very high heat, stirring continuously, for 2–3 minutes until the lettuce is just beginning to soften. Season and serve immediately.

To braise, trim the lettuce, removing the outer leaves if necessary. Wash thoroughly but leave whole. Blanch in boiling salted water for 1 minute; drain. Fry a chopped onion in 25 g (1 oz) butter for 10 minutes. Add the lettuce with chopped parsley, seasoning and 150 ml ($\frac{1}{4}$ pint) chicken stock. Cover and simmer gently for 20–25 minutes, until tender. Place the lettuce on a heated serving dish. Reduce the stock by half by boiling rapidly and pour over the lettuce.

Lettuce in cream sauce

25 g (1 oz) butter
1 clove garlic, skinned
1 Webb or cos lettuce, shredded
30 ml (2 tbsp) chopped fresh parsley
150 ml ($\frac{1}{4}$ pint) single cream
salt and freshly ground pepper
50 g (2 oz) cooked ham, chopped
chopped fresh chives or parsley to garnish

Melt the butter in a large pan, add the garlic, lettuce and parsley and cook over a high heat for 1–2 minutes, stirring. Remove the clove of garlic, reduce the heat and stir in the cream, seasoning and ham. Reheat gently, stirring occasionally. Turn the lettuce into a warmed serving dish and sprinkle with chives or parsley.

Individual tuna coleslaws

1 red-skinned eating apple, cored and sliced
1 green-skinned eating apple, cored and sliced
15 ml (1 tbsp) lemon juice
1 Webb or cos lettuce, shredded
2 medium carrots, peeled and grated
2 stalks celery, trimmed and sliced
198-g (7-oz) can tuna fish, roughly flaked
50 g (2 oz) walnuts, chopped

For the dressing
1 egg yolk
1.25 ml ($\frac{1}{4}$ level tsp) salt
freshly ground black pepper
2.5 ml ($\frac{1}{2}$ level tsp) dry mustard
pinch of caster sugar
150 ml ($\frac{1}{4}$ pint) salad or olive oil
15 ml (1 tbsp) lemon juice

Put the apple slices in a bowl of water with the lemon juice added to prevent discolora-tion. Put the lettuce in a large bowl. Stir in the carrots, celery, tuna and walnuts. Reserve four slices of red and green apple and add the rest to the bowl. Mix well.

For the dressing, beat together the egg yolk, seasoning, mustard and sugar in a bowl until thick. Add the oil, a little at a time, whisking vigorously between each addition. Stir in the lemon juice. Add the dressing to the salad ingredients and mix well. Place the coleslaw in four individual salad bowls and decorate each with one green and one red slice of apple.

Marrow

To prepare
Wash the outside skin and, if very thick, peel thinly. Cut in half lengthways if the marrow is to be stuffed, or cut into smaller pieces. Scoop out the seeds and centre fibres unless the marrow is very young. Cut into 2.5-cm (1-in) cubes or slices. If preferred, place the pieces of marrow in a colander or sieve and sprinkle liberally with salt. Leave to drain for about 30 minutes. Rinse well under cold water and pat dry with kitchen paper towel.

Basic cooking
Marrow may be cooked for a few minutes in boiling salted water, but for best results either fry or steam.
To fry, cook prepared marrow in a large covered pan with 25–50 g (1–2 oz) butter for 5–10 minutes until tender but still crisp.
To steam, place marrow pieces in a steamer and cook for 20–40 minutes according to size.

Marrow in cider

25 g (1 oz) butter
1 medium onion, skinned and chopped
1 cooking apple, peeled, cored and chopped
1 marrow, about 900 g (2 lb), peeled, seeded and diced
150 ml ($\frac{1}{4}$ pint) dry cider
2.5 ml ($\frac{1}{2}$ level tsp) salt
freshly ground black pepper
15 ml (1 level tbsp) cornflour

Melt the butter in a large saucepan, add the onion and fry gently for 5 minutes until soft but not browned. Stir in the apple, marrow, cider and seasoning. Cover and simmer gently for 10–15 minutes. Blend the cornflour with a little water and add to the marrow. Bring to the boil, stirring, to thicken the sauce. Spoon into a warmed serving dish.

Marrow with herby tomato sauce

1 marrow, about 900 g (2 lb), peeled, sliced and seeded
150 ml ($\frac{1}{4}$ pint) chicken stock
6 tomatoes, skinned and sliced
5 ml (1 level tsp) dried mixed herbs
5 ml (1 level tsp) salt
freshly ground black pepper
15 ml (1 level tbsp) cornflour

Place the marrow in a large saucepan with the stock, tomatoes, herbs and seasoning. Cover and simmer gently for 10–15 minutes until the marrow is tender. Blend the cornflour with a little water in a small bowl and add to the pan. Bring to the boil, stirring, to thicken the sauce. Place in a warmed serving dish.

Marrow and tomato au gratin

450 g (1 lb) marrow, peeled, seeded and chopped
salt and freshly ground pepper
450 g (1 lb) tomatoes, skinned
5 ml (1 level tsp) dried mixed herbs
5 ml (1 level tsp) dry mustard
5 ml (1 tsp) water
150 ml ($\frac{1}{4}$ pint) natural yogurt
175 g (6 oz) Gouda cheese, grated
1 egg yolk

Cook the marrow in boiling salted water for 10 minutes, until tender. Drain very well and keep warm. Put the tomatoes in a saucepan. Add the herbs and boil uncovered to give a thick pulp. Cream the mustard with the water. Put the yogurt, 75 g (3 oz) of the cheese, the egg yolk, mustard and seasoning in a saucepan. Beat together, then cook gently until the mixture thickens.

Arrange a ring of marrow around the edge

of a warm 900-ml (1½-pint) ovenproof dish. Fill the bottom with half the remaining marrow pieces. Season well. Add 40 g (1½ oz) of the cheese in an even layer. Top with the remaining marrow. Season and add the remaining cheese. Spoon the hot tomato mixture over. Pour about half the yogurt sauce over the tomatoes. Grill to heat through and brown the topping. Serve the extra yogurt sauce with each portion.

Marrow chutney

1.4 kg (3 lb) marrow, peeled, seeded and chopped
salt
225 g (8 oz) shallots, skinned and sliced
225 g (8 oz) apples, peeled, cored and sliced
12 peppercorns
100 g (4 oz) dried whole root ginger
225 g (8 oz) sultanas
100 g (4 oz) demerara sugar
900 ml (1½ pints) malt vinegar

Put the marrow pieces in a bowl and sprinkle liberally with salt. Cover and leave for 12 hours. Drain well and place in a pan with the shallots and apples. Tie the peppercorns and ginger in muslin. Put in the pan with the sultanas, sugar and vinegar. Bring to the boil, reduce the heat and simmer uncovered until the consistency is thick, with no free liquid. Remove the muslin bag. Pot and cover.
Makes about 1.8 kg (4 lb)

Danish stuffed marrow rings

1 marrow, about 900 g (2 lb), peeled
175 g (6 oz) fresh white breadcrumbs
150 g (5 oz) Danish blue cheese, crumbled
4 spring onions, trimmed and chopped
50 g (2 oz) walnuts, chopped
salt and freshly ground black pepper
1 egg, beaten
600 ml (1 pint) tomato sauce (see page 106)
watercress to garnish

Cut the marrow into eight rings and remove the seeds. Place the marrow rings in the bottom of a large ovenproof dish. Mix together the breadcrumbs, cheese, onion, nuts and seasoning. Bind together with the egg. Fill the centres of the marrow rings with the stuffing. Pour the tomato sauce around the marrow. Cover and bake in the oven at 190°C

(375°F) mark 5 for 55–60 minutes until the marrow is tender. Place the marrow rings on a heated serving dish and pour the sauce around. Garnish with watercress.

Spiced marrow and beef supper

50 g (2 oz) dried red kidney beans, soaked overnight
1 large marrow, peeled, seeded and diced
25 g (1 oz) beef dripping
1 large onion, skinned and chopped
450 g (1 lb) minced beef
30 ml (2 level tbsp) tomato paste
5 ml (1 level tsp) salt
freshly ground pepper
15 ml (1 level tbsp) cornflour

For the marinade
15 ml (1 tbsp) wine vinegar
15 ml (1 tbsp) vegetable oil
2.5 ml (½ level tsp) chilli powder
1.25 ml (¼ level tsp) ground cumin
1.25 ml (¼ level tsp) ground cardamom
1.25 ml (¼ level tsp) turmeric
2.5 ml (½ level tsp) ground ginger
60 ml (4 tbsp) dry red wine
15 ml (1 tbsp) Worcestershire sauce
15 ml (1 tbsp) lemon juice

Drain the kidney beans. Mix the marinade ingredients together and pour over the marrow in a large bowl. Cover and leave in the refrigerator for 30 minutes.

Heat the dripping in a large saucepan and fry the onion for 5 minutes, until soft. Add the mince and fry for a further 5 minutes. Stir in the tomato paste, seasoning, kidney beans, marrow and the marinade. Bring to the boil, then cover and simmer gently for 35–40 minutes.

Mix the cornflour to a smooth paste with a little cold water and stir into the marrow mixture. Cook for 2–3 minutes until thickened. Serve with boiled rice or pasta.

Marrow and ginger jam

1.8 kg (4 lb) peeled and seeded marrow, prepared weight
1.8 kg (4 lb) sugar
25 g (1 oz) root ginger, bruised
thinly pared rind and juice of 3 lemons

Cut the marrow into pieces about 1 cm (½ in) square. Place in a basin, sprinkle with about

450 g (1 lb) of the sugar and leave overnight. Next day, bruise the ginger with a weight to release the flavour and tie in muslin with the lemon rind. Place in a pan with the marrow and lemon juice. Simmer for 30 minutes, then add the rest of the sugar and boil gently until the marrow looks transparent and setting point is reached. Remove the muslin bag, then pot and cover in the usual way.
Makes about 2.7–3 kg (6–6½ lb)

ᴄMelon

To prepare
Cut the melon in half, scoop out the seeds and discard. To serve melon as a starter, cut the flesh from the skin with a small sharp knife and cut into sections crossways. Leave the skin underneath the flesh. Serve with sugar and ginger, topped with an orange slice and cherry on a cocktail stick. For melon cocktails as a starter or for dessert, cut balls of melon flesh from the two halves with a parisienne cutter.

Melon with jellied blackberries

1.4-kg (3-lb) ripe honeydew melon, halved
  lengthways and seeded
600 ml (1 pint) raspberry jelly tablet
225 g (8 oz) fresh blackberries

Strain the melon seeds and reserve any melon juice. Make the melon juice up to 175 ml (6 fl oz) with water. Dissolve the jelly tablet in the melon juice and water and chill until just on the point of setting. Spoon the blackberries through the jelly and turn into the

Melon with jellied blackberries

melon halves. Chill until completely set. Cut into wedges and serve.
Serves 4–6

Spiced melon with dates

1 honeydew melon, halved and seeded
350 g (12 oz) slice of watermelon, seeded
50 g (2 oz) stoned dates
300 ml (½ pint) sweet white wine
1 lemon
3 whole cloves
pinch of ground cinnamon
50 g (2 oz) caster sugar

Using a parisienne cutter or baller, scoop out the honeydew and watermelon flesh and place in a bowl. Add the dates to the bowl and pour over the wine. Cut four 2.5-cm (1-in) strips from the lemon rind and place in the bowl with the cloves. Sprinkle over the cinnamon and sugar, cover and chill for 1–2 hours. Just before serving, remove the cloves and lemon rind.

Melon and pear compote

100 g (4 oz) granulated sugar
300 ml (½ pint) water
60 ml (4 tbsp) Kirsch
45 ml (3 tbsp) lemon juice
4 large ripe pears
1 medium ripe honeydew melon

Dissolve the sugar in the water in a shallow pan. Bring to the boil and add the Kirsch and strained lemon juice. Peel, quarter, core and slice the pears into the syrup. Cover and poach gently for about 20 minutes until tender.

Meanwhile, divide the melon into eighths and discard the seeds. Remove the flesh from the skin in one piece and cut across into thin slices. Place in a large mixing bowl. While still hot, pour the pears with their syrup over

the melon and mix well together. Cool, cover and chill well, preferably overnight.
NOT SUITABLE FOR FREEZING
Serves 6

Honeydew ice-cream with melon balls

450 g (1 lb) honeydew melon, peeled and seeded
150 ml (¼ pint) milk
50 g (2 oz) caster sugar
2 eggs, beaten
15 ml (1 tbsp) port or sweet sherry
150 ml (¼ pint) double cream, whipped
green food colouring
225 g (8 oz) watermelon, seeded

Purée the honeydew melon flesh in an electric blender or rub through a sieve. Heat the milk and sugar in a saucepan, remove from the heat and pour over the eggs. Return the egg custard to the pan and continue cooking for 2–3 minutes until the custard thickens. Strain and leave to cool. Add the port or sherry, melon purée, whipped cream and a few drops of green food colouring to the cooled custard. Pour into a freezing tray and freeze until mushy. Turn out and whisk until smooth. Return to the tray and re-freeze.

Meanwhile, using a parisienne cutter or baller, cut the watermelon into balls. To serve, scoop out the ice-cream and place in individual dishes with a few watermelon balls. Serve immediately.

ℳilk

To prepare
Store the milk, covered, in the refrigerator or a cool place until required. Keep well away from any strong smelling foods.

Basic cooking
To scald, pour the milk into a saucepan, bring to the boil, stirring, and cool immediately.
White sauce, melt 20 g (¾ oz) butter in a saucepan, add 30 ml (2 level tbsp) flour and stir with a wooden spoon until smooth. Cook over a gentle heat for 1–2 minutes, stirring, until the mixture (called a roux) begins to bubble. Remove from the heat and gradually add 300 ml (½ pint) milk, stirring after each addition to prevent lumps forming. Bring the sauce to the boil, stirring continuously, and when it has thickened, cook for a further 1–2 minutes. Season to taste.

Bacon toad in the hole

225 g (8 oz) flour
2 eggs
300 ml (½ pint) milk
300 ml (½ pint) water
350 g (12 oz) lean hock or collar bacon
50 g (2 oz) fresh white breadcrumbs
15 ml (1 level tbsp) tomato paste
2.5 ml (½ tbsp) tomato paste
2.5 ml (½ tsp) Worcestershire sauce
45 ml (3 tbsp) chopped fresh parsley
freshly ground black pepper
25 g (1 oz) lard or dripping

Sift the flour and beat in the eggs, with the milk and water. Beat until the batter is smooth. If preferred this can be done in an electric blender. Finely mince the bacon and mix with the breadcrumbs, tomato paste, Worcestershire sauce, parsley and pepper to taste, no salt. Form the mixture into 8 similar sized balls.

Bacon toad in the hole

Heat the lard or dripping in a shallow, round 23-cm (9-in) metal dish. Place the bacon balls evenly apart in the dish. Bake in the oven at 200°C (400°F) mark 6 for 15 minutes. Loosen the bacon balls but leave in place. Pour the batter into the hot fat around the bacon. Return to the oven for about a further 45 minutes, until well-risen and golden.

NOT SUITABLE FOR FREEZING

Cheesy leek pancakes

For the pancakes
225 g (8 oz) flour
pinch of salt
2 eggs
300 ml ($\frac{1}{2}$ pint) milk

For the filling
900 g (2 lb) leeks, trimmed and sliced
25 g (1 oz) butter
25 g (1 oz) flour
300 ml ($\frac{1}{2}$ pint) milk
75 g (3 oz) cheese, grated
salt and freshly ground pepper
watercress to garnish

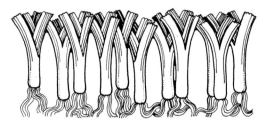

Make the pancake batter by sifting the flour and salt together into a bowl. Beat in the eggs and half of the milk. Add the rest of the milk and mix in well. Cook 8 pancakes and keep warm.

For the filling, cook the leeks in boiling salted water for about 10–15 minutes until tender but still firm. Drain well. Melt the butter, add the flour and cook for 1 minute. Remove from the heat and gradually stir in the milk. Bring to the boil and simmer for 2 minutes. Add the cheese to the sauce and stir well. Season and add the leeks. Divide the hot filling between the pancakes. Roll up and place on a large warmed serving dish. Serve garnished with watercress.

Mushroom

To prepare
Mushrooms should never be washed as they absorb water quickly and lose their delicate flavour and firm texture. If they are dirty, wipe them carefully with a damp cloth. Peel large mushrooms only if really necessary, as much of the flavour is in the skin. Trim the stalk base only as this contains much of the flavour.

Basic cooking
To poach, cook in a little salted water, with a squeeze of lemon juice added to keep the mushrooms really white, for 3–5 minutes, then drain thoroughly.

To sauté, cook in butter, with a little lemon juice added, in an uncovered pan for 5–10 minutes until golden brown.

To steam, place whole or sliced mushrooms in a steamer and cook for 5–10 minutes.

Mushroom salad in lemon dressing

450 g (1 lb) button mushrooms, sliced
15 ml (1 level tbsp) capers
1 small onion, skinned and chopped

For the dressing
90 ml (6 tbsp) vegetable oil
45 ml (3 tbsp) wine vinegar
grated rind and juice of 1 lemon
15 ml (1 level tbsp) French mustard
30 ml (2 level tbsp) chopped fresh parsley
salt and freshly ground pepper

Mix together in a large bowl the mushrooms, capers and onion. For the dressing, in a small bowl beat together the oil and vinegar. Add the lemon rind, lemon juice, French mustard, parsley and seasoning. Mix well, pour over the mushrooms and toss in the dressing. Place in a serving dish and chill for 30 minutes.

Pickled mushrooms

450 g (1 lb) young mushrooms, stalks removed
vinegar
2 blades mace
2.5 ml ($\frac{1}{2}$ level tsp) white pepper
5 ml (1 level tsp) salt
5 ml (1 level tsp) ground ginger
$\frac{1}{4}$ onion, skinned and chopped

Wash the mushrooms in salted water and
drain well. Place in a pan. Add sufficient
vinegar to cover and stir in the remaining ingredients. Cook slowly, on top of the stove or
in the oven at 170°C (325°F) mark 3, until
the mushrooms are quite tender and have
shrunk. Lift them out, put into jars and pour
the hot vinegar over. Cover as usual.
Makes 450 g (1 lb)

Mushroom and chicken savoury

40 g (1$\frac{1}{2}$ oz) butter
1 medium onion, skinned and chopped
450 g (1 lb) button mushrooms, sliced
25 g (1 oz) flour
400 ml ($\frac{3}{4}$ pint) milk
5 ml (1 level tsp) dried mixed herbs
salt and freshly ground black pepper
450 g (1 lb) cooked chicken meat, diced
450 g (1 lb) mashed potatoes
1.25 ml ($\frac{1}{4}$ level tsp) grated nutmeg
100 g (4 oz) Gruyère cheese, grated

Melt 25 g (1 oz) of the butter in a large saucepan and fry the onion for 5 minutes. Add the
mushrooms and cook for 2 minutes, then remove from the pan. Stir in the flour and
cook for 3 minutes. Remove from the heat
and gradually stir in the milk. Return to the
heat and bring to the boil, stirring. Add the
mushrooms, onion, mixed herbs, seasoning
and chicken.

Beat the remaining butter into the potatoes
with the nutmeg and 75 g (3 oz) of the
cheese. Pipe or spoon the potato mixture
around the edge of an ovenproof dish. Spoon
the mushroom and chicken sauce into the
centre of the dish. Sprinkle over the remaining cheese. Bake in the oven at 190°C (375°F)
mark 5 for 25–30 minutes, until heated
through and golden brown.

Mushroom quiche

210-g (7$\frac{1}{2}$-oz) packet frozen puff pastry, thawed
300 ml ($\frac{1}{2}$ pint) single cream
4 egg yolks
salt and freshly ground pepper
225 g (8 oz) button mushrooms, sliced
1 clove garlic, skinned and crushed

Roll out the dough and use to line a 23-cm
(9-in) plain flan ring. Beat together the cream,
egg yolks and seasoning. Stir in the mushrooms and garlic and pour into the flan
case. Bake in the oven at 230°C (450°F)
mark 8 for 10 minutes. Reduce the oven
temperature to 190°C (375°F) mark 5 and
continue baking for 20–25 minutes until the
pastry is golden and the filling set. Serve hot
with a mixed salad.
Serves 6

Onion

To prepare
Cut the stalk end from the onion and peel
away the outer skin. To chop, cut the onion
in half lengthways and place, cut side down,
on a work surface. Make four or five cuts,
towards the root but not through it, hori-
zontally and vertically, and then finally slice.
The onion will fall into even size dice,

Basic cooking
Where onion is used as a flavouring in soup,

casseroles or stews, it should first be fried in
vegetable oil or butter to soften.
To fry, fry sliced onions in hot oil or butter
for 5–10 minutes until golden brown. Drain
on kitchen paper towel.
To boil, cook whole onions in boiling salted
water for 30–40 minutes. Drain and serve
with butter or white sauce (see page 77),
if liked.
To braise, fry chopped carrot and celery in
25 g (1 oz) butter. Add whole onions to the

79

pan with enough stock to cover. Simmer gently for 30–40 minutes.

To bake, leave the skin on the onions and bake in the oven at 180°C (350°F) mark 4 for 1–1½ hours. Serve with butter, if liked.

To steam, place in a steamer and cook whole onions for 40 minutes and sliced onion for 15 minutes.

Spanish onion salad

450 g (1 lb) Spanish onions, skinned and thinly
   sliced
3 stalks celery, trimmed and sliced
30 ml (2 tbsp) chopped fresh mint
15 ml (1 tbsp) chopped fresh parsley
225 g (8 oz) Cheddar cheese, cubed
50 g (2 oz) seedless raisins
1 red apple, cored and diced
1 green apple, cored and diced
15 ml (1 tbsp) lemon juice

For the dressing
90 ml (6 tbsp) vegetable oil
45 ml (3 tbsp) cider vinegar
salt and freshly ground pepper
2.5 ml (½ level tsp) sugar
2.5 ml (½ level tsp) dry mustard

Blanch the onions in boiling water for 2–3 minutes. Drain and plunge into cold water until cool. Drain. Stir the onions, celery and herbs together.

   Place the dressing ingredients in a screw-top jar and shake until well blended. Pour over the onion mixture and toss gently. Cover and leave in the refrigerator for about 30 minutes. Stir in the cheese, raisins, apples and lemon juice just before serving.

Beef stuffed onions

6 even-sized onions, about 175 g (6 oz) each,
   skinned
30 ml (2 tbsp) vegetable oil
50 g (2 oz) red pepper, seeded and finely chopped
10 ml (2 level tsp) hot Madras curry powder
5 ml (1 level tsp) ground cardamom
350 g (12 oz) minced beef
40 g (1½ oz) fresh white breadcrumbs
30 ml (2 tbsp) chopped fresh parsley
5 ml (1 level tsp) salt
freshly ground pepper

Cut a slice from the top of each onion. Remove the centre of each, leaving a 'shell'

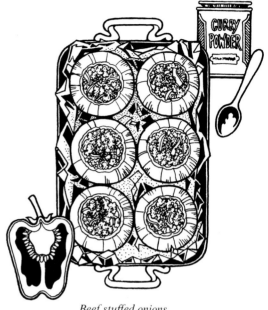

Beef stuffed onions

about 1 cm (½ in) thick. Finely chop 50 g (2 oz) of the scooped-out onion (the rest may be used in another dish). Heat the oil and fry the chopped onion gently for 5 minutes. Add the red pepper with the spices and cook for 2 minutes. Add the mince and cook for 5 minutes. Add the breadcrumbs, parsley and seasoning. Spoon the mince mixture into the onion shells. Place on a large sheet of foil and fold over to enclose, sealing the ends. Steam for 45 minutes or until tender. Serve with soured cream spooned over, if wished.

Rich rabbit and onion casserole

1 rabbit, jointed
300 ml (½ pint) dry cider
150 g (5 oz) prunes
100 g (4 oz) streaky bacon, in one piece
25 g (1 oz) butter
225 g (8 oz) button onions, skinned
30 ml (2 level tbsp) flour
150 ml (¼ pint) chicken stock
salt and freshly ground pepper
1 large cooking apple

Place the rabbit in a bowl and pour the cider

Prawn stuffed tomatoes (page 104), Cucumber and mint salad (page 59), Chunky beef with celery (page 51).

over. Cover the prunes with water. Leave both to soak overnight.

Drain and dry the rabbit, reserving the marinade. Drain and stone the prunes. Cut the bacon into 2-cm (¾-in) dice. Melt the butter in a frying pan and fry the rabbit with the bacon and onions for 10 minutes, until brown. Place in a casserole. Stir the flour into the fat and cook for 1 minute. Gradually blend in the stock and cider marinade and simmer for 3 minutes. Season and pour over the rabbit. Cover and cook in the oven at 150°C (300°F) mark 2 for 1–1½ hours.

Half an hour before the end of cooking time, peel, core and slice the apple and add with the prunes to the casserole. Cover and continue cooking. Garnish with triangles of fried bread.
Serves 4–6

Pickled onions

Choose small, even-sized onions; the silver-skin kinds are best. Place, without skinning, in a brine made from 450 g (1 lb) salt to every 4.5 litres (1 gallon) of water. Leave for 12 hours. Skin, then cover with fresh brine and leave for a further 24–36 hours. Remove the onions from the brine and drain thoroughly. Pack into jars or bottles and cover with cold spiced vinegar. Cover in the usual way. Leave for 3 months before using.

Orange

To prepare
Slices of orange complete with skin are often used as garnish for sweet or savoury dishes. Segments of orange free from all white pith and skin are used in both sweet and savoury recipes. Cut a slice with a small sharp knife from the top and bottom of the orange to reveal the flesh. Stand the orange on a flat surface with one cut side down. Using a downward movement cut away the skin complete with the pith, curving the knife to the shape of the orange. Place the orange in the palm of the hand and cut out each segment by inserting the knife between the flesh and membrane – on both sides of each section. Remove all pips.

Orange and pork duchesse

700 g (1½ lb) pork fillet
60 ml (4 tbsp) vegetable oil
225 g (8 oz) leeks, trimmed and sliced
45 ml (3 level tbsp) flour
300 ml (½ pint) dry cider
300 ml (½ pint) chicken stock
2 large oranges
salt and freshly ground black pepper
900 g (2 lb) potatoes, peeled
150 ml (¼ pint) creamy milk

Cut the pork into 1-cm (½-in) pieces and fry in hot oil in a heavy based pan for 5 minutes until golden brown. Remove from the pan. Fry the leeks in the oil for 5 minutes until golden brown. Stir in the flour, cider and stock. Finely grate in the rind of both oranges and season to taste. Bring to the boil, replace the meat, cover and simmer gently for about 1¼ hours or until the meat is tender.

Orange and pork duchesse

Potato crusted chilli pie (page 93), Parsnip and carrot purée (page 83), Turnips braised with bacon (page 106).

Meanwhile, boil the potatoes, drain and mash with the milk. Keep warm. Remove the pith from the oranges with a serrated knife and slice thinly. Spoon the meat into a 1.7-litre (3-pint) shallow oven-proof dish. Pipe the potato on top, leaving space in the centre for a garnish of orange slices. Cook gently under a hot grill until golden brown. Garnish with the orange slices.
Serves 6

Glazed orange cheesecake

Illustrated in colour facing page 65

225 g (8 oz) digestive biscuits, crushed
100 g (4 oz) butter or block margarine, melted
225 g (8 oz) cream cheese
2 large thin-skinned oranges
50 g (2 oz) caster sugar
2 large eggs, separated
15 g ($\frac{1}{2}$ oz) powdered gelatine
200 ml ($\frac{1}{3}$ pint) water
300 ml ($\frac{1}{2}$ pint) whipping cream
75 g (3 oz) granulated sugar

Mix the biscuits with the melted fat. Press into the bottom of a 23-cm (9-in) loose-bottomed flan tin.

Beat the cheese thoroughly to soften. Add the finely grated rind and strained juice of one orange with the caster sugar and egg yolks and beat well. Dissolve the gelatine in 60 ml (4 tbsp) of the water in a heatproof bowl over a pan of hot water. Fold into the cheese mixture. Whip the cream and fold in. Beat the egg whites until stiff and fold in. Pour into the crumb shell and chill until set. Remove from the tin.

Meanwhile, thinly slice the second orange. Place the granulated sugar and remaining water in a large pan. Heat gently to dissolve the sugar and then bring to the boil. Add the orange slices, cover and poach gently until the peel is tender (about 50 minutes). When the orange is cool, drain and use to decorate the cake. Boil down the syrup to a glaze

and brush over the orange. Chill well before serving.
Serves 6–8

Seville orange marmalade

1.4 kg (3 lb) Seville oranges
90 ml (6 tbsp) lemon juice
3.4 litres (6 pints) water
2.7 kg (6 lb) sugar

Wash and halve the oranges. Squeeze out the juice and tie the pips and any loose pulp in muslin. Slice the peel thinly or thickly as preferred. Place the peel in a pan with the orange juice, lemon juice, pips and water. Simmer gently for about 2 hours or until the peel is soft and the contents of the pan reduced by about half.

Remove the muslin bag, squeezing well into the pan. Add the sugar and stir until dissolved. Boil rapidly until setting point is reached. Leave to stand for about 15 minutes, to prevent peel rising in the jars. Stir gently, then pot and cover in the usual way.
Makes about 4.5 kg (10 lb)

Whole fruit method

(For ingredients and yield, see Orange Marmalade above). Wash the fruit, then place in a saucepan with the water. Cover and simmer gently for about 2 hours until a fork pierces the peel easily. Remove the fruit from the pan, cool a little, then cut it up with a knife and fork. Tie the pips in muslin and return them to the liquid in the saucepan. Add the lemon juice and boil for 5 minutes.

Put the cut-up fruit in a preserving pan and add the liquid from the saucepan, discarding the muslin bag. Boil off the excess liquid until the contents weigh 2 kg ($4\frac{1}{2}$ lb). Add the sugar, stir until dissolved, then bring to the boil and boil rapidly until setting point is reached. Cool for about 15 minutes. Stir gently to distribute the peel before potting and covering in the usual way.

Parsnip

To prepare

Trim the top and bottom of each parsnip and peel thinly. Leave young parsnips whole. Cut large, old ones into slices or quarters and cut out the core if it is woody.

Basic cooking

To boil, place prepared parsnips in a pan with cold salted water. Bring to the boil and simmer for 10–15 minutes. Drain and toss in melted butter.

To roast, place prepared parsnips in a pan with cold salted water. Bring to the boil, cook for 1–2 minutes and drain. Place around a roasting joint of meat or in a roasting tin with dripping and cook at 200°C (400°F) mark 6 for 40 minutes.

To sauté, blanch as above and sauté in melted butter for 10–12 minutes until golden brown.

To steam, place sliced parsnips in a steamer and cook for 10 minutes.

Buttered parsnips with nutmeg

450 g (1 lb) parsnips, peeled and quartered
40 g (1½ oz) butter
salt and freshly ground black pepper
1.25 ml (¼ level tsp) grated nutmeg
chopped fresh parsley to garnish

Cook the parsnips in a saucepan of boiling salted water for 10–15 minutes until tender. Drain well and return to the pan. Add the butter, seasoning and nutmeg and toss well. Place in a warmed serving dish and garnish with parsley.

Sautéed parsnip straws

450 g (1 lb) parsnips, peeled
seasoned flour
50 g (2 oz) dripping
chopped fresh chives to garnish

Thinly slice the parsnips and cut into thin sticks. Toss in the seasoned flour. Melt the dripping in a large frying pan and gently fry the parsnip straws for 10–12 minutes until golden brown and crisp. Drain on kitchen paper towel. Place in a warmed serving dish and sprinkle with chives.

Parsnip and carrot purée

Illustrated in colour facing page 81

700 g (1½ lb) parsnips, peeled and sliced
700 g (1½ lb) carrots, peeled and sliced
50 g (2 oz) butter
salt and freshly ground black pepper
1.25 ml (¼ level tsp) grated nutmeg
chopped fresh parsley to garnish

Cook the parsnips and carrots in a large saucepan of boiling salted water for 45 minutes, until very tender. Drain well, return to the pan and mash. Add the butter, seasoning and nutmeg. Cook over a high heat, stirring frequently, to drive off any moisture. Spoon the vegetable purée into a warmed serving dish and garnish with chopped parsley.

Parsnip and almond loaf

450 g (1 lb) parsnips, peeled
25 g (1 oz) butter
1 large onion, skinned and finely chopped
175 g (6 oz) fresh white breadcrumbs
75 g (3 oz) blanched almonds, chopped
salt and freshly ground pepper
3 eggs, beaten
300 ml (½ pint) milk

Cut the parsnips into 0.5-cm (¼-in) dice and cook in boiling salted water for 5 minutes. Drain well. Melt the butter in a pan and fry the onion for 5 minutes. Stir the parsnips, onion, breadcrumbs, almonds, seasoning, eggs and milk together. Turn the mixture into a greased 900-g (2-lb) loaf tin and cook in the oven at 180°C (350°F) mark 4 for about 1½ hours, until set and golden brown.

Pea

To prepare

Shell peas, discarding any blemished or discoloured ones, and wash under cold running water.

Basic cooking

To boil, cook in lightly salted boiling water, with a sprig of fresh mint added, for 10–15 minutes until just tender. Drain well and add a knob of butter, if liked.

To steam, place peas in a steamer and cook for 3–5 minutes until just tender.

Peas in parsley cream sauce

450 g (1 lb) shelled peas
300 ml (½ pint) chicken stock
5 ml (1 level tsp) sugar
salt and freshly ground black pepper
15 ml (1 tbsp) lemon juice
15 ml (1 level tbsp) cornflour
30 ml (2 tbsp) water
60 ml (4 tbsp) double cream
45 ml (3 tbsp) chopped fresh parsley
15 ml (1 tbsp) brandy
chopped fresh parsley to garnish

Simmer the peas gently in the stock with the sugar, seasoning and lemon juice for 10–15 minutes until tender. Mix the cornflour to a smooth paste with the water. Stir into the peas and continue cooking until the liquid thickens. Add the cream, parsley and brandy and cook for 2 minutes. Serve garnished with chopped parsley.

Chilled chicken and pea mousse

Illustrated in colour facing page 48

25 g (1 oz) powdered gelatine
45 ml (3 tbsp) water
450 g (1 lb) cooked peas, mashed
225 g (8 oz) cooked chicken meat, minced
300 ml (½ pint) chicken stock
90 ml (6 tbsp) single cream
150 ml (¼ pint) mayonnaise
2 eggs, separated
salt and freshly ground black pepper
juice of 1 lemon
1.25 ml (¼ level tsp) ground mace
watercress, 25 g (1 oz) cooked peas and lemon
   slices to garnish

Dissolve the gelatine in the water and cool.

In a bowl mix together the peas, chicken and stock. Stir together the single cream, mayonnaise, egg yolks, seasoning, lemon juice and mace and stir into the chicken mixture. Stir in the cooled gelatine. Whisk the egg whites until stiff and fold into the pea mixture. Pour into a 1.1-litre (2-pint) ring mould and leave to set.

Turn out on to a flat serving plate and garnish the centre with watercress. Place the peas around the base of the mousse with the lemon slices.
Serves 6

Layered lamb and pea bake

450 g (1 lb) shelled peas
5 ml (1 level tsp) sugar
15 g (½ oz) butter
2 onions, skinned and chopped
900 g (2 lb) shoulder of lamb, minced
5 ml (1 tsp) chopped fresh rosemary
salt and freshly ground black pepper
25 g (1 oz) flour
150 ml (¼ pint) chicken stock

For the sauce
25 g (1 oz) butter
25 g (1 oz) flour
568 ml (1 pint) milk
100 g (4 oz) Cheddar cheese, grated
salt and freshly ground pepper
5 ml (1 level tsp) dry mustard

For the topping
grated Parmesan cheese

Simmer the peas with the sugar in boiling salted water for 10–15 minutes. Drain and reserve. Melt the butter in a pan, add the onions and fry for 5 minutes until soft. Stir in the minced lamb, rosemary and seasoning and cook for 5 minutes until brown. Drain off any excess fat. Stir in the flour and cook for 2 minutes. Add the stock, bring to the boil and cook for 5 minutes.

For the sauce, melt the butter in a pan, add the flour and cook for 1–2 minutes. Gradually stir in the milk, bring to the boil and cook for 2–3 minutes. Remove from the heat and add the Cheddar cheese, seasoning and mustard.

Place half the peas in the bottom of an ovenproof dish and top with half the lamb mixture. Pour over half the cheese sauce.

Layer the remaining peas and lamb and pour over the remaining sauce. Sprinkle with Parmesan cheese. Bake in the oven at 190°C (375°F) mark 5 for 40–45 minutes, until the top is golden brown.
Serves 4–6

Peach

To prepare
The furry skin of the peach is quite unpleasant to eat and should be removed. Immerse the peaches in a bowl of boiling water for 1–2 minutes. Plunge immediately into cold water, then drain. The skin will peel away quite easily. Cut the flesh away from the stone either into segments or cut in half.

Basic cooking
To poach, peaches that are not quite ripe can be used for fruit salads, sweets, etc., if poached in a sugar syrup for 5–10 minutes. Place 150 ml ($\frac{1}{4}$ pint) water in a saucepan with 25–50 g (1–2 oz) sugar and bring to the boil. Simmer gently until the sugar has dissolved, then add the skinned and sliced or halved peaches. Poach for 5–10 minutes.

Nut meringue with peach compote

200 g (7 oz) icing sugar, sifted
3 egg whites
100 g (4 oz) blanched almonds, chopped
450 g (1 lb) peaches, skinned, stoned and sliced
150 ml ($\frac{1}{4}$ pint) water
10 ml (2 level tsp) sugar
45 ml (3 tbsp) brandy
10 ml (2 level tsp) arrowroot
300 ml ($\frac{1}{2}$ pint) double cream
60 ml (4 tbsp) milk

Line two baking sheets with non-stick paper, then draw twelve 7.5-cm (3-in) circles well apart.

Place the icing sugar and egg whites in a deep heatproof bowl over a saucepan of hot water. Whisk for 5–10 minutes until the mixture forms stiff peaks. Remove from the heat and fold in the nuts. Spoon or pipe the meringue on to the circles on the non-stick paper. Cook in the oven at 150°C (300°F) mark 2 for about 30 minutes, until crisp on the outside and cream-coloured. Cool for a few minutes, then carefully slide off the paper on to a wire rack.

Put the peaches in a saucepan with any juice, the water, sugar and brandy. Bring to the boil gently and simmer for 2 minutes. Blend the arrowroot to a smooth paste with a little cold water, stir into the peaches and continue cooking until the liquid is clear. Remove from the heat and chill well.

Whip the cream and milk together until stiff enough to hold its shape. Pipe a border of cream around each meringue and serve the peach compote separately.
Serves 6

Peach jam

This preserve has a light set.

1 lemon
1.8 kg (4 lb) peaches, skinned, quartered and stoned
400 ml ($\frac{3}{4}$ pint) water
1.2 kg ($2\frac{3}{4}$ lb) white sugar
450 g (1 lb) demerara sugar

Halve the lemon and squeeze out the juice. Cut up the peel and tie in muslin. Put the peaches, lemon juice and peel into a pan with the water. Bring to the boil, then simmer for 30–45 minutes until tender. Remove the muslin bag, squeezing well. Add the sugars and stir until dissolved. Bring to the boil and boil rapidly until setting point is reached. Stir once more, then pot and cover in the usual way.
Makes about 2.7 kg (6 lb)

Peach syllabub

150 ml ($\frac{1}{4}$ pint) dry white wine
75 g (3 oz) caster sugar
30 ml (2 tbsp) lemon juice
10 ml (2 tsp) finely grated lemon rind
6 ripe peaches, skinned, stoned and sliced
300 ml ($\frac{1}{2}$ pint) double cream

Combine the wine, sugar, lemon juice and rind together in a large basin. Add the peaches and marinate for several hours.

Drain the peaches and reserve the marinade. Divide the peach slices between 6–8 stemmed glasses. Add the cream to the wine marinade and whisk until thick enough to stand in peaks. Spoon over the peaches. Serve on the day of making.
Serves 6–8

Pear

To prepare
Carefully cut away the peel with a small sharp knife or potato peeler and place in water with 15 ml (1 tbsp) lemon juice added to prevent discoloration while preparing other pears. Cut each pear in half, then in quarters and cut out the core and stalk. For pear halves, cut out the stalk with a small knife and carefully scoop out the core with a teaspoon.

Basic cooking
To poach, place 300 ml ($\frac{1}{2}$ pint) water in a saucepan with 50–75 g (2–3 oz) sugar. Bring to the boil and simmer gently until the sugar has dissolved. Add the prepared pears and simmer very gently for 5–10 minutes until tender.

Chicken and pear casserole

Illustrated in colour facing page 32

1.4-kg (3-lb) roasting chicken
30 ml (2 tbsp) vegetable oil
1 large onion, skinned and sliced
210-g (7$\frac{1}{2}$-oz) can prunes
450 g (1 lb) Conference pears, peeled, quartered and cored
30 ml (2 level tbsp) flour
1 chicken stock cube
150 ml ($\frac{1}{4}$ pint) dry white wine
grated rind of 1 lemon
salt and freshly ground pepper

Trim and wipe the chicken and cut into quarters. Heat the oil in a large frying pan and brown the chicken pieces. Drain and place in a shallow casserole. Fry the onion in the reheated oil for 5 minutes until transparent. Drain and add to the chicken. Reserve the juices in the pan.

Drain the prunes, reserve the can syrup and make it up to 150 ml ($\frac{1}{4}$ pint) with water. Spoon the prunes and pears over the chicken. Stir the flour into the pan juices and cook for 1–2 minutes. Add the crumbled stock cube, prune syrup mixture and wine. Bring to the boil, stirring and cook for 1–2 minutes. Add the lemon rind, adjust the seasoning and pour over the chicken. Cover and cook in the oven at 190°C (375°F) mark 5 for about 1 hour.

Pear and walnut pie

75 g (3 oz) self raising flour
75 g (3 oz) plain flour
pinch of salt
50 g (2 oz) caster sugar
100 g (4 oz) butter, at room temperature
50 g (2 oz) walnuts, grated
1 egg yolk
few drops vanilla essence
15 ml (1 tbsp) water
45 ml (3 level tbsp) semolina
grated rind and juice of 1 small orange
25 g (1 oz) demerara sugar
900 g (2 lb) ripe eating pears, peeled, halved and cored
few walnut halves
warm golden syrup

Sift the flours and salt into a basin. Add the sugar, butter, grated walnuts, egg yolk, essence and the water. Work to a soft dough with the fingertips. Chill to a manageable consistency.

Roll out half the dough and use to line a 23-cm (9-in) china fluted flan dish. Sprinkle the bottom with 15 ml (1 tbsp) of the semolina. Combine the remaining semolina with the orange rind and juice and demerara sugar. Reserve 6 pear halves. Chop the re-

Pear and walnut pie

maining fruit and scatter over the bottom of the flan case. Arrange the pear halves on top, spoon the orange mixture over and top with the remaining dough.

Bake in the oven at 200°C (400°F) mark 6 for 50–60 minutes. (Cover the pastry edges with foil when a golden brown.) Fill the centre with walnut halves and glaze with syrup. Serve warm, not hot, with whipped cream flavoured with orange rind.
Serves 6

Pear mayonnaise

99-g (3½-oz) can tuna steak, drained
1 stalk celery, trimmed and diced
1 large spring onion, trimmed and diced
150 ml (¼ pint) thick mayonnaise
30 ml (2 tbsp) white vinegar
freshly ground black pepper
2 ripe eating pears, halved and cored
1 small lettuce, washed
2 tomatoes, sliced

Flake the tuna into a basin. Add the celery, onion, 60 ml (4 tbsp) of the mayonnaise and 15 ml (1 tbsp) of the vinegar and season to taste with black pepper. Mix well. Cut a small slice from the skin side of each pear to ensure

the pears sit flat on the plate. Pile the tuna mixture in the centre hollow. Combine the remaining mayonnaise and vinegar and spoon over the tuna. Serve the pear halves garnished with lettuce and tomato and hand round brown bread and butter separately.

Pears brûlée with orange cream

thinly pared rind and juice of 1 large juicy orange
50 g (2 oz) caster sugar
300 ml (½ pint) water
4 firm ripe eating pears, peeled, halved and cored
30 ml (2 level tbsp) soft brown sugar
5 ml (1 level tsp) arrowroot
25 g (1 oz) butter
150 ml (¼ pint) double cream

Boil the orange rind strips in water until soft. Drain. Place the caster sugar in a saucepan with the measured water and heat gently until the sugar has dissolved. Bring to the boil, then reduce the heat and simmer gently. Place the pears in the syrup, cover and simmer gently for about 10 minutes until tender.

Remove the pears from the syrup and place, cut sides down, in a flameproof dish. Sprinkle with the soft brown sugar and grill quickly until the sugar melts. Meanwhile, add the orange juice to the syrup and reduce by boiling to 150 ml (¼ pint). Reserve 45 ml (3 tbsp) of the syrup and chill. Blend the arrowroot to a smooth paste with a little cold water, add to the remaining syrup and boil until clear. Stir in the butter, then pour over the pears and chill.

Place the cream and reserved orange syrup in a bowl and whisk until it holds its shape. Spoon over the pears and decorate with the orange rind strips.

Pear and lemon chutney

1.8 kg (4 lb) pears, peeled, cored and chopped
450 g (1 lb) onions, skinned and chopped
350 g (12 oz) seedless raisins, chopped
50 g (2 oz) preserved stem ginger, chopped
grated rind and juice of 2 lemons
225 g (8 oz) brown sugar
30 ml (2 level tbsp) salt
1.1 litres (2 pints) vinegar
2 cloves garlic, skinned and crushed
6 dried chillies, crushed
4 whole cloves

Place the pears, onions, raisins, ginger, lemon rind and juice, sugar, salt and vinegar in a preserving pan. Tie the garlic, chillies and cloves in a muslin bag. Add to the pan. Bring to the boil and simmer gently until no free liquid remains – about 2 hours. Pot in the usual way with vinegar-proof covers.
Makes 1.8 kg (4 lb)

Pear jam

1.4 kg (3 lb) cooking or firm eating pears, peeled,
  cored and chopped
thinly pared rind of 1½ lemons
150 ml (¼ pint) water
45 ml (3 tbsp) lemon juice
600 g (1 lb 5 oz) sugar

Put the pear cores and peel in a saucepan with the lemon rind and water and boil for 10 minutes. Strain and return the liquid to the pan with the pear flesh and lemon juice. Simmer gently until the pears are tender. Add the sugar, stir over a low heat until dissolved, and bring to the boil. Boil until setting point is reached. Pot and cover in the usual way.
Makes about 900 g–1.1 kg (2–2½ lb)

Pepper

To prepare
For salads, peppers are more digestible if skinned. Place the peppers under a hot grill and cook until the skin is charred all over. Plunge into cold water, then rub off the skin.

Cut the stalk end off the pepper and, if stuffing, cut out the seeds and membrane. If the pepper is to be sliced or diced, cut in half lengthways to scoop out the seeds more easily.

Basic cooking
Peppers are usually added to casseroles, vegetable dishes, sauces etc.
To steam, place whole peppers in a steamer and cook for 12 minutes.

Sautéed peppers in soured cream

25 g (1 oz) butter
2 medium onions, skinned and sliced
1 clove garlic, skinned and crushed
2 red peppers, seeded and sliced
2 green peppers, seeded and sliced
5 ml (1 level tsp) salt
freshly ground black pepper
75 ml (5 level tbsp) soured cream

Melt the butter in a large saucepan, add the onion and garlic and fry gently for 3 minutes.

Add the peppers and seasoning, cover and cook for 15 minutes. Stir in the soured cream and heat for a further minute. Place in a warmed serving dish.

Fiesta peppered chicken

4 chicken portions, skinned
salt and freshly ground black pepper
25 g (1 oz) flour
45 ml (3 tbsp) vegetable oil
2 large onions, skinned and sliced
1 clove garlic, skinned and crushed
225 g (8 oz) green pepper, seeded and diced
225 g (8 oz) red pepper, seeded and diced
50 g (2 oz) smoked ham, chopped
4 tomatoes, skinned and sliced
30 ml (2 level tbsp) tomato paste
300 ml (½ pint) chicken stock
8 black olives, halved and stoned

Coat the chicken joints in seasoned flour. Heat the vegetable oil in a large frying pan and fry the chicken for 5 minutes until brown on all sides. Remove the chicken and place in a casserole. Add the onions, garlic, green and red pepper, ham, tomatoes, tomato paste and seasoning to the frying pan. Fry gently for 8–10 minutes. Stir in any remaining flour, then add the stock. Bring to the boil, stirring.

Pour over the chicken. Cover and cook in the oven at 180°C (350°F) mark 4 for 1–1½ hours until the chicken is tender. Sprinkle over the olives and serve.

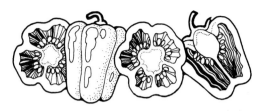

Spiced pepper chutney

3 red peppers, seeded and finely chopped or minced
3 green peppers, seeded and finely chopped or minced
450 g (1 lb) tomatoes, quartered
350 g (12 oz) onions, skinned and chopped
450 g (1 lb) cooking apples, peeled, cored and
  chopped
225 g (8 oz) demerara sugar
5 ml (1 level tsp) ground allspice
400 ml (¾ pint) malt vinegar
5 ml (1 level tsp) peppercorns
2.5 ml (½ level tsp) mustard seed

Place the peppers in a preserving pan with the tomatoes, onions, apples, sugar, allspice and vinegar. Tie the peppercorns and mustard seed in a piece of muslin. Add to the pan. Bring to the boil and simmer un-covered for about 1½ hours over a moderate heat until soft and pulpy. Pot as usual, after removing the muslin bag.
Makes about 1.6 kg (3½ lb)

Pineapple

To prepare
Cut off the leaf top and cut the pineapple into 1-cm (½-in) slices, crossways. Using a small sharp knife cut away the skin from each slice, removing all the woody eyes. Cut the core from each slice with a small pastry or cocktail cutter.
For a pineapple shell, cut the pineapple in half lengthways, complete with leaves. Scoop out the flesh; cut out the core and discard. Brush the inside of the shell with lemon juice to prevent discoloration. Add the pineapple flesh to a fruit cocktail or ice-cream and serve in the pineapple shells.

Pineapple in caramel syrup

450 g (1 lb) caster sugar
2.5-cm (1-in) vanilla pod
1 large pineapple
15 ml (1 tbsp) Kirsch
4 glacé cherries and toasted flaked almonds to
  decorate

Place the sugar in a saucepan with 200 ml (8 fl oz) water and the vanilla pod. Heat gently until the sugar has dissolved, then bring to the boil. Remove the vanilla pod and continue boiling the syrup until a deep caramel colour.

Remove from the heat and slowly add 150 ml (¼ pint) warm water, stirring. Return to the heat to dissolve the caramel. Pour into a bowl and cool.

Cut the pineapple into eight slices. Remove the hard centre core of each slice using an apple corer or a small pastry cutter. Arrange the slices in a serving dish. Add the Kirsch to the cooled caramel syrup and pour over the pineapple. Chill for 2 hours. Just before serving sprinkle with cherries and flaked almonds.
Serves 4–6

Pineapple mint frappé

225 g (8 oz) sugar
400 ml (¾ pint) water
1 ripe medium pineapple
150 ml (¼ pint) Freezomint crème de menthe
  liqueur

Dissolve the sugar in the water in a saucepan, bring slowly to the boil and boil uncovered for 5 minutes. Leave to cool. Peel the pine-apple, discard the core and purée the flesh in an electric blender to give 350 g (12 oz). Add to the syrup with the crème de menthe. Blend well and pour into an ice-cube tray without dividers. Freeze until the mixture has started to set round the edges.

Beat well, return to the freezer and continue to freeze until the frappé is firm. To serve, scoop out with a spoon into stemmed glasses.
Serves 6–8

Pineapple bûché

1 ripe medium pineapple
75-g (2⅔-oz) packet macaroons
300 ml (½ pint) whipping or double cream
30 ml (2 tbsp) Kirsch
pistachio nuts to decorate

Cut away the top and base of the pineapple. Carefully cut away the skin, removing the 'eyes'. Cut the pineapple in half lengthways and remove the central core. Cut each half into six 'half-moon' slices. Reserve the leaf top.

Roughly crush the macaroons. Whip together the cream and Kirsch until it just holds its shape. Reserve one-third of the cream and stir the macaroons into the remaining two-thirds. Spread each slice of pineapple with the macaroon cream and arrange on a serving dish, pressing them together to form a 'log'. Finish each end with a slice of pineapple. Use the remaining cream to coat the 'log'. Using a knife, mark out diamond shapes over the cream and decorate the centre of each with a sliver of pistachio nut. Refrigerate for 2–3 hours before serving. Decorate each end of the log with the leaf top sliced into two.
Serves 4–6

Pineapple jam

1.4 kg (3 lb) pineapple flesh, shredded
400 ml (¾ pint) water
45 ml (3 tbsp) lemon juice or 5 ml (1 level tsp) citric or tartaric acid
1.1 kg (2½ lb) sugar

Put the pineapple in a pan with the water and lemon juice or acid and simmer for 45 minutes–1 hour, until the pineapple is tender and the water has almost evaporated. Add the sugar and, when dissolved, bring to the boil. Boil for 10–12 minutes or until setting point is reached. Pot and cover in the usual way.
Makes about 1.8 kg (4 lb)

Plum

To prepare

Remove the stalks and wash the fruit. Remove the stone from each plum by cutting around the middle. The plum will separate if very ripe and the stone can be removed. If under-ripe, the stone may not be removable until after cooking.

Basic cooking

To poach, place the prepared fruit in a saucepan with water to cover the bottom of the pan and 25–50 g (1–2 oz) sugar to taste. Cover, bring to the boil and simmer gently for 10–15 minutes. Remove any stones that come to the surface of the juice.

Plum almond crisp

100 g (4 oz) plain flour
50 g (2 oz) rice flour
75 g (3 oz) caster sugar
100 g (4 oz) butter or margarine, softened
50 g (2 oz) trifle sponges, crumbled
10 ml (2 level tsp) ground ginger
700 g (1½ lb) ripe plums, halved and stoned
whole blanched almonds
175 g (6 oz) plum jam

Combine the flours and sugar together. Rub in the butter or margarine until the mixture resembles fine breadcrumbs. Lightly butter a 28 × 15 cm (11 × 6 in) ovenproof dish. Press the rubbed-in crumbs onto the bottom. Blend the cake crumbs with the ground ginger and sprinkle over the pressed-in mixture. Place the plums on the crumbs, cut sides up. Place an almond on each. Bake uncovered in the oven at 200°C (400°F) mark 6 for about 50 minutes.

Heat the jam in a saucepan, sieve if necessary and brush over the fruit to glaze. Allow to cool before serving just warm, with pouring cream.
Serves 6

Choux puffs with plum rum sauce

For the choux pastry
50 g (2 oz) butter
150 ml ($\frac{1}{4}$ pint) water
65 g (2$\frac{1}{2}$ oz) flour
25 g (1 oz) caster sugar
2 eggs
oil for deep frying
icing sugar

For the sauce
100 g (4 oz) granulated sugar
600 ml (1 pint) water
700 g (1$\frac{1}{2}$ lb) eating plums, stoned and quartered
15 ml (1 level tbsp) cornflour
90 ml (6 tbsp) rum
30 ml (2 tbsp) lemon juice
4 firm bananas, chopped

For the choux pastry, melt the butter in the water and bring to the boil. Remove the pan from the heat and add all the flour and sugar at once. Beat until the paste is smooth. Cool. Beat in the eggs a little at a time. Spoon the paste into a piping bag fitted with a medium star vegetable nozzle and chill while making the sauce.

For the sauce, dissolve the granulated sugar in the water and fast boil for 1–2 minutes. Add one third of the plums and purée in an electric blender or rub through a sieve. Blend the cornflour with the rum and lemon juice, add to the puréed plums and bring to the boil to thicken, stirring. Add the rest of plums and the bananas. Keep warm.

Heat the oil for deep frying to 182°C (360°F). Pipe 3.5-cm (1$\frac{1}{2}$-in) lengths of the choux dough into the oil. Fry, in about three batches, for 2–3 minutes, turning once, until puffed and golden. Drain on kitchen paper

towel and keep warm. To serve, dredge with icing sugar and accompany with the sauce.
Serves 6

Creamy plum tart

For the pastry
200 g (7 oz) plain flour
100 g (4 oz) butter
50 g (2 oz) caster sugar
grated rind of 1 lemon
1 egg yolk

For the filling
450 g (1 lb) plums, halved and stoned
2 eggs, beaten
150 ml ($\frac{1}{4}$ pint) double cream
100 g (4 oz) caster sugar
caster sugar to decorate

For the pastry, place the flour in a bowl and rub in the butter until the mixture resembles fine breadcrumbs. Stir in the sugar and lemon rind. Add the egg yolk and enough cold water to mix to a soft dough. Cover and leave to relax in the refrigerator or cold place for 30 minutes.

Roll out the dough and use to line a 25.5-cm (10-in) fluted flan ring. Leave to relax for 20 minutes, then bake blind in the oven at 190°C (375°F) mark 5 for 25 minutes.

For the filling, place the plums in the flan, cut sides up. Beat the eggs into the double cream with the sugar and pour into the flan case. Return to the oven to bake for 25–30 minutes until set. Serve warm or cold, sprinkled with caster sugar.
Serves 6–8

Crunchy plum trifle

450 g (1 lb) plums, halved and stoned
60 ml (4 tbsp) water
15 g ($\frac{1}{2}$ oz) powdered gelatine
150 g (5 oz) caster sugar
300 ml ($\frac{1}{2}$ pint) cold custard
30 ml (2 tbsp) sherry
175 g (6 oz) macaroons
150 ml ($\frac{1}{4}$ pint) double cream, whipped
little grated chocolate to decorate

Place the plums in a pan with 15 ml (1 tbsp) of the water, cover and simmer gently for 10–15 minutes until soft. Purée in an electric blender or rub through a sieve. Cool.

Dissolve the gelatine in the remaining water and cool. Stir the sugar, custard and sherry into the plum purée and fold in the cooled gelatine. Place the plum mixture in a refrigerator or cool place until beginning to set.

Meanwhile, crumble the macaroons and place in the bottom of a serving dish. Pour over the plum mixture and leave to set completely in the refrigerator. When set, spread the cream over the top in swirls and sprinkle with grated chocolate.

Plum syllabub

Illustrated in colour facing page 32

450 g (1 lb) plums, halved and stoned
100 g (4 oz) caster sugar
150 ml (¼ pint) water
30 ml (2 tbsp) brandy
2 egg whites
300 ml (½ pint) double cream, whipped

Place the plums in a pan with the sugar and water. Stir over a gentle heat to dissolve the sugar, then cover and simmer gently until very soft and pulpy. Rub the plums through a sieve. Cool the puréed fruit completely. When cold, stir in the brandy.

Reserve 30 ml (2 level tbsp) of the purée for decoration. Whisk the egg whites until stiff but not dry and fold evenly into the remaining plum purée with the cream. Turn into between 6–8 stemmed glasses or a bowl. Using a teaspoon, trail a little of the reserved plum purée over the fruit. With the handle of the spoon swirl into a feather pattern. Chill.
Serves 6–8

Plum jam

2.7 kg (6 lb) plums, halved and stoned
900 ml (1½ pints) water
2.7 kg (6 lb) sugar

Crack some of the plum stones and remove the kernels. Put the plums, kernels and water in a pan and simmer gently for about 30 minutes until really soft and well reduced. Add the sugar, stir until dissolved, then boil rapidly until setting point is reached. Pot and cover in the usual way.

If preferred, you can cook the plums without stoning. In this case, remove the stones when they come to surface as the jam boils.
Makes about 4.5 kg (10 lb)

Potato

To prepare
Where possible, scrub the potatoes and cook in their skins. Either serve in the skin or remove after cooking. If the skin must be removed, scrape early or new potatoes and thinly peel maincrop potatoes. Cut large potatoes into smaller pieces or slice or dice, or do this after cooking.

Basic cooking
To boil, early or new potatoes, place in cold salted water with a sprig of fresh mint. Bring to the boil and cook for 10–15 minutes, according to size.

For maincrop potatoes, scrub or peel and cut larger potatoes into smaller pieces. Place in cold salted water, bring to the boil and cook for 15–20 minutes, according to size.
To mash, cook as above, then mash to a

smooth purée with a fork or potato masher. Season, return to a low heat and dry for 2–3 minutes, stirring.

To cream, cook as above and mash to a smooth purée with a fork or potato masher. Beat in a knob of butter, a little hot milk and seasoning. Reheat over a low heat, beating until fluffy.

To roast, peel the potatoes thinly and cut into even-sized pieces. Place in cold salted water, bring to the boil and cook for 2–3 minutes. Drain thoroughly. Heat lard or dripping in a roasting tin in the oven at 220°C (425°F) mark 7. Add the potatoes, baste with the fat and cook in the oven for about 45 minutes, until golden brown. Turn once or twice during cooking. Alternatively, cook the potatoes around the roasting joint for the same length of time.

To bake, choose even-sized potatoes. Scrub well, dry and prick all over with a fork. Brush the skins with oil or melted butter. Bake near the top of the oven at 200°C (400°F) mark 6 for 1–1¼ hours until tender when pierced with a knife. Cut a cross in the top, or cut large ones in half lengthways. Serve topped with a large knob of butter or spoonful of soured cream.

To sauté, boil the potatoes for 15 minutes until they are just cooked. Drain, remove the skins and cut into 0.5-cm (¼-in) slices. Fry slowly in hot butter or oil until golden brown and crisp on both sides. Drain well on kitchen paper towel and sprinkle with salt.

To deep fry (chips or French fries), peel potatoes thinly and cut into 0.5–1 cm (¼–½ in) slices and then into 0.5–1 cm (¼–½ in) sticks. Place in cold water and leave for at least 30 minutes to remove the excess starch. Drain well and pat dry. Heat the oil or lard to 190°C (375°F) in a deep fat fryer. If you haven't a thermometer, test by dropping in a chip. It should rise to the surface immediately and be surrounded with bubbles. Quarter fill the basket with prepared chips, lower into the oil, cover immediately and cook for 6–7 minutes, until just beginning to colour. Remove the basket from the pan, shake to remove excess fat and drain the chips on kitchen paper towel. Proceed until all the chips have been 'blanched'. Reheat the oil and fry the same quantity for 3 minutes, until golden brown and crisp. Drain well. Repeat until all the chips are cooked. Serve sprinkled with salt.

French style potatoes

900 g (2 lb) potatoes, peeled and sliced
30 ml (2 level tbsp) Dijon mustard
30 ml (2 level tbsp) chopped chives
300 ml (½ pint) milk or chicken stock
salt and freshly ground pepper
25 g (1 oz) butter, melted

Layer half the potato slices in a casserole. Combine the mustard, chives, milk or stock and seasonings. Pour half of this mixture over the potatoes. Add the remaining potatoes and pour over the rest of the mustard mixture. Brush melted butter over the surface of the potatoes. Season with salt and pepper. Cover and cook in the oven at 180°C (350°F) mark 4 for 1¾ hours.
Serves 6

Potato crusted chilli pie

Illustrated in colour facing page 81

900 g (2 lb) cooked lamb or beef
1 large onion, skinned and chopped
60 ml (4 tbsp) vegetable oil
5 ml (1 level tsp) mild chilli powder
30 ml (2 level tbsp) flour
400 ml (¾ pint) thick gravy
5 ml (1 level tsp) salt
freshly ground black pepper
432-g (15¼-oz) can red kidney beans, drained
396-g (14-oz) can tomatoes, drained
900 g (2 lb) medium even-sized potatoes
50 g (2 oz) butter, melted

Discard all the gristle and fat from the meat and mince. Fry the onion in the oil in a saucepan for 5 minutes, until soft. Add the chilli powder and flour and cook for 2–3 minutes. Mix in the gravy and seasoning, bring to the boil and simmer for 10–15 minutes. Add the minced meat and kidney beans and turn into an ovenproof dish. Arrange the tomatoes in a layer over the mince mixture.

Parboil the potatoes in their skins for 15 minutes. Skin and slice and arrange over the surface of the meat mixture. Brush with the melted butter and cook in the oven at 200°C (400°F) mark 6 for 30–40 minutes, until golden.

Note: if you have no gravy, use an extra 30 ml (2 level tbsp) flour and 400 ml (¾ pint) beef stock, adding more oil if necessary.

Raspberry

To prepare
Remove the hulls and wash carefully. If storing in the refrigerator, leave unwashed.

Basic cooking
To poach, place 450 g (1 lb) prepared raspberries in a saucepan with water to cover the bottom of the pan and 50–75 g (2–3 oz) sugar to taste. Cover the pan, bring to the boil and simmer gently for 10–15 minutes until tender. Rub through a sieve to purée and remove the pips.

Raspberry shortcake gâteau

275 g (10 oz) plain flour
50 g (2 oz) ground rice
100 g (4 oz) caster sugar
finely grated rind of 1 lemon
225 g (8 oz) butter
50 g (2 oz) walnuts, finely chopped
1 egg yolk
300 ml (½ pint) double cream
450 g (1 lb) raspberries, hulled
icing sugar

Place the flour, ground rice, caster sugar and lemon rind in a large mixing bowl and rub in the butter until the mixture resembles fine breadcrumbs. Add the walnuts and egg yolk and knead together to form a soft dough. Wrap in polythene and chill for 30 minutes.

Roll out two-thirds of the dough to form a rectangle 30.5 × 15 cm (12 × 6 in) and place carefully on a baking sheet. Mark in half lengthways. Roll out the remaining dough and cut into six 7.5-cm (3-in) rounds with a fluted pastry cutter. Cut each round in half. Place on another baking sheet. Bake in the oven at 180°C (350°F) mark 4, allowing 30 minutes for the rectangle and 20 minutes for the semi-circles, until all are light golden and firm. While the rectangle is still warm break it in half lengthways. Cool.

Whip the cream until stiff. Pipe two-thirds of the cream down the centre of one rectangle of shortbread. Arrange most of the raspberries over the cream. Place the second rectangle of shortbread on top and press down lightly. Pipe the remaining cream in whirls down the centre. Arrange the semi-circles along the cream and place whole raspberries in between. Sprinkle with icing sugar.
Serves 6

Fresh raspberry caramel

12 small macaroon biscuits
60 ml (4 tbsp) medium dry sherry
4 ripe bananas
30 ml (2 level tbsp) caster sugar
350 g (12 oz) raspberries, hulled
300 ml (½ pint) soured cream
soft dark brown sugar

Place the macaroons to cover the bottoms of four individual flameproof dishes. Spoon the sherry over the biscuits and allow to absorb. Mash the bananas and caster sugar together. Divide half the raspberries between the dishes and top with the banana mixture. Cover with the remaining berries. Stir the soured cream and spoon evenly over the raspberries. Sprinkle generously with brown sugar. Place under a hot grill and cook for 5 minutes to caramelize the sugar. Serve immediately.
Serves 4

Raspberry whirls

225 g (8 oz) raspberries, hulled
75 g (3 oz) granulated sugar
300 ml (½ pint) water
600-ml (1-pint) raspberry jelly tablet
150 ml (¼ pint) crushed ice or iced water
15–30 ml (1–2 tbsp) lemon juice
150 ml (¼ pint) double cream
grated chocolate

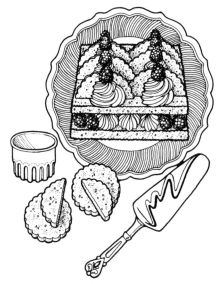

Raspberry shortcake gâteau

94

Poach the fruit gently with the sugar and water. Divide the jelly into cubes and dissolve in the hot fruit mixture. While still warm, purée in an electric blender with the crushed ice or iced water. Strain through a nylon sieve and add lemon juice to taste. Cool the mixture until almost set, then whisk well to make it light and airy. Turn into four tall glasses. Swirl a little unwhipped cream through each and refrigerate until set. Decorate with the remaining cream, whipped, and coarsely grated chocolate.

To freeze: wrap and freeze before decorating.

To use, leave at room temperature about 3 hours, then decorate.

Raspberry jam

1.8 kg (4 lb) raspberries, hulled
1.8 kg (4 lb) sugar

Simmer the raspberries very gently in their own juice for about 15–20 minutes or until really soft. Add the sugar, stir until dissolved, then boil rapidly until setting point is reached. Pot and cover in the usual way.
Makes about 2.7–3.2 kg (6–7 lb)

Redcurrant

To prepare
Remove the berries from the stalks and wash carefully in cold water. Drain well.

Basic cooking
To poach, place the prepared redcurrants in a saucepan with water to cover the bottom of the pan and 50–100 g (2–4 oz) sugar to taste. Cover, bring to the boil and simmer gently for 5–10 minutes until tender.

Redcurrant griestorte

3 large eggs, separated
100 g (4 oz) caster sugar
grated rind and juice of $\frac{1}{2}$ lemon
50 g (2 oz) fine semolina
15 ml (1 level tbsp) ground almonds
150 ml ($\frac{1}{4}$ pint) double cream
15 ml (1 tbsp) milk
100–175 g (4–6 oz) redcurrants
icing sugar, sifted

Grease and line a 33 × 23-cm (13 × 9-in) Swiss roll tin. Dust with caster sugar and flour. Whisk the egg yolks and sugar together in a bowl until thick and pale. Whisk in the lemon juice. Stir together the lemon rind, semolina and ground almonds and fold into the egg mixture. Whisk the egg whites until stiff and carefully fold into the mixture. Pour the mixture into the prepared tin and bake in the oven at 180°C (350°F) mark 4 for about 30 minutes, until well risen and golden brown.

Place a piece of greaseproof paper on a damp teatowel and dust with caster sugar. Turn the cake on to it. Remove the lining paper and trim the four edges. Roll up loosely with the paper inside and leave to cool.

Whip the cream and milk together. Unroll the cake and spread with the whipped cream. Reserve a few redcurrants for decoration and sprinkle the remainder over the cream. Roll up the griestorte, sprinkle with icing sugar and decorate with the reserved redcurrants. Serve on the day of baking.

Redcurrant raspberry water ice

100 g (4 oz) caster sugar
300 ml ($\frac{1}{2}$ pint) water
15 ml (1 tbsp) Cointreau
15 ml (1 tbsp) lemon juice
225 g (8 oz) redcurrants
225 g (8 oz) raspberries, hulled
2 egg whites

Dissolve the sugar in the water in a small saucepan. Bring to the boil, add the Cointreau, lemon juice and fruits and simmer gently for 5–10 minutes until soft. Cool slightly.

Purée the fruit with the syrup in an electric blender. Rub through a sieve to remove the pips and pour into ice trays (without dividers). Freeze until mushy. Turn out into a large bowl. Whisk the egg whites until stiff and fold into the fruit mixture. Return to the ice tray and freeze until firm. Allow the ice to 'come to' at room temperature for about 15 minutes before serving.

To freeze: treat as for ice-cream.
Serves 6

Redcurrant choux puffs

For the pastry
100 g (4 oz) butter
300 ml ($\frac{1}{2}$ pint) water
150 g (5 oz) plain flour
4 eggs, beaten

For the filling
400 ml ($\frac{3}{4}$ pint) double cream
225 g (8 oz) redcurrants
60 ml (4 level tbsp) caster sugar
15 ml (1 tbsp) calvados or brandy
icing sugar, sifted
redcurrants on the stem to decorate

Redcurrant choux puffs

Melt the butter in the water and bring to the boil. Remove from the heat and add the flour all at once. Beat until smooth. Cool slightly. Beat in the eggs, a little at a time, and beat until the mixture is shiny.

Draw two 2.5-cm (8-in) circles on non-stick paper-lined baking sheets. Put two-thirds of the choux mixture into a piping bag filled with a vegetable star nozzle. Pipe rosettes close together within one circle. Pipe the remaining mixture through a plain vegetable nozzle in the second ring. Bake in the oven at 200°C (400°F) mark 6 for about 30 minutes, until golden brown. Cool on the baking sheet.

Whip 150 ml ($\frac{1}{4}$ pint) of the cream and use to sandwich the rings together. Place on a serving plate. Crush the redcurrants lightly with half the sugar. Whip the rest of the cream with the calvados or brandy, and remaining sugar. Layer with the fruit in the centre of the ring. Decorate with icing sugar and redcurrants.
Serves 6

Redcurrant and raspberry jam

700 g (1$\frac{1}{2}$ lb) redcurrants
700 g (1$\frac{1}{2}$ lb) raspberries, hulled
600 ml (1 pint) water
1.4 kg (3 lb) sugar

Put the fruits in a pan with the water. Simmer gently for about 20 minutes or until really soft. Add the sugar, stir until dissolved, then boil rapidly until setting point is reached. Pot and cover in the usual way.
Note: to reduce the amount of pips, cook the fruits separately, each in 300 ml ($\frac{1}{2}$ pint) water. Sieve the redcurrants before adding to the raspberries. The yield will be slightly less.
Makes about 2.3 kg (5 lb)

Rhubarb

To prepare
Cut off the root ends and leaves. Older rhubarb may be coarser and any tough strings of skin must be peeled off. Wash and drain well, then cut into required lengths.

Basic cooking
To poach in the oven, cut 450 g (1 lb) of rhubarb into 2.5-cm (1-in) lengths and place in an ovenproof dish. Sprinkle over 75–100 g (3–4 oz) sugar and 30 ml (2 tbsp) water.

Cover the dish and bake in the oven at 180°C (350°F) mark 4 for 30–35 minutes until tender.

Rhubarb and orange chiffon pie

175 g (6 oz) ginger biscuits, crushed
75 g (3 oz) butter, melted
450 g (1 lb) rhubarb, trimmed
50 g (2 oz) sugar
2 medium oranges
10 ml (2 level tsp) powdered gelatine
30 ml (2 tbsp) water
60 ml (4 tbsp) double cream, whipped

Mix together the biscuit crumbs and butter and use to line a 20.5-cm (8-in) flan ring, reserving a few crumbs for decoration. Chill.

Cut the rhubarb into 2.5-cm (1-in) pieces and simmer gently with the sugar for 10–15 minutes, until tender. Cool. Purée the cooked fruit in an electric blender with the juice of one orange. Turn out into a bowl.

Sprinkle the gelatine over the water in a small heatproof bowl and stand in a pan of hot water to dissolve. Stir the gelatine into the rhubarb with the lightly whipped cream. Spoon into the flan case and refrigerate to set.

Remove the rind and all the pith from the second orange and cut the flesh into segments, discarding the pips. Use the orange segments to decorate the pie. Do not do this too far in advance of serving or the segments will weep into the rhubarb chiffon. Neaten the edges of the pie with the reserved crumbs.

NOT SUITABLE FOR FREEZING
Serves 6

Hot rhubarb meringue

1 egg, separated
120 ml (4 fl oz) sweet sherry
16 boudoir biscuits
450 g (1 lb) rhubarb, trimmed
30 ml (2 tbsp) water
75 g (3 oz) caster sugar

Beat together the egg yolk and sherry. Moisten the boudoir biscuits in the egg and sherry mixture and arrange round the sides of a 900-ml (2-pint) ovenproof dish. Cut the rhubarb into 2.5-cm (1-in) lengths and place in the centre of the dish with the water and half the sugar. Cover with foil. Bake in the oven at 200°C (400°F) mark 6 for 25 minutes.

Whisk the egg white until stiff. Whisk in half the remaining sugar, then fold in the rest. Remove the foil cover from the rhubarb. Pipe or spoon the meringue around the edge of the dish and return to the oven to bake for 10 minutes until crisp and golden.

Rhubarb and port compote

900 g (2 lb) pink rhubarb, trimmed
2 large oranges
50 g (2 oz) stoned dates, halved
150 ml ($\frac{1}{4}$ pint) tawny port
50 g (2 oz) soft light brown sugar
1.25 ml ($\frac{1}{4}$ level tsp) ground cinnamon
25 g (1 oz) flaked almonds, toasted

Cut the rhubarb into 2.5-cm (1-in) pieces and place in an ovenproof dish. Peel one orange and cut into segments. Grate the rind and squeeze the juice from the second orange. Add the segments, rind and juice to the rhubarb with the dates, port, sugar and cinnamon. Stir well. Cover and cook in the oven at 170°C (325°F) mark 3 for 45 minutes, until the fruit is tender. Sprinkle with the almonds and serve with whipped cream.

Rhubarb and ginger upside down pudding

50 g (2 oz) butter or margarine
50 g (2 oz) soft brown sugar
350 g (12 oz) rhubarb, trimmed

For the sponge
100 g (4 oz) soft tub margarine
100 g (4 oz) soft brown sugar
2 eggs, beaten
45 ml (3 tbsp) milk
175 g (6 oz) self raising flour
10 ml (2 level tsp) ground ginger

Cream the butter or margarine and brown sugar together and spread over the bottom of an 18-cm (7-in) round cake tin. Cut the rhubarb into 2.5-cm (1-in) lengths and place on top of the sugar and butter layer.

For the sponge, cream the margarine and sugar together until pale and fluffy. Beat in the eggs and milk a little at a time, then fold in the flour and ginger. Spread on top of the fruit layer and bake in the oven at 180°C 350°F) mark 4 for about 45 minutes until the sponge is well risen and golden brown.

Rhubarb ginger jam

1.1 kg (2½ lb) trimmed rhubarb, prepared weight
1.1 kg (2½ lb) sugar
75 ml (5 tbsp) lemon juice
25 g (1 oz) root ginger, bruised
100 g (4 oz) preserved or crystallised ginger, finely
  chopped

Cut the rhubarb into pieces and place in a large basin in alternate layers with the sugar. Add the lemon juice, cover and leave overnight. Next day, bruise the root ginger with a weight or hammer to release the flavour, tie in muslin and place in a pan, together with the rhubarb and sugar contents of the basin. Bring to the boil and boil rapidly for 15 minutes. Remove the muslin bag, add the chopped ginger and boil for a further 5 minutes, or until setting point is reached. Pot and cover in the usual way.

Makes about 1.8 kg (4 lb)

Rhubarb and orange chutney

1.1 kg (2½ lb) rhubarb, trimmed
thinly pared rind and juice of 2 oranges
3 onions, skinned and chopped
900 ml (1½ pints) malt vinegar
900 g (2 lb) demerara sugar
450 g (1 lb) seedless raisins
15 ml (1 level tbsp) mustard seeds
5 ml (1 level tsp) peppercorns
5 ml (1 level tsp) whole allspice berries

Cut the rhubarb into 2.5-cm (1-in) lengths. Shred the orange rind finely. Place the rhubarb, orange rind and juice in a large preserving pan with the onions, vinegar, sugar and raisins. Add the spices, tied in muslin. Bring to the boil and simmer uncovered for about 1½ hours until thick and pulpy. Remove the muslin bag. Pour into hot jars and seal.

Makes about 3.6 kg (8 lb)

Spinach

To prepare

Grit really clings to spinach leaves and only several changes of washing water will remove it. The leaves damage very easily so they should be handled gently. Trim the base of the stalks of summer spinach. Winter or perpetual spinach should have the coarser stalks and centre ribs removed.

Basic cooking

To steam, summer spinach leaves should be cooked without any water except that which clings to them after washing. Add a knob of butter, season and steam in an open pan for 5–10 minutes until tender. Drain, if necessary, and serve sprinkled with grated nutmeg.
To boil, the coarser winter and perpetual spinach is best cooked in boiling salted water for 5–10 minutes. Drain well and press the excess water from the leaves. Rub the spinach through a sieve or chop finely. Return to the pan with a knob of butter or a little cream, salt and pepper and a sprinkling of grated nutmeg.

Spinach layer pie

450 g (1 lb) lean minced beef
1 large onion, skinned and chopped
30 ml (2 level tbsp) tomato paste
5 ml (1 level tsp) dried mixed herbs
salt and freshly ground pepper
450 g (1 lb) spinach, trimmed and chopped
pinch of grated nutmeg
300 ml (½ pint) natural yogurt
2 egg yolks
pinch of dry mustard
50 g (2 oz) Edam cheese, grated

Place the minced beef and onion in a large saucepan and cook over a medium heat until the fat starts to run. Increase the heat and cook for 10 minutes, until brown. Stir in the tomato paste, herbs and seasoning. Place the spinach in a saucepan without water, cover and cook gently for about 5–10 minutes. Drain very well. Stir in the nutmeg and season to taste.

Layer the meat mixture and the spinach in an ovenproof dish. Combine the yogurt, egg yolks, mustard and cheese and pour over the top. Cook in the oven, uncovered, at 190°C (375°F) mark 5 for about 45 minutes until the topping is bubbling and golden.

Spinach soufflé

75 g (3 oz) butter
1 medium onion, skinned and chopped
450 g (1 lb) spinach, trimmed and chopped
salt and freshly ground pepper
1.25 ml ($\frac{1}{4}$ level tsp) grated nutmeg
25 g (1 oz) flour
300 ml ($\frac{1}{2}$ pint) milk
3 large eggs, separated
40 g (1$\frac{1}{2}$ oz) Parmesan cheese, grated

Melt 25 g (1 oz) of the butter in a pan and cook the onion for 5 minutes, until tender. Add the spinach and cook for a further 5–10 minutes. Stir in the seasoning and nutmeg. Melt the remaining butter in another pan, stir in the flour and cook for 1 minute. Gradually stir in the milk, bring to the boil and cook for 2–3 minutes. Season the sauce and add half to the spinach mixture. Turn into a greased 900-ml (1$\frac{1}{2}$-pint) soufflé dish.

Beat the egg yolks and most of the cheese into the remaining sauce. Whisk the egg whites until stiff and fold into the sauce carefully. Spoon over the spinach mixture and sprinkle the remaining cheese on the top. Cook in the oven at 190°C (375°F) mark 5 for about 40 minutes, until well risen and golden brown.

Sage Derby florentine

900 g (2 lb) spinach, trimmed
salt and freshly ground pepper
25 g (1 oz) butter
100 g (4 oz) sage Derby cheese, grated
4 eggs

Place the spinach in a large saucepan, cover and cook in the water remaining on the leaves for 5–10 minutes. Drain well and roughly chop the spinach. Season well, add the butter and stir in three quarters of the cheese. Spoon the spinach into a shallow ovenproof dish. Make four wells in the centre. Break the eggs one at a time and pour into the wells. Sprinkle the top with the remaining cheese. Bake in the oven at 180°C (350°F) mark 4 for 15 minutes until the eggs are just set. Serve immediately.

Strawberry

To prepare
Remove the stalks and hulls and wash carefully. If storing in the refrigerator, leave unwashed.

Basic cooking
To poach, place 450 g (1 lb) prepared strawberries in a saucepan with water to cover the bottom of the pan and 50–75 g (2–3 oz) sugar to taste. Cover the pan, bring to the boil and simmer gently for 10–15 minutes until tender. The strawberries may be rubbed through a sieve to purée and remove the pips.

Caramelled strawberries

350 g (12 oz) sugar
400 ml ($\frac{3}{4}$ pint) water
450 g (1 lb) strawberries, hulled

Place the sugar and water in a pan and heat gently until the sugar is dissolved. Bring to the boil without stirring and boil until the syrup is golden brown. Remove from heat.

Pierce each whole strawberry with a cocktail stick, dip into the caramel and quickly twist the strawberry to cover completely with caramel. Immerse the strawberries in a bowl of iced water for 30 seconds to set the caramel, then place on greaseproof paper and remove the cocktail sticks, if wished. Pile up the caramel strawberries in a serving dish and serve immediately with cream.

Strawberry cream sorbet

350 g (12 oz) ripe strawberries, hulled and sliced
100 g (4 oz) caster sugar
450-g (15.9-oz) carton strawberry yogurt
45 ml (3 tbsp) lemon juice
150 ml ($\frac{1}{4}$ pint) double cream
2 egg whites

Put the strawberries into an electric blender, add the sugar, yogurt and lemon juice and purée until smooth. Turn the mixture into a 1.7-litre (3-pint) container and freeze until almost firm – this will take about 1 hour.

Just before taking the sorbet mixture from the freezer, whip the cream to the 'floppy' stage. In a separate bowl, whisk the egg whites until stiff but not dry. Turn the strawberry mixture into a mixing bowl and break up quickly, using a fork or a potato masher, until of a snow consistency. Fold in the cream followed by the egg whites. Return to the container, cover and leave in the freezer until firm or until needed.

About 1 hour before serving transfer to the body of the refrigerator to bring to serving consistency.
Serves 8

Strawberry cheese creams

Illustrated in colour facing page 64

225 g (8 oz) cream cheese
60 ml (4 tbsp) soured cream
45 ml (3 level tbsp) golden syrup
450 g (1 lb) strawberries, hulled
15 g ($\frac{1}{2}$ oz) caster sugar
30 ml (2 tbsp) calvados or brandy

Beat together the cream cheese, soured cream and golden syrup in a bowl and chill. Reserve

Strawberry cheese creams

12 whole strawberries for decoration and halve the remainder. Sprinkle the halved strawberries with the sugar and calvados or brandy. Cover and chill for about 2 hours, turning the strawberries in the liqueur twice.

Divide the strawberries between four individual glasses. Spoon the cream cheese mixture over them and top with the remaining whole strawberries.

Strawberry hazel nut meringue flan

For the pastry
200 g (7 oz) plain flour
pinch of salt
100 g (3$\frac{1}{2}$ oz) butter
25 g (1 oz) sugar
25 g (1 oz) toasted hazel nuts, finely chopped
1 egg yolk
15–30 ml (1–2 tbsp) water

For the filling
50 g (2 oz) butter
50 g (2 oz) flour
300 ml ($\frac{1}{2}$ pint) milk
2 egg yolks
65 g (2$\frac{1}{2}$ oz) caster sugar
15 ml (1 tbsp) sherry
450 g (1 lb) strawberries, hulled and halved

For the meringue
3 egg whites
100 g (4 oz) caster sugar

For the pastry, sift the flour and salt into a bowl. Rub in the butter until the mixture resembles fine breadcrumbs. Stir in the sugar and hazel nuts, then add the egg yolk and enough water to mix to a firm dough. Cover and leave to relax in a cool place for 30 minutes. Roll out the dough on a floured surface and use to line a 20.5-cm (8-in) flan ring. Bake blind in the oven at 190°C (375°F) mark 5 for 30 minutes. Cool.

For the filling, melt the butter in a saucepan, stir in the flour and cook for 1–2 minutes. Gradually stir in the milk and cook for 2–3 minutes. Beat in the egg yolks, 50 g (2 oz) of the sugar and the sherry. Cool.

Place the flan case on a baking sheet and pour in the cooled filling. Cover with the strawberries and sprinkle with the remaining caster sugar.

For the meringue, whisk the egg whites

until stiff, add half the sugar and whisk until shiny. Fold in the remaining sugar. Spread the meringue over the top of the strawberries to cover completely. Bake in the oven at 200°C (400°F) mark 6 for 3–4 minutes until crisp and light golden brown.

Strawberry shortbread gâteau

200 g (7 oz) plain flour
25 g (1 oz) cornflour
100 g (4 oz) caster sugar
100 g (4 oz) butter, softened
2 eggs
225 g (8 oz) strawberries, hulled
300 ml ($\frac{1}{2}$ pint) double cream
45 ml (3 tbsp) milk
icing sugar, sifted

Sift together 150 g (5 oz) of the flour, the cornflour and 50 g (2 oz) of the sugar. Rub in the butter and knead to a soft dough. Roll out on a lightly floured board and trim, using a pan lid as a guide, to give a 21.5-cm (8$\frac{1}{2}$-in) round. Transfer to a baking sheet. Bake in the oven at 170°C (325°F) mark 3 for about 25 minutes until pale golden brown. Cut the shortbread into eight sections while still warm. Leave to cool on a wire rack.

Make a whisked sponge by whisking together the eggs and remaining sugar until pale and thick. Fold in the remaining flour and turn into a 21.5-cm (8$\frac{1}{2}$-in) sandwich tin.

Bake in the oven at 190°C (375°F) mark 5 for about 15 minutes until golden. Turn out and cool on a wire rack.

Slice all but one of the strawberries. Whip the cream with the milk until it holds its shape. Sweeten to taste with a little icing sugar, if desired. Using a larger star vegetable nozzle, pipe whirls of cream around the outside edge of the sponge. Fold the sliced strawberries through the remaining cream and pile into the centre of the sponge. Dust four pieces of the shortbread with icing sugar and arrange alternate plain and sugared pieces at an angle on top of the cream. Top with the whole strawberry.
Serves 8

Strawberry jam

1.6 kg (3$\frac{1}{2}$ lb) small strawberries, hulled
45 ml (3 tbsp) lemon juice
1.4 kg (3 lb) sugar

Put the strawberries into a pan with the lemon juice and simmer gently, without adding water, for 20–30 minutes until really soft. Add the sugar, stir until dissolved, then boil rapidly until setting point is reached. Allow to cool for about 15–20 minutes, to prevent the fruit rising in the jars, then pot and cover in the usual way.
Makes about 2.3 kg (5 lb)

Swede

To prepare
Scrub and peel swedes thickly to remove all the tough skin and roots. Cut into suitable sized pieces, or dice or slice thickly.

Basic cooking
To boil, place the prepared swedes in salted water, bring to the boil and cook for about 20 minutes. Serve in pieces or mashed with a little butter and seasoning.
To steam, cut the swedes into large dice and steam for 15–20 minutes.
To roast, cut into chunks or fingers and cook around the joint or in a separate roasting

tin, with sufficient fat or oil for basting, in the oven at 200°C (400°F) mark 6 for 1–1$\frac{1}{4}$ hours, according to size.

Creamy swede soup

25 g (1 oz) butter
350 g (12 oz) swede, peeled and chopped
1 onion, skinned and sliced
175 g (6 oz) carrot, peeled and sliced
175 g (6 oz) celery, trimmed and thinly sliced
1.1 litres (2 pints) beef stock
salt and freshly ground black pepper
150 ml ($\frac{1}{4}$ pint) soured cream
chopped fresh chives to garnish

Melt the butter in a large saucepan and add the swede, onion, carrot and celery. Fry for 5 minutes. Pour in the stock and season. Cover and simmer for 45 minutes until the vegetables are really soft. Purée the soup in an electric blender or rub through a sieve and return to the pan to reheat. Adjust the seasoning and stir in the soured cream. Pour into a warmed tureen and serve garnished with chives.
Serves 4–6

Cheesy topped swede casserole

350 g (12 oz) swede, peeled and thinly sliced
1 onion, skinned and thinly sliced
100 g (4 oz) carrots, peeled and thinly sliced
50 g (2 oz) celery, trimmed and thinly sliced
1 large potato, peeled and thinly sliced
15 ml (1 level tbsp) cornflour
300 ml ($\frac{1}{2}$ pint) chicken or beef stock
bouquet garni
salt and freshly ground black pepper
100 g (4 oz) Cheddar cheese, grated

Place the sliced vegetables in layers in a 2.3-litre (4-pint) casserole. Blend the cornflour with a little of the stock, stir in the remainder and pour over the vegetables. Add the bouquet garni and seasoning. Cover and bake in the oven at 180°C (350°F) mark 4 for 1 hour.

Remove the bouquet garni and sprinkle over the cheese. Return to the oven, uncovered, and bake for a further 20 minutes until the top is golden brown. Serve with buttered crusty bread.

Swede and lentil purée

100 g (4 oz) lentils
25 g (1 oz) butter or margarine
450 g (1 lb) swede, peeled and thinly sliced
1 small onion, skinned and thinly sliced
1.1 litres (2 pints) beef stock
salt and freshly ground black pepper
150 ml ($\frac{1}{4}$ pint) soured cream
chopped parsley to garnish

Place the lentils in a bowl, cover with boiling water and soak for 2 hours. Melt the fat in a large saucepan, add the swede and onion and fry gently for 10 minutes. Stir in the stock, drained lentils and seasoning. Bring to the boil, cover and simmer for 45 minutes until the vegetables are soft.

Purée the vegetables in an electric blender or rub through a sieve. Return to the pan to heat through. Adjust the seasoning. A little more stock may need to be added. Pour into a warmed serving dish. Serve accompanied with the soured cream garnished with chopped parsley.
Serves 4–6

Sweetcorn

To prepare
For corn on the cob, cut the stalk from the cob, remove the leaves and fine silk. Trim the tip of the cob if not fully formed. To remove corn from the cob, hold the cob upright on a working surface and, with a sharp knife, cut away the corn with a downward movement. Work around the lower half of the cob and, when all the corn has been removed, turn the cob upside down and repeat.

Basic cooking
To boil, place corn on the cob in a pan of unsalted boiling water and cook for 5–15 minutes, according to size and age (the older the corn, the longer it will take to cook). When the corn is cooked a kernel can be easily removed from the base.

Drain well and serve immediately with plenty of melted butter and coarse salt. Each end of the cob is pierced with a small corn holder for easy eating, although two small forks or skewers may be used if you don't have special corn holders.

Corn off the cob is cooked in a little boiling water for 5–10 minutes. Drain well and serve tossed in melted butter.

Sweetcorn, cheese and chive soufflé

450 g (1 lb) sweetcorn kernels
25 g (1 oz) butter, melted
7.5 ml (1½ level tsp) salt
freshly ground black pepper
30 ml (2 tbsp) double cream
4 eggs, separated
175 g (6 oz) Cheddar cheese, grated
2.5 ml (½ level tsp) dry mustard
30 ml (2 tbsp) chopped fresh chives

Cook the sweetcorn kernels in boiling salted water for 5–10 minutes. Drain. Reserve 175 g (6 oz) of whole sweetcorn kernels and purée the remaining kernels in an electric blender or rub through a sieve. Place the sweetcorn purée and whole kernels in a large mixing bowl. Stir in the melted butter, seasoning, double cream, egg yolks, cheese, mustard and chives. Whisk the egg whites until stiff and fold into the sweetcorn mixture. Spoon into a lightly buttered 15-cm (6-in) soufflé dish. Bake in the oven at 190°C (375°F) mark 5 for 35 minutes until well risen and golden brown. Serve immediately.

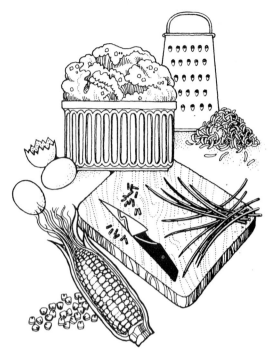

Sweetcorn, cheese and chive soufflé

Sweetcorn and bacon fritters

100 g (4 oz) flour
5 ml (1 level tsp) salt
15 ml (1 tbsp) corn oil
150 ml (¼ pint) water
225 g (8 oz) bacon, rinded and finely chopped
1 egg white
350 g (12 oz) sweetcorn kernels, cooked
oil for deep frying
grated Parmesan cheese

Mix together the flour and salt in a bowl. Make a well in the centre and add the oil and water. Beat until smooth. Fry the bacon in its own fat until crisp and golden. Drain. Whisk the egg white until stiff and fold into the batter with the bacon and sweetcorn kernels.

Heat the oil to 180°C (350°F). Drop spoonfuls of the batter into the hot oil and cook for 4 minutes until golden brown and crisp. Drain the fritters on kitchen paper towel and place in a warmed serving dish. Serve sprinkled with Parmesan cheese.
Makes 16

Sweetcorn relish

This relish is a very tasty accompaniment for cold meats or cheese.

6 corn cobs, trimmed and leaves and silk removed
½ small white cabbage, trimmed
2 medium onions, skinned
1½ red peppers, seeded
10 ml (2 level tsp) salt
30 ml (2 level tbsp) flour
2.5 ml (½ level tsp) turmeric
175 g (6 oz) sugar
10 ml (2 level tsp) dry mustard
600 ml (1 pint) distilled vinegar

Cook the corn cobs in boiling salted water for 3 minutes. Drain. Cut the corn from the cobs, using a sharp knife. Coarsely mince the cabbage, onions and red peppers. Combine with the corn.

Blend the salt, flour, turmeric, sugar and mustard together in a saucepan, then gradually add the vinegar. Bring to the boil, stirring. Add the vegetables and simmer for 25–30 minutes, stirring occasionally. Pour into hot jars and seal at once.
Makes about 2.3 kg (5 lb)

103

Tomato

To prepare

For cooking, most recipes require skinned tomatoes. The skin can be removed by holding the tomato on a fork over a low gas flame until the skin is blistered all over. The skin can then be easily peeled away. Alternatively, place the tomatoes in a bowl, cover with boiling water and leave to stand for 1–2 minutes. Plunge the tomatoes into cold water, drain and peel away the skins.

Basic cooking

To fry, cut tomatoes in half or slice thickly and cook in hot oil or butter for 3–4 minutes. Turn and cook the other side. Serve sprinkled with salt and freshly ground pepper and a little sugar if liked.

To grill, cut the tomatoes in half, sprinkle with salt, freshly ground pepper, a little sugar and chopped parsley, marjoram or basil. Cook under a hot grill for 4–5 minutes.

To bake, leave the tomatoes whole and cut a cross in the smooth end, or cut in half. Dot with a knob of butter, sprinkle with salt and freshly ground pepper and cook in the oven at 180°C (350°F) mark 4 for about 15 minutes until cooked.

To steam, place whole tomatoes in the steamer and cook for 7 minutes.

Prawn stuffed tomatoes

Illustrated in colour facing page 80

8 large tomatoes, skinned
5 ml (1 level tsp) salt
freshly ground pepper
5 ml (1 level tsp) sugar
1 small lettuce
100 g (4 oz) prawns in shells
fresh parsley sprigs

For the filling
1 egg yolk
1.25 ml ($\frac{1}{4}$ level tsp) salt
freshly ground pepper
2.5 ml ($\frac{1}{2}$ level tsp) dry mustard
pinch of caster sugar
150 ml ($\frac{1}{4}$ pint) salad or olive oil
10 ml (2 tsp) sherry
15 ml (1 tbsp) lemon juice
5 ml (1 level tsp) tomato paste
15 ml (1 tbsp) chopped fresh chives
1 hard-boiled egg, finely chopped
175 g (6 oz) peeled prawns

Carefully slice a lid from each tomato. With a teaspoon, scoop out the seeds and flesh and discard. Sprinkle the insides of the tomatoes with salt, pepper and sugar.

For the filling, beat the egg yolk in a bowl until thick. Add the seasoning, mustard and sugar. Add the oil, drop by drop, whisking vigorously between each addition. Gradually whisk in the sherry, lemon juice and tomato paste and whisk until thick. Stir in the chives, egg and peeled prawns.

Fill the tomatoes with the prawn mixture. Place the lettuce leaves on a serving plate. Arrange the tomatoes on the bed of lettuce and garnish with unpeeled prawns and parsley sprigs.

Tomatoes baked in garlic butter

100 g (4 oz) butter
350 g (12 oz) flat mushrooms, stalks removed
700 g (1$\frac{1}{2}$ lb) tomatoes, skinned and sliced
2 large cloves garlic, skinned and crushed
45 ml (3 tbsp) chopped fresh parsley
2.5 ml ($\frac{1}{2}$ level tsp) dried oregano
salt and freshly ground pepper
15 ml (1 tbsp) chopped fresh chives

Melt the butter in a frying pan and gently fry the mushrooms for 5 minutes, until tender. Remove with a slotted spoon and arrange them in alternate layers with the tomato slices in a large ovenproof dish. Add the garlic to the remaining butter in the pan and fry for 2–3 minutes. Stir in the parsley and oregano and pour over the vegetables. Season well, cover and bake in the oven at 200°C (400°F) mark 6 for 25–30 minutes. Serve sprinkled with the chopped chives.

Tomato quiche

175 g (6 oz) shortcrust pastry (see page 63)
50 g (2 oz) butter
1 medium onion, skinned and finely chopped
50 g (2 oz) fresh white breadcrumbs
100 g (4 oz) mature Cheddar cheese, grated
5 ml (1 level tsp) dried mixed herbs
2.5 ml ($\frac{1}{2}$ level tsp) garlic salt
2.5 ml ($\frac{1}{2}$ level tsp) dry mustard
freshly ground pepper
2 eggs, beaten
30 ml (2 tbsp) milk
450 g (1 lb) tomatoes, skinned and sliced

Roll out the dough and use to line a 25.5-cm (10-in) plain flan ring or fluted loose-bottomed flan tin. Bake blind in the oven at 200°C (400°F) mark 6 for 25 minutes or until the pastry is golden brown.

Melt 25 g (1 oz) of the butter and fry the onion for 5 minutes until soft. Off the heat combine with the breadcrumbs, cheese, herbs, garlic salt, mustard and pepper. Beat the eggs and milk together and mix into the breadcrumb mixture. Spread over the bottom of the flan case.

Scatter the end pieces of the tomatoes over the breadcrumb mixture. Arrange the slices neatly overlapping over the surface. Sprinkle with pepper and bake for a further 20 minutes. Melt the remaining 25 g (1 oz) butter and brush over the tomatoes. Serve hot or cold.
Serves 6

Tomato fish bake

1 large mackerel, filleted
450 g (1 lb) white fish fillet, skinned
100 g (4 oz) button mushrooms, sliced
1 small onion, skinned and sliced
225 g (8 oz) tomatoes, skinned and sliced
30–45 ml (2–3 tbsp) lemon juice
salt and freshly ground pepper

For the topping
200 g (7 oz) self raising flour
25 g (1 oz) butter
150 ml ($\frac{1}{4}$ pint) soured cream
15 ml (1 tbsp) chopped fresh parsley
milk to glaze

Cut the fish into 4-cm (1$\frac{1}{2}$-in) pieces and layer in a 2-litre (3$\frac{1}{2}$-pint) shallow ovenproof dish with a lip. Add the mushrooms, onion, tomatoes, lemon juice and seasoning.

For the topping, sift the flour into a bowl and rub in the butter. Stir in the soured cream and parsley and mix to a firm 'scone' type dough. Roll out the dough and use to make a lid on top of the fish. With a sharp knife, mark the topping into 4–6 segments and glaze with milk. Place the dish on a baking sheet. Bake in the oven at 220°C (425°F) mark 7 for 15 minutes, then reduce the temperature to 180°C (350°F) mark 4 and bake for a further 15 minutes.
Serves 4–6

Tomato and potato au gratin

450 g (1 lb) potatoes, peeled and thinly sliced
50 g (2 oz) butter
1 large onion, skinned and sliced
1 clove garlic, skinned and crushed
225 g (8 oz) streaky bacon, rinded and chopped
700 g (1$\frac{1}{2}$ lb) tomatoes, skinned and sliced
175 g (6 oz) double Gloucester cheese, grated
salt and freshly ground pepper
5 ml (1 level tsp) dried thyme
150 ml ($\frac{1}{4}$ pint) double cream
75 g (3 oz) fresh white breadcrumbs

Blanch the potatoes in boiling salted water for 3 minutes. Drain. Melt the butter in a frying pan and fry the onion, garlic and bacon for 5 minutes. Remove with a slotted spoon and reserve. Add the potato slices, half at a time, to the frying pan and fry for about 10 minutes, until just tender and golden brown.

Layer the tomatoes, potatoes, onion and bacon mixture and half the cheese in an ovenproof dish. Sprinkle each layer with salt, pepper and thyme. Pour the double cream over the vegetables. Stir the breadcrumbs and the remaining cheese together and spoon over the vegetables. Bake in the oven, uncovered, at 190°C (350°F) mark 5 for 25–30 minutes, until the topping is crisp and golden brown.

Green tomato and apple chutney

This chutney is delicious with cheese and cold meat.

1.1 kg (2$\frac{1}{2}$ lb) green tomatoes, chopped
1.1 kg (2$\frac{1}{2}$ lb) cooking apples, peeled, cored and chopped
550 g (1$\frac{1}{4}$ lb) shallots, skinned and chopped
225 g (8 oz) seedless raisins
450 g (1 lb) demerara sugar
2.5 ml ($\frac{1}{2}$ level tsp) ground ginger
5 ml (1 level tsp) ground mixed spice
15 g ($\frac{1}{2}$ oz) salt
600 ml (1 pint) malt vinegar

Put all the ingredients in a large pan. Bring to the boil, then reduce the heat and simmer uncovered until the chutney is well reduced. Stir occasionally. Pot and cover in the usual way.
Makes about 3.2 kg (7 lb)

Tomato sauce

25 g (1 oz) butter
1 small onion, skinned and chopped
1 small carrot, peeled and chopped
2 rashers bacon, rinded and chopped
15 g (½ oz) flour
300 ml (½ pint) chicken stock
450 g (1 lb) tomatoes, quartered
1 small bay leaf
1 sprig fresh rosemary
salt and freshly ground pepper
5 ml (1 level tsp) caster sugar

Melt the butter in a saucepan, add the onion, carrot and bacon and fry for 5 minutes. Stir in the flour and cook for 2 minutes. Gradually stir in the stock, then add the tomatoes, bay leaf, rosemary, seasoning and sugar. Bring to the boil, stirring, and simmer for 30–35 minutes, until the vegetables are tender. Sieve the sauce and return to the heat. Adjust the seasoning and reheat gently.
Makes about 400 ml (¾ pint)

Turnip

To prepare
Early turnips should be trimmed and peeled thinly if used raw. Maincrop turnips should be peeled quite thickly to remove all the tough fibrous skin and cut into smaller pieces, or diced or sliced.

Basic cooking
To boil, early turnips can be cooked whole in their skins in salted water. Bring to the boil and cook for 20–30 minutes according to size, until tender. Drain and rub off the skins. Maincrop turnips should be cooked in salted water for 20–30 minutes, depending on preparation. Mash maincrop turnips with milk and butter and serve, or combine with equal quantities of mashed carrot, parsnip or potato.

To steam, cut into large dice, place in the steamer and cook for 15 minutes.

Mustard turnips

450 g (1 lb) turnips, peeled and quartered
1 lemon
50 g (2 oz) butter
5 ml (1 level tsp) sugar
10 ml (2 level tsp) dry mustard
lemon slices to garnish

Cook the turnips in boiling salted water with a slice of lemon for 20–30 minutes until tender. Drain and remove the lemon slice. Return the turnips to the pan with the butter, sugar and mustard blended with a little lemon juice. Heat gently for 5 minutes. Serve in a warmed dish garnished with lemon slices.

Turnips braised with bacon

Illustrated in colour facing page 81

450 g (1 lb) small turnips, peeled
1 onion, skinned and thinly sliced
50 g (2 oz) streaky bacon, rinded and chopped
15 ml (1 tbsp) vegetable oil
1 sprig parsley
1 small clove garlic, skinned and crushed
2–3 peppercorns
30 ml (2 level tbsp) tomato paste
300 ml (½ pint) stock
parsley sprig to garnish

Cook the turnips in boiling salted water for 15 minutes. Meanwhile, fry the onion and bacon in the oil in a large frying pan for 10 minutes until browned. Add the parsley sprig, garlic, peppercorns, tomato paste and stock. Cover and simmer gently for 10 minutes. Remove parsley and peppercorns.

Drain the turnips and add to the onion mixture. Adjust the seasoning, cover and cook for a further 10–15 minutes until the turnips are tender. Serve in a warmed dish garnished with parsley.

Zucchini *see* Courgette

Freezing and Other Methods of Preserving

Drying, Salting, Bottling,
Jams, Jellies and Marmalades,
Pickles and Chutneys

Freezing

How to freeze poultry

Commercial quick-frozen raw poultry is so readily available that it is only an advantage to freeze chicken at home when the price is very favourable. If the birds are your own, starve them for 24 hours before killing, and, if possible, set to and pluck out the feathers while the corpse is still warm – they come out much easier that way.

How you freeze your birds depends on how you are going to cook them. Obviously if you are going to make a chicken casserole, you will be wasting freezer space if you freeze a chicken whole, instead of cutting it up into more convenient pieces. And talking of wastage, remember that chicken fat is excellent rendered down for frying chips, and that any odd scraps and bones can make tasty concentrated stocks for soups and sauces.

More sizeable remnants of cold roast chicken (carved or not) and poached chicken may be frozen satisfactorily, too.

Whole chickens

Wipe and dry the bird after plucking and drawing it. Pack the giblets separately instead of inside, because they will only keep for a quarter of the time the chicken can be stored. Don't stuff the chicken, as it takes too long to freeze and thaw. If you wish, package any stuffing separately. To truss the bird see page 56.

Chicken portions

Divide small birds – about 1–1.5 kg (2–3 lb) – into quarters. With young birds, this can be done with poultry shears or a sharp knife. Cut the bird in half, through and along the breastbone. Open the bird out, and then cut along the length of the backbone.

If you want to remove the backbone entirely, cut along either side of it, then lift it out – and don't forget to use it for making stock. If you are using a knife, you will have to tap the back sharply with a heavy weight to cut through the bony sections. Either way, once the bird is in two halves, lay these skin side up. Divide each in half again by cutting diagonally across between wing and thigh, allocating more breast meat to the wing than to the thigh, to even out the amount of meat per portion.

Smaller chicken joints

When these are to be used in casseroles, etc., cut the thigh loose along the rounded edge and pull the leg away from the body to isolate the joint. Break the thigh backwards so that the knife can cut through the socket of each thigh joint, and loosen the wings from the breast meat from the breastbone. Both breast portions may be halved, and the back is divided into two or three pieces or used to supplement the stock pot.

Packing for the freezer

Before packing whole birds in heavy-duty polythene bags, first pad the legs with foil so that they can't spike their way through the wrapping. Exclude as much air as possible before sealing the bag.

With chicken quarters or joints, pack individually in foil or polythene bags, and then combine into a larger package to save time hunting for individual packs.

Cold roast or poached chicken should be cooled as rapidly as possible after cooking. Parcel in foil, with any stuffing packed separately, and freeze at once.

Storage times
Chicken: 12 months
Giblets: 2–3 months

Thawing
All poultry must be completely thawed before cooking.
Slow thawing: leave the bird in its packaging and thaw in the refrigerator overnight. As a guide 450 g (1 lb) of food can take up to 6 hours to thaw in the refrigerator so allow plenty of time. Allow 6 hours for chicken portions.
Quick thawing: poultry can be thawed in about half the time if thawed in its packaging at room temperature. However, once the food is thawed don't leave it at room temperature for any longer than necessary as it will start to perish very quickly. Allow about 9–10 hours for whole birds and about 3 hours for chicken portions.

How to freeze bacon

It is most important to freeze bacon that is perfectly fresh, so if possible the bacon should be frozen on the day it is supplied to the

FREEZING—AT A GLANCE

Food (storage time)	Preparation	Packaging	Thawing and serving
Bacon Joints (see page 110)	Select vacuum-packed or very fresh joints. Check vacuum packaging is intact.	Overwrap vacuum-packed joints in foil or with a polythene bag. Wrap fresh joints in foil and overwrap with a polythene bag.	Thaw overnight in the refrigerator. Remove packaging as soon as possible during thawing process.
Rashers, chops and steaks (see page 110)	Select very fresh bacon. Pack rashers in 225 g (8 oz) quantities.	Wrap rashers in kitchen foil or cling film, then overwrap with a polythene bag. Wrap bacon chops and steaks individually or interleave with waxed or non-stick paper. Pack bacon chops and steaks together in polythene bags. Overwrap vacuum-packed bacon rashers, chops or steaks with a polythene bag.	Thaw overnight in the refrigerator or in hot water for a few minutes.
Cheese (6 months)	Soft cheeses and cream cheese are suitable for freezing. Hard cheeses become crumbly if stored for too long but are fine grated for cooking. Cottage cheese is not suitable for freezing.	Wrap in freezer film or polythene bag.	Thaw for 24 hours in refrigerator and allow to come to room temperature before serving. Use grated cheese straight from frozen.
Chicken (12 months)	Use fresh birds only; prepare and draw in the usual way. Do not stuff before freezing. Cover protruding bones with greaseproof paper or foil.	Pack trussed bird inside polythene bag and exclude as much air as possible before sealing. Freeze giblets separately. If wished, freeze in joints, wrap individually, and then overwrap.	Thaw in wrapping, preferably in refrigerator. Thaw a small bird over-night; birds up to 1.8 kg (4 lb) up to 12 hours; 1.8–5.5 kg (4–12 lb) up to 24 hours; over 5.5 kg (12 lb) for 48–72 hours. Joints 6 hours.
Eggs (separated 8–10 months)	Freeze only fresh eggs – yolks and whites separately.	Pack in waxed or rigid containers. Yolks – to every 6 yolks add 5 ml (1 level tsp) salt or 10 ml (2 level tsp) sugar; to single yolks add 2.5 ml ($\frac{1}{2}$ level tsp) salt or sugar.	Thaw in refrigerator or rapidly thaw at room temperature for about $1\frac{1}{2}$ hours.
Herbs (6 months)	Wash and trim if necessary. Dry thoroughly.	Freeze in small bunches in a rigid foil container or polythene bag. Alternatively, herbs, especially parsley, can be chopped and frozen in ice cube trays.	Can be used immediately. Crumble whilst still frozen.
Milk (1 month)	Ordinary pasteurised milk does not freeze well. Homogenised is satisfactory.	Pack in rigid containers; allow 2.5 cm (1 in) headspace. Do not freeze in bottle.	Thaw in refrigerator. Thawing may be accelerated if milk is to be used in cooking.

retailer. The longer the bacon has been cut or kept in the shop, the shorter its storage life in the freezer.

Smoked bacon can be stored for longer periods than unsmoked before any risk of rancidity arises.

Storage times

Smoked bacon joints wrapped in foil and polythene:	up to 8 weeks
Unsmoked bacon joints wrapped in foil and polythene:	up to 5 weeks
Vacuum-packed bacon joints, smoked and unsmoked:	up to 20 weeks
Vacuum-packed rashers or steaks, smoked or unsmoked:	up to 20 weeks
Smoked rashers, chops and gammon steaks wrapped in foil and polythene:	up to 8 weeks
Unsmoked rashers, chops and gammon steaks wrapped in foil and polythene:	2–3 weeks

Packing for the freezer

Commercial vacuum-packing is generally accepted as the most suitable wrapping, since the maximum amount of air is extracted, so if possible buy bacon for freezing ready-packed in this way. Again, the bacon should be frozen on or very near the day when it was vacuum-packed. However, quite acceptable results have been achieved when top-quality bacon has been wrapped in foil or cling film and overwrapped in polythene bags.

If you wish, rashers can be interleaved for easier separation – use waxed or non-stick paper or Cellophane. This is not necessary if the packs are made up to suit individual cooking needs. Wrap bacon chops individually in foil, then pack together in a polythene bag. Joints up to 1.5–2 kg (3–4 lb) should be wrapped in foil, then overwrapped in a polythene bag. It is also wise to overwrap vacuum-packed bacon, and to check each package carefully to make sure the vacuum is intact and that the bacon does not move about within the pack. Freeze quickly.

Thawing

All bacon must be thawed before cooking.

Bacon joints: allow plenty of time to thaw slowly in the refrigerator – the more slowly the meat is thawed the better the quality will be when cooked. The wrapping material should be opened and removed completely as soon as possible during the thawing process.

Bacon rashers: packets of bacon rashers, steaks or chops may be thawed overnight in the refrigerator but for immediate use, can be thawed in hot water for a few minutes. Dry well on kitchen paper towel before frying or grilling. Frozen bacon rashers can be rather salty, so it is advisable to dip each rasher in hot water and dry before cooking.

How to freeze fruit

Freezing fruits at their best means freezing them just as they become ready for eating, but if you haven't managed to pick them in time, slightly over-ripe fruits can be made into purées and used for sauces, fool-type desserts and baby foods. Purées take up less room in the freezer than whole fruits.

Tough-skinned fruits such as redcurrants, blackcurrants, gooseberries or blackberries can be frozen just as they are. Even juicy ones such as strawberries and raspberries only need to be sprinkled with sugar when packing or open-frozen on trays and then packed.

Firm-textured fruits such as peaches and apricots retain their shape and flavour if frozen in a syrup. To help keep their colour

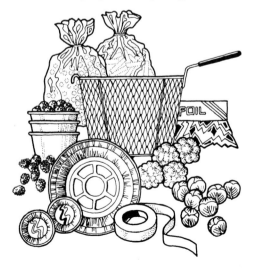

FREEZING FRUIT

Fruit	*Preparation*
Apple, sliced	Peel, core and drop into cold water. Cut into approx. 0.5-cm ($\frac{1}{4}$-in) slices. Blanch for 2–3 minutes and cool in ice-cold water before packing. Useful for pies and flans.
purée	Peel, core and stew in the minimum amount of water – sweetened or unsweetened. Sieve or liquidise. Leave to cool before packing.
Apricot	Plunge into boiling water for 30 seconds to loosen the skins, then peel. (a) Cut in half or slice into syrup made with 450 g (1 lb) sugar to 1.1 litres (2 pints) water, with some ascorbic acid (vitamin C) added to prevent browning; for each 450-g (1-lb) pack allow 200–300 mg ascorbic acid. Immerse the apricots by placing a piece of clean, crumpled, non-absorbent paper on the fruit, under the lid. (b) Leave whole and freeze in cold syrup. After long storage, an almond flavour may develop round the stone.
Berry, etc. (including currants and cherries)	All may be frozen by the dry pack method, but the dry sugar pack method is suitable for soft fruits, e.g. raspberries. *Dry pack* : sort the fruit; some whole berries may be left on their sprigs or stems for use as decoration. Spread the fruit on paper-lined trays or baking sheets, put into the freezer until frozen, then pack. *Dry sugar pack* : pack dried whole fruit with the stated quantity of sugar 100–175 g (4–6 oz) to 450 g (1 lb) fruit, mix together and seal.
Blackberry	Dry pack or dry sugar pack – allow 225 g (8 oz) sugar to 900 g (2 lb) fruit. Leave a headspace, and pack in rigid containers.
Gooseberry	Wash and thoroughly dry fruit. Pack (a) by dry method in polythene bags, without sugar; use for pie fillings; (b) in cold syrup using 900 g (2 lb) sugar to 1.1 litres (2 pints) water; (c) as purée: stew fruit in a very little water, press through a nylon sieve and sweeten to taste; useful for fools and mousses.
Strawberry and **raspberry**	Choose firm, clean, dry fruit; remove stalks. Pack (a) by dry method; (b) by dry sugar method – 100 g (4 oz) sugar to each 450 g (1 lb) fruit; (c) as purée: pass through a nylon sieve or liquidise, sweeten to taste – about 50 g (2 oz) sugar per 225 g (8 oz) purée – and freeze in small containers; useful for ice-creams, sorbets, sauces or mousses.
Blackcurrant	Wash, top and tail. (a) Dry and use dry pack method for whole fruit. (b) Purée: cook to a purée with very little water and brown sugar, according to taste.
Redcurrant	Wash and dry the whole fruit, then freeze on a paper-lined tray in a single layer until frozen. Pack in rigid containers.
Cherry	Remove the stalks. Wash and dry. Use any of these methods: (a) dry pack method; (b) dry sugar pack – 225 g (8 oz) sugar to 900 g (2 lb) stoned cherries, pack in containers cooked or uncooked; best used stewed for pie fillings; (c) cover with cold syrup – 450 g (1 lb) sugar to 1.1 litres (2 pints) water, mixed with 2.5 ml ($\frac{1}{2}$ tsp) ascorbic acid per 1.1 litres (2 pints) syrup; leave headspace. Take care not to open packet until required, as fruit loses colour rapidly on exposure to the air.
Damson	Wash in cold water. The skins are inclined to toughen during freezing. Best packing methods are: (a) in a purée, to be used later in pies; (b) halve, remove the stones and pack in cold syrup – 450 g (1 lb) sugar to 1.1 litres (2 pints) water, they will need cooking after freezing – can be used as stewed fruit; (c) poached and sweetened.
Grapefruit	Peel fruit, removing all pith; segment and pack (a) in cold syrup – equal quantities of sugar and water; use any juice from the fruit to make up the syrup; (b) in dry sugar pack – allowing 225 g (8 oz) sugar to 450 g (1 lb) fruit, sprinkled over fruit; when juices start to run, pack in rigid containers.
Greengage	Wash in cold water, halve, remove stones and pack in syrup – 450 g (1 lb) sugar to 1.1 litres (2 pints) water, with ascorbic acid added (see Apricots). Place in rigid containers. Do not open pack until required, as fruit loses colour rapidly. Skins tend to toughen during freezing.

FREEZING FRUIT (continued)

Fruit	Preparation
Lemon	There are various methods. (a) Squeeze out juice and freeze it in ice-cube trays; remove frozen cubes to polythene bags for storage. (b) Leave whole, slice or segment before freezing. (c) Remove all pith from the rind, cut into julienne strips, blanch for 1 minute, cool and pack; use for garnishing dishes. (d) Mix grated lemon rind and a little sugar to serve with pancakes. (e) Remove slivers of rind, free of pith, and freeze in foil packs to add to drinks.
Melon	Cantaloup and honeydew melons freeze quite well (though they lose their crispness when thawed), but the seeds of watermelon make it more difficult to prepare. Cut in half and seed, then cut flesh into balls, cubes or slices and put straight into cold syrup – 450 g (1 lb) sugar to 1.1 litres (2 pints) water. Alternatively, use dry pack method, with a little sugar sprinkled over. Pack in polythene bags.
Orange	Prepare and pack as for grapefruit or squeeze out and freeze the juice; add sugar if desired and freeze in small quantities in containers or as frozen orange cubes. Grate rind for orange sugar as for lemon sugar. Seville oranges may be scrubbed, packed in suitable quantities and frozen whole until required for making marmalade. (It is not recommended to thaw whole frozen fruit in order to cut it up before cooking as some discoloration often occurs – use whole fruit method for marmalade. It is advisable to add one eighth extra weight of Seville or bitter oranges or tangerines when freezing for subsequent marmalade making in order to offset pectin loss.)
Peach	Really ripe peaches are best peeled and stoned under running water, as scalding them to ease skinning will soften and slightly discolour the flesh. Firm peaches are treated in the usual way. Brush over with lemon juice. (a) Pack halves or slices in cold syrup – 450 g (1 lb) sugar to 1.1 litres (2 pints) water, with ascorbic acid added (see Apricots); pack in rigid containers, leaving 1-cm (½-in) headspace. (b) Purée peeled and stoned peaches by using a nylon sieve or liquidiser; mix in 15 ml (1 tbsp) lemon juice and 100 g (4 oz) sugar to each 450 g (1 lb) fruit; suitable for sorbets and soufflé-type desserts.
Pear	It is really only worthwhile freezing pears if you have a big crop from your garden, as they discolour rapidly, and the texture of thawed pears can be unattractively soft. Peel, quarter, remove core and dip in lemon juice immediately. Poach in syrup – 450 g (1 lb) sugar to 1.1 litres (2 pints) water for 1½ minutes. Drain, cool and pack in the cold syrup.
Pineapple	Peel and core, then slice, dice, crush or cut into wedges. (a) Pack unsweetened in boxes, separated by non-stick paper. (b) Pack in syrup – 450 g (1 lb) sugar to 1.1 litres (2 pints) water – in rigid containers; include any pineapple juice from the preparation. (c) Pack the crushed pineapple in rigid containers, allowing 100 g (4 oz) sugar to about 350 g (12 oz) fruit.
Plum	Wash, halve and discard stones. Freeze in syrup with ascorbic acid (see Apricots); use 450 g (1 lb) sugar to 1.1 litres (2 pints) water. Pack in rigid containers. Do not open packet until required, as the fruit loses colour rapidly.
Rhubarb	Wash, trim and cut into 1–2.5 cm (½–1 in) lengths. Heat in boiling water for 1 minute and cool quickly. Pack in cold syrup, using equal quantities of sugar and water, or dry-pack, to be used later for pies and crumbles.

Fruits not suitable for freezing: Banana.

(this also applies to apples and pears) add a little ascorbic acid – vitamin C – or soak in a solution of lemon juice. Either way, this increases the food value, and if the syrup is eaten with the fruit, even the natural fruit sugars and vitamins are not wasted.

The syrup

When preparing fruits for the freezer, make plenty of syrup and cool before packing. As a guide use 300 ml (½ pint) syrup to each 450 g (1 lb) fruit – make the syrup with the quantities of sugar and water given in the chart under the individual fruit.

To make the syrup, dissolve the sugar in the water, bring to the boil, remove from the heat, cover and leave to cool. Pour the syrup over the fruit or place the fruit in a container with the syrup. Light-weight fruits which tend to rise in liquids can be held below the surface by means of a dampened and crumpled piece of non-absorbent paper. To serve fruit frozen in syrup, open when ready to use and keep stoned fruit submerged in the syrup as long as possible.

Storage time
Packed in sugar or syrup: 9–12 months
Whole fruits: 6–8 months
Fruit purées: 6–8 months
Fruit juices: 4–6 months

Thawing
Fruit that is to be eaten without further preparation should be thawed as slowly as possible, particularly if the fruit is to be used without syrup. Slow thawing minimises the amount of natural juice leakage and prevents the fruit from becoming too soft and mushy. Ideally thaw in the refrigerator.

If the fruit is to be served complete with syrup thaw slowly over a gentle heat.

How to freeze vegetables

If possible select vegetables in prime condition for freezing, as freezing cannot improve their quality. It is advisable to blanch vegetables before freezing to destroy the enzymes and reduce the micro-organisms, and in turn preserve the colour, flavour, texture and vitamin content of the vegetables. When dealing with a glut of vegetables they can be frozen without blanching, but as a result their storage time is reduced to about one quarter of the storage time of blanched vegetables.

Prepare the vegetables as normal and blanch 450 g (1 lb) vegetables in not less than 3.5 litres (6 pints) boiling water. Bring the water back to the boil within 1 minute of adding the vegetables. Follow the blanching times given in the chart. Careful timing ensures the best results, so a pinger timer or watch with a second hand is useful. Blanching times should be timed from the moment when the water returns to the boil.

FREEZING VEGETABLES

Vegetable	Preparation and Packing	Blanching time
Artichoke, globe	Remove all coarse outer leaves and stalks, and trim tops and stems. Wash well in cold water. Blanch, a few at a time, adding a little lemon juice to the blanching water. Cool and drain upside-down on kitchen paper towel. Pack in rigid boxes.	7–10 minutes
Asparagus	Grade into thick and thin stems. Wash in cold water, blanch, cool and drain. Tie into small bundles, packed tips to stalks, separated by non-stick paper.	Thin stems: 2 minutes Thick stems: 4 minutes
Aubergine	Peel and cut roughly into 2.5 cm (1 in) slices. Blanch, cool and dry on kitchen paper towel. Pack in layers, separated by non-stick paper.	4 minutes
Avocado	Prepare in pulp form. Peel and mash, allowing 15 ml (1 tbsp) lemon juice for each avocado. Pack in small polythene containers. Also good frozen with cream cheese to use as a party dip.	
Bean	Select young, tender beans; wash thoroughly. Broad: shell and blanch. French: trim ends and blanch. Runner: slice thickly and blanch. Cool, drain and pack in polythene bags.	Broad: 3 minutes French: 2–3 minutes Runner: 2 minutes

Beetroot	Choose small beetroots. Wash well and rub skin off after scalding. Beetroots under 2.5 cm (1 in) in diameter may be frozen whole; large ones should be sliced or diced. Cool, drain and pack in cartons. *Note:* Short blanching and long storage can make beetroot rubbery.	Small whole:
		  5–10 minutes
		Large: 45–50 minutes
		  until tender

FREEZING VEGETABLES (continued)

Vegetable	*Preparation and packing*	*Blanching time*
Broccoli	Trim off any woody parts and large leaves. Wash in salted water and cut into small sprigs. Blanch, cool and drain well. Pack in boxes in 1–2 layers, tips to stalks, or polythene bags.	Thin stems: 3 minutes Medium stems: 4 minutes Thick stems: 5 minutes
Brussels sprout	Use small compact heads. Remove outer leaves and wash. Blanch, cool and drain well before packing in polythene bags.	Small: 3 minutes Medium: 4 minutes
Cabbage	Use only young, crisp cabbage. Wash thoroughly and shred finely. Blanch, cool and drain. Pack in small quantities in polythene bags.	1½ minutes
Carrot	Scrape, then slice or cut into small dice. Blanch, cool, drain and pack in polythene bags.	3–5 minutes
Cauliflower	Heads should be firm, compact and white. Wash, break into small sprigs, about 5 cm (2 in) in diameter. Add the juice of a lemon to the blanching water to keep them white. Cool, drain and pack in polythene bags.	3 minutes
Celery	Trim, removing any strings, and scrub well. Cut into 2.5 cm (1 in) lengths. Blanch, cool, drain and pack in polythene bags.	3 minutes
Courgette	Choose young ones. Wash and cut into 1 cm (½ in) slices. Either blanch and cool, or sauté in a little butter and drain. Pack in polythene bags.	1 minute
Leek	Cut off tops and roots; remove coarse outside leaves. Slice into 1 cm (½ in) slices and wash well. Sauté in butter or oil for 4 minutes. Drain, cool and pack in polythene bags.	
Marrow	Cut marrow in 1–2.5 cm (½–1 in) slices. Blanch, cool, drain and pack in polythene bags.	3 minutes
Mushroom	Choose small button mushrooms and leave whole; wipe clean but don't peel. Sauté in butter for 1 minute. Drain, cool and pack in polythene bags. Mushrooms larger than 2.5 cm (1 in) in diameter are suitable only for slicing and using in cooked dishes.	
Onion	Skin, finely chop and blanch. Cool and pack in small polythene containers for cooking later; packages should be overwrapped, to prevent the smell filtering out. *Note:* Small onions may be blanched whole and used later in casseroles.	Chopped: 2 minutes Small whole: 4 minutes
Parsnip	Trim and peel young parsnips and cut into narrow strips. Blanch, cool, dry and pack in polythene bags.	2 minutes
Pea	Use young, sweet green peas, not old or starchy. Shell and blanch, then shake the blanching basket from time to time to distribute the heat evenly. Cool, drain and pack in polythene bags.	1–2 minutes
Pepper	Freeze red and green peppers separately. Wash well, remove stems and all traces of seeds and membranes. Can be blanched as halves for stuffed peppers, or in thin slices for stews and casseroles. Cool, drain and pack halves in containers and slices in polythene bags.	3 minutes
Potato	Best frozen in the cooked form, as partially-cooked chips (fully cooked ones are not satisfactory), croquettes or duchesse potatoes. New: choose small even-sized potatoes. Scrape, cook fully with mint and cool. (Appearance similar to that of canned potatoes.) Pack in polythene container or bags. Chipped: part-fry in deep fat or oil for 2 minutes, cool and freeze in polythene bags for final frying.	

FREEZING VEGETABLES (continued)

Vegetable	Preparation and packing	Blanching time
Spinach	Select young leaves. Wash very thoroughly under running water; drain. Blanch in small quantities, cool quickly and press out excess moisture. Pack in rigid polythene containers or bags, leaving 1 cm (½ in) headspace.	2 minutes
Sweetcorn	Select young yellow kernels, not starchy, over-ripe or shrunken. Remove husks and silks. Blanch, cool, dry and pack in polythene bags. *Note:* There may be loss of flavour and tenderness after freezing. Thaw before cooking.	Small: 4 minutes Medium: 6 minutes Large: 8 minutes
Tomato	Tomatoes are most useful if frozen as purée or as juice, although whole ones can be used in casseroles. *Whole:* wash, dry and pack in polythene containers or bags. *Purée:* skin and core tomatoes and simmer in their own juice for 5 minutes until soft. Pass them through a nylon sieve or liquidise, cool and pack in small containers. *Juice:* trim, quarter and simmer for about 10 minutes. Press through a nylon sieve and season with salt: 5 ml (1 level tsp) salt to every 1.1 litres (2 pints). Cool and pack in small polythene containers.	
Turnip	Use small, young turnips. Trim and peel. Cut into small dice, about 1 cm (½ in). Blanch, cool, drain and pack in polythene bags. *Note:* turnips may be fully cooked and mashed before freezing.	2½ minutes

Unsuitable for freezing: cucumber, lettuce, Jerusalem artichokes (suitable only as soups and purées).

After blanching, quickly remove the vegetables from the boiling water and immediately plunge into ice-cold water to cool as quickly as possible. Drain and dry well before packaging.

Storage time

Whole or prepared vegetables 10–12 months
Vegetable purées   6–8   months
Mushrooms   6   months

Thawing

Frozen vegetables should not be thawed before cooking but added to boiling salted water and cooked for just a few minutes. Alternatively frozen vegetables can be cooked in a covered pan with just a knob of butter and a little seasoning or herbs, or added to soups or stews without prior cooking. The final cooking should be as brief as possible so that the vegetables retain their texture.

Drying

Drying is one of the early methods of preservation that can still be used in modern day life. Some foods, such as apples, pears, plums, mushrooms, herbs and onions, are more suitable than others for drying and can be dried at home using basic kitchen equipment. However, if this method of preservation appeals to you, you may want to invest in an electrical 'food dehydrator' that dries larger quantities of foods in each batch.

In the home, any source of heat can be utilised for drying, providing it is applied with ventilation. Unfortunately the average oven does not have a low enough temperature setting to dry foods slowly and instead tends to bake and shrivel the food. However, the heat left in the oven after cooking can be used to dry food. This method of using residual heat means the food has to be dried over a longer period.

A warm airing cupboard or the area over a central heating boiler is ideal because you have a continuous supply of gentle heat and the air can circulate freely. The prepared food should be placed on an open rack; a wire rack or cooling tray is ideal.

Select good quality fruit that is just ripe. Avoid any with blemishes or bruises, or cut out the blemishes.

How to dry fruit

Apples and pears: prepare by peeling and coring. Slice apples into rings about 0.5 cm ($\frac{1}{4}$ in) thick, and cut pears in half or into quarters using a stainless steel knife. Put the prepared fruit in a solution of 50 g (2 oz) salt to 4.5 litres (1 gallon) of water, to prevent discoloration. Leave in the solution for 5 minutes, then dry on a cloth.

Spread the fruit on trays, or thread the rings on thin sticks, and dry in a very cool oven, at the lowest setting, in an airing cupboard or over the central heating boiler until leathery in texture. This will take about 6–8 hours. When dried, remove from the heat and allow to cool. Pack into jars, tins, or paper-lined boxes – they needn't be airtight containers – and store in a cool, dry, well-ventilated place.

Plums and apricots: for best results cut the fruit in half and remove the stones, although smaller fruit can be dried whole. Wash the fruit, dry carefully and arrange, cut sides up, on trays. Dry as above.

To cook dried fruit: soak in cold water overnight or for several hours before use. Drain well before using for stewed fruit or in puddings and pies.

How to dry vegetables

Mushrooms: wipe with a damp cloth; do not wash. Leave whole or cut into slices or quarters. Dry as above. Add dried mushrooms to soups, stews and casseroles. Soak in water for 30 minutes for frying or grilling.

Onions: remove the skins and cut into 0.5-cm ($\frac{1}{4}$-in) slices. Separate into rings and dip each ring into boiling water for 30 seconds. Drain, dry and spread on trays or thread on to thin sticks. Dry as above. Soak dried onions in hot water for 30 minutes. Drain and dry on kitchen paper towel before frying or grilling.

How to dry garden-grown herbs

Herbs should be picked on a dry day shortly before they flower – usually in June or July. Wash and pick off any damaged leaves. Dry the herbs by hanging them in the sun or by placing on a flat tin in a cool oven or warm airing cupboard. When the leaves crumble easily the herbs are ready. Crumble the leaves, put in jars and store in a cool, dry, dark place. Alternatively, tie them in bunches with a paper bag fastened over the leaves to keep off dust.

Parsley and mint will keep green if dipped in boiling water for 1 minute and then dried fairly quickly.

You can make your own bouquets garni by placing a bay leaf, a sprig of parsley and a sprig of thyme on a small square of muslin and tying into a small bag with string. Dry and add to soups, stews and casseroles.

Mixed dried herbs
50 g (2 oz) parsley
25 g (1 oz) winter savory
25 g (1 oz) lemon-scented thyme
25 g (1 oz) sweet marjoram

Weigh the herbs before drying. When dry, mix well and sift. Store in a labelled jar.

Spiced black pepper
15 g ($\frac{1}{2}$ oz) black pepper
15 g ($\frac{1}{2}$ oz) dried marjoram
15 g ($\frac{1}{2}$ oz) dried thyme
15 g ($\frac{1}{2}$ oz) dried rosemary
15 g ($\frac{1}{2}$ oz) winter savory
15 g ($\frac{1}{2}$ oz) ground mace

Mix all the ingredients together well, sift them and store in a labelled bottle.

Herb spice
25 g (1 oz) dried bay leaves
25 g (1 oz) dried thyme
25 g (1 oz) dried marjoram
25 g (1 oz) dried basil
22 ml (1$\frac{1}{2}$ level tbsp) ground mace
7.5 ml (1$\frac{1}{2}$ level tsp) nutmeg
7.5 ml (1$\frac{1}{2}$ level tsp) freshly ground pepper
7.5 ml (1$\frac{1}{2}$ level tsp) ground cloves

Mix and sift the herbs and spices together. Put into clean, dry glass jars and label. This herb spice may be used for flavouring meat or sausage dishes, stuffing and so on.

Salting

Salting is another old-fashioned method of preserving that is still useful today. Really good results can be achieved when salting beans – French or runner – and nuts.

How to salt beans

If you have a glut of beans in the garden and run out of freezer space, salt the surplus beans but be sure to use them within 6 months. French and runner beans can be stored in kitchen salt, but free-running table salt is not suitable. Use glass or stone jars, not glazed earthenware. The beans must be small, young and fresh – it isn't worth preserving old stringy ones.

Cut off the stalks. Break the French beans if they're long; runners should be sliced. Pack into containers with alternate layers of salt, allowing at least 450 g (1 lb) of salt to 1.4 kg (3 lb) of beans. Finish with a good layer of salt, press down firmly and cover with a moisture-proof lid or several layers of paper. Leave for a few days to settle down. The beans will shrink considerably as the salt draws out the moisture from them, making a brine, and so the jars can be filled up with more beans and salt – always finishing with salt.

To cook salted beans: rinse them several times in cold water, then soak for 2 hours in cold water. Cook as for fresh beans, but in unsalted water.

How to salt and store nuts

You can store nuts – hazel nuts, filberts, walnuts and chestnuts, for example – for several months, providing they are quite dry and in good condition when gathered.

Hazel nuts and filberts: pack tightly into a jar within 1 cm ($\frac{1}{2}$ in) of the top and cover with salt. Store in a cool, dry place.

Walnuts and chestnuts: pack into a box or crock with alternate layers of perfectly dry sand. These, too, should be stored in a cool, dry place. If the walnuts are not in best condition, crack them and remove the nuts. Then dry the nuts by putting them on a baking tin in a cool oven. Store in jars.

Bottling

Bottling may not be everyone's favourite method of preserving, but if you don't own a freezer and have plenty of cool, dark storage space, it's well worth devoting the time to storing fruit in this way, especially when there is a glut. Although you have to buy special preserving jars, these can be used over and over again, with new sealing rings.

Almost any type of fruit will bottle, providing you follow the general rules for preparing and processing. As with any other preserving process, the fruit must be fresh, sound, free of disease, clean and properly ripe – neither too soft nor too hard. Choose fruits of a similar shape, size and ripeness for any one bottle.

Preparing fruit for bottling

Pick over, removing any damaged fruit, or leaves, stems and so on. Some fruits require special preparation, as indicated in the chart below.

Jars for bottling

Use special bottling jars with glass caps or metal discs, secured by screw-bands or clips. If the cap or disc has no fitted rubber gasket, thin rubber rings are inserted between it and the top of the bottle. Neither the rubber rings nor the metal discs with fitted seals should be used more than once.

Before use, check jars and fittings for any flaw and test to make sure they will be airtight. To do this, fill with water, put fittings in place, then turn upside down. Any leak will show in 10 minutes.

Jars must be absolutely clean, so wash them and rinse in clean hot water. There is no need to dry them – the fruit slips into place more easily if the jar is wet.

BOTTLING FRUIT

Fruit	Preparation
Apple	*Normal pack:* peel, core and cut into thick slices or rings; during preparation put into a brine solution of 15 g ($\frac{1}{2}$ oz) salt to 1.2 litres (2 pints) water. Rinse quickly in cold water before packing into jars. *Solid pack:* prepare slices as above, remove from brine and blanch in boiling water, in small quantities for $1\frac{1}{2}$–3 minutes, until the fruit is just tender and pliable. Pack in jars tightly.
Apricot	*Whole:* remove stalks and wash fruit. *Halves:* make a cut round each fruit up to the stone, twist the two halves apart and remove the stone. Crack some stones to obtain the kernels and include with the fruit. Pack quickly, to prevent browning.
Blackberry	Pick over, removing damaged fruits. Wash carefully.
Blackberry with apple	Prepare apples as for solid pack above before mixing with the blackberries.
Blackcurrant	String, pick over and wash.
Cherry	*Whole:* remove stalks and wash fruit. *Stoned:* use a cherry stoner or small knife to remove the stones. Collect any juice and include with the fruit, if liked. Add 7 g ($\frac{1}{4}$ oz) citric acid to each 4.5 litres (1 gallon) of syrup (with either black or white cherries) to improve the colour and flavour.
Damson	Remove stems and wash fruit.
Gooseberry	Small green fruits are used for pies and made-up dishes; larger, softer ones are served as stewed fruit. Top and tail, cutting off a thin slice; this prevents shrivelling.
Greengage	*Whole:* see Apricot. *Halves:* see Apricot.
Pear, dessert	Peel, halve and remove cores with a teaspoon. During preparation, keep in a solution of 15 g ($\frac{1}{2}$ oz) salt and 7 g ($\frac{1}{4}$ oz) citric acid per 1.1 litres (2 pints) water. Rinse quickly in cold water before packing. Add 1.25 ml ($\frac{1}{4}$ level tsp) citric acid or 10 ml (2 tsp) lemon juice to each 450-g (1-lb) jar.
Pear, cooking	Prepare as for dessert pears then, before packing, stew gently in a sugar syrup – 100–175 g (4–6 oz) sugar to 600 ml (1 pint) water – until just soft. Add 1.25 ml ($\frac{1}{4}$ level tsp) citric acid or 10 ml (2 tsp) lemon juice to each 450-g (1-lb) jar.
Pineapple	Peel, trim off leaves and remove central core and as many 'eyes' as possible. Cut into rings or chunks.
Plum	*Whole:* see Apricot. *Halves:* see Apricot.
Raspberry	See Blackberry.
Redcurrant	See Blackcurrant.
Rhubarb	The thicker sticks are generally used for made-up dishes; the more delicate, forced rhubarb is used as stewed fruit. Cut rhubarb into 5-cm (2-in) lengths. To pack it more economically and make it taste sweeter when bottled, pour hot syrup over and leave overnight; use this syrup to top up the packed jars.
Strawberry	These do not bottle well.

Using water or syrup
You can use either water or syrup, but syrup gives a better flavour and colour. The usual proportion is 225 g (8 oz) sugar to 600 ml (1 pint) water, but the amount can be varied according to the sweetness of the particular fruit.

Use granulated sugar. Dissolve in half the required amount of water, bring to the boil and boil for 1 minute. Then add the remainder of the water. This method reduces the time needed for the syrup to cool. If the syrup is to be used while still boiling (see below), keep a lid on the pan to prevent evaporation, which would alter the syrup's strength.

Golden syrup can be used to make bottling syrup, using the same proportions – 225 g (8 oz) syrup to 600 ml (1 pint) of water. In this case, put the golden syrup and water into a pan, bring to the boil and simmer for 5 minutes before use. The flavour will, of course, be altered.

Packing the fruit
Put the fruit in the jars layer by layer, using a packing spoon or the handle of a wooden spoon to push down the fruit. When a jar is full, the fruit should be firmly and securely wedged in place, without bruising or squashing. The more closely the fruit is packed, the less likely it is to rise after the shrinkage which may occur during processing.

After processing by one of the methods described below, allow the jars to cool, then test for correct sealing by removing the screw-band or clip and trying to lift the jar by the cap or disc. If this holds firm, it shows that a vacuum has been formed as the jar cooled and it is hermetically sealed. If cap or disc come off, there is probably a flaw in the rim of the jar or on the cap. If, however, several bottles are unsealed the processing procedure may have been faulty. Use the fruit from the jars at once; it can be re-processed but the result is loss of quality. Store without clips or screw-bands. If you do leave the latter on, then oil each one and screw on loosely.

Processing

Oven method
The advantages of the oven method are that

jars can be processed at one time and no special equipment is needed. It is, however, not quite so exact as the water bath method, as it is not so easy to maintain a constant temperature throughout the oven and it is easier to overcook the fruit.

The oven method is not recommended for tall jars. If you use this method, use only one shelf of the oven, placed in the centre. Don't overcrowd the jars or the heat will not penetrate the fruit evenly.

Wet pack: heat the oven to 150°C (300°F) mark 2. Fill the packed jars with boiling syrup or water to within 2.5 cm (1 in) of the top. Put on rubber rings, glass caps or metal discs but not screw-bands or clips. Place the jars 5 cm (2 in) apart on a solid baking sheet, lined with newspaper to catch any liquid which may boil over. Put in the centre of the oven and process for the time stated in the table. Remove the jars one by one and put on clips or screw-bands as tightly as possible. Allow to become quite cold before testing for air-tightness.

Dry pack: heat the oven to 130°C (250°F) mark ½. Pack the bottles with fruit but do not

add any liquid. Put on caps, but not rubber rings, discs with rings, screw-bands or clips. Place the jars 5 cm (2 in) apart on a baking sheet lined with newspaper. Process for the time stated in the table, then remove the jars one at a time. Use the contents of one jar to top up the others if the fruit has shrunk during the cooking. Fill up at once with boiling syrup, place rubber bands, caps or metal discs in position and secure with clips or screw the bands on tightly. Cool before testing.

When the jars have been filled with fruit and syrup, all air bubbles should be dispelled by jarring each bottle on the palm of the hand. Alternatively, pack the fruit and add liquid alternately until the jar is full. Fill the jars to the brim before putting on the fittings. **Note:** the dry pack oven method is not recommended for fruits which discolour in the air,

such as apples, pears and peaches. From the chart it will be seen that with both oven methods the time required varies not only with the type of fruit, but also with the tightness of the pack and the total load in the oven at any one time; the load is calculated according to the total capacity (in g/lb) of the jars. With fruits such as strawberries and raspberries, these can be rolled in caster sugar before packing dry; the flavour will be delicious but the appearance less attractive.

Water bath method
This is the more exact method of processing, but it calls for some special equipment – a large vessel, about 5 cm (2 in) deeper than the height of the bottling jars, a thermometer and bottling tongs. The vessel can be a very large saucepan, a zinc bath or

OVEN METHOD PROCESSING TIMES
These are the temperatures and processing times recommended by the Long Ashton Research Station.

Type of fruit	Wet Pack		Dry Pack	
	Preheat oven to 150°C (300°F) mark 2. Process time varies with quantity in oven, as below.		Preheat oven to 130°C (250°F) mark ½. Process time varies with quantity in oven, as below.	
	Quantity in g (lb)	Time in minutes	Quantity in g (lb)	Time in minutes
Soft fruit, normal pack: Blackberries, Currants, Raspberries, Gooseberries and Rhubarb (for made-up dishes), Apples, sliced	450 g–1.8 kg (1–4 lb) 2.3–4.5 kg (5–10 lb)	30–40 45–60	450 g–1.8 kg (1–4 lb) 2.3–4.5 kg (5–10 lb) Not recommended	45–55 60–75
Soft fruit, tight packs: as above including Gooseberries and Rhubarb (for stewed fruit)	450 g–1.8 kg (1–4 lb) 2.3–4.5 kg (5–10 lb)	40–50 55–70	450 g–1.8 kg (1–4 lb) 2.3–4.5 kg (5–10 lb)	55–70 75–90
Stone Fruit, dark, whole: Cherries, Damsons, Plums	As above		As above	
Stone fruit, light, whole: Apricots, Cherries, Gages, Plums	As above		Not recommended	
Apples, solid packs; **Apricots,** halved; **Peaches; Pineapples; Plums,** halved	450 g–1.8 kg (1–4 lb) 2.3–4.5 kg (5–10 lb)	50–60 65–80	Not recommended	
Pears	As above		Not recommended	

WATER BATH METHOD PROCESSING TIMES

Type of fruit	Slow method	Quick method
	Raise from cold in 90 minutes and maintain as below	Raise from warm 38°C (100°F) to simmering 88°C (190°F) in 25–30 minutes and maintain as below
Soft fruit, normal pack: Blackberries, Currants Raspberries, Gooseberries and Rhubarb (for made up dishes), Apples, sliced	74°C (165°F) for 10 minutes	2 minutes

Soft fruit, tight pack:
as above, including
  Gooseberries and Rhubarb
  to serve as stewed fruit,
  stone fruit, whole Apricots,
  Cherries, Damsons, Gages,
  Plums
	82°C (180°F) for 15 minutes	10 minutes

Apples, solid pack; **Apricots,** halved; **Peaches,** **Pineapple,** **Plums,** halved	82°C (180°F) for 15 minutes	20 minutes
Pears	88°C (190°F) for 30 minutes	40 minutes

a zinc bucket. It must have a false bottom such as a metal grid, strips of wood nailed together trellis-fashion, or even a folded coarse cloth. A sugar-boiling thermometer will be satisfactory. Bottling tongs are not essential, but they make it easier to remove the jars from the water bath.

Slow water bath: pack the jars with fruit, then fill up the jars with cold syrup. Put the rubber bands and heat-resisting glass discs (or metal discs) and screw-bands in place, then turn the screw-bands back a quarter turn. Place the jars in the large vessel and cover with cold water, immersing the jars completely, if possible, but at least up to the necks. Heat gently on top of the cooker, checking the temperature of the water regularly; raise the temperature to 54°C (130°F) in 1 hour, then to the processing temperature given in the chart below in a further 30 minutes. Maintain the temperature for the time given in the chart. Remove the jars with tongs (or bale out enough water to remove them with the aid of an oven

cloth). Place the jars on a wooden surface one at a time, and tighten the screw-bands straight away.

Quick water bath: if you have no thermometer, this is a good alternative method. Fill the packed jars with hot (not boiling) syrup, cover and place in the vessel of warm water. Bring the water to simmering point in 25–30 minutes, and keep simmering for the time stated in the table.

Pulped fruit

Soft and stone fruits can be bottled as pulp. Prepare as for stewing, then cover with the minimum of water and stew until just cooked. If desired, the fruit can be sieved at this point. While still boiling, pour into hot jars and place the rubber bands and heat-resisting discs (or metal discs) and screw-bands in position.

Immerse the jars in a deep pan and add hot water up to the necks. Raise the temperature to boiling point and maintain for 5 minutes. Remove the jars and allow to cool.

121

Bottling fruit in a pressure cooker
This shortens the processing time and also ensures that the temperature is controlled exactly. The cooker must have a low (5 lb) pressure control. Any pressure cooker will take 450 g (1 lb) bottling jars, but you will need a pan with a domed lid for larger jars.

Prepare the fruit as for ordinary bottling, but look at the additional notes in the chart on pressure cooking. Pack the fruit into clean, warm bottles, filling them right to the top. Cover with boiling syrup or water to within 0.5 cm ($\frac{1}{4}$ in) of the top of the bottles. Put on the rubber bands and caps or metal discs, clips or screw-bands, screwing these tight, then turning them back a quarter-turn. Next,

PREPARATION AND PROCESSING OF FRUIT IN A PRESSURE COOKER
Prepare the fruit as for ordinary fruit bottling, unless otherwise stated. Bring to pressure as described above, and process for the time given in the chart.

Fruit	Processing time (in minutes) at low (5 lb) pressure
Apples (quartered)	1
Apricots or plums (whole)	1
Blackberries	1
Raspberries	1
Cherries	1
Red and blackcurrants	1
Damsons	1
Gooseberries	1
Pears, eating	5
Pears, cooking (very hard ones can be pressure-cooked for 3–5 minutes before being packed in jars)	5
Plums or apricots (stoned and halved)	3
Rhubarb [in 5-cm (2-in) lengths]	
Strawberries	Not recommended
Soft fruit, solid pack: put the fruit in a large bowl, cover with boiling syrup [175 g (6 oz) sugar to 600 ml (1 pint) water] and leave overnight. Drain, pack jars and cover with same syrup. Process as usual.	3
Pulped fruit, e.g. apples: prepare as for stewing. Pressure cook with 150 ml ($\frac{1}{4}$ pint) water at high (15 lb) pressure for 2–3 minutes, then sieve. While still hot, fill jars and process.	1

as an extra precaution, heat the jars by standing them in a bowl of boiling water.

Put the inverted trivet into the pressure cooker and add 900 ml (1$\frac{1}{2}$ pints) water, plus 15 ml (1 tbsp) vinegar to prevent the pan from becoming stained. Bring the water to the boil. Put the bottles into the cooker, making sure they do not touch each other by packing newspaper between. Fix the lid in place, put the pan on the heat without weight and heat until steam comes steadily from the vent. Put on the low (5 lb) pressure control and bring to pressure on a medium heat. Reduce the heat and maintain the pressure for the time given in the last column in the chart. Any change in pressure will cause liquid to be lost from the jars and under-processing may follow.

Remove the pan carefully from the heat and reduce the pressure at room temperature for about 10 minutes before taking off the lid. Lift out the jars one by one, tighten the screw-bands and leave to cool.

Bottling tomatoes

Preparation
Whole unskinned tomatoes (recommended for oven sterilising): choose small or medium evenly-sized fruit, ripe yet firm. Remove the stalks and wash or wipe the tomatoes. Pack into jars and fill up with a brine made with 15 g ($\frac{1}{2}$ oz) salt per 1.2 litres (2 pints) of water instead of syrup (see water bath and oven methods). Add 1.25 ml ($\frac{1}{4}$ level tsp) citric acid or 10 ml (2 tsp) lemon juice to each 450-g (1-lb) jar.
Solid pack, with no liquid added: any size of fruit may be used, but they must be firm. Skin the tomatoes. Small tomatoes may be left whole, but larger ones should be halved or quartered so that they may be packed really tightly, with no air spaces, making it unnecessary to add water. The flavour is improved if about 5 ml (1 level tsp) salt and 5 ml (1 level tsp) sugar are sprinkled among the fruit in each 450-g (1-lb) jar. Add 1.25 ml ($\frac{1}{4}$ level tsp) citric acid or 10 ml (2 tsp) lemon juice to each 450-g (1-lb) jar.
In their own juice: skin the tomatoes, then pack tightly into jars. Stew some extra tomatoes in a covered pan, with 7 g ($\frac{1}{4}$ oz)

salt to each 900 g (2 lb) fruit, strain the juice and use to fill up the jars. Add 1.25 ml ($\frac{1}{4}$ level tsp) citric acid or 10 ml (2 tsp) lemon juice to each 450-g (1-lb) jar.

Processing by oven method

	Wet pack		Dry pack	
	Preheat oven to 150°C (300°F) mark 2. Process time varies with quantity in oven, as below		Preheat oven to 130°C (250°F) mark $\frac{1}{2}$. Process time varies with quantity in oven, as below	
	Quantity in g (lb)	*Time in minutes*	*Quantity in g (lb)*	*Time in minutes*
Whole tomatoes	450 g–1.8 kg (1–4 lb)	60–70	450 g–1.8 kg (1–4 lb)	80–100
	2.3–4.5 kg (5–10 lb)	75–90	2.3–4.5 kg (5–10 lb)	105–125
Solid pack (halved or quartered)	450 g–1.8 kg (1–4 lb)	70–80	Not recommended	
	2.3–4.5 kg (5–10 lb)	85–100		

Processing by water bath method

	Slow method	Quick method
	Raise from cold in 90 minutes and maintain as below	Raise from warm 38°C (100°F) to simmering 88°C (190°F) in 25–30 minutes and maintain for:
Whole tomatoes	88°C (190°F) for 30 minutes	40 minutes
Solid pack tomatoes (halved or quartered)	88°C (190°F) for 40 minutes	50 minutes

Processing by pressure cooker method

Whole or halved tomatoes in brine (prepare them as for ordinary bottling) should be processed for 5 minutes at low (5 lb) pressure; for solid pack allow 15 minutes.

Bottled tomato purée

This method enables you to use poorly shaped tomatoes – although they must still be sound and ripe. Wash, place in a covered pan with a little water and salt and cook until soft. Rub the pulp through a sieve and return it to the pan, then bring to the boil. Pour it at once, while boiling, into hot jars and put the rubber bands, caps or metal discs, screw-bands or clips in place. It is vital that this process should be carried out quickly; the pulp deteriorates if left exposed to the air. Immerse the bottles in a pan of hot water – padded at the bottom with thick cloth or newspaper – bring to the boil and boil for 10 minutes. Finish and test as usual.

Tomato juice

Simmer ripe tomatoes until soft and rub through a nylon sieve. To each 1.1 litres (2 pints) pulp, add 300 ml ($\frac{1}{2}$ pint) water, 5 ml (1 level tsp) salt, 25 g (1 oz) sugar and a pinch of pepper. Process the juice as for tomato purée.

Jams, jellies and marmalades

Equipment for jam-making

Some special utensils and tools, though by no means indispensable, make jam-making easier.

Preserving pan

Choose one made from heavy aluminium, stainless steel or tin-lined copper. It should have a fairly thick base or the jam will tend to burn. The pan should be wide enough across the top to allow for good evaporation of the water and deep enough to allow the jam to boil rapidly without splashing all over the cooker. The best overall size will depend on how much jam you make at a time – the jam should preferably not come more than halfway up the pan.

Old-style preserving pans made from un-lined copper or brass can be used for jams, jellies and marmalades, providing they are perfectly clean; any discoloration or tarnish must be removed with a patent cleaner and the pan should then be thoroughly washed. Jams made in copper or brass pans will contain less vitamin C than those made in aluminium or stainless steel pans. The preserve must not be left standing in such a pan

for any length of time, and a copper or brass pan must not be used for pickles or chutneys, as they are too acidic and would react with the metal.

If you haven't a preserving pan, use a big thick-based saucepan, remembering that since most saucepans are not as wide across as a preserving pan, you may need to allow a longer simmering and boiling period for the fruit.

Other equipment

Slotted spoon

Useful for skimming off any stones as they rise to the surface when you are making jam from fruit such as damsons. A funnel with a wide tube for filling the jars is useful. Failing this, use a jug or large cup.

Any sieve that is used in jam-making should be of nylon, not of metal, which might discolour the fruit.

Jam jars

You will need a good supply of jars, which should be free from cracks, chips or other flaws. Jars holding 450 or 900 g (1 or 2 lb) are the most useful sizes, as covers are sold for these sizes. Wash them well in warm soapy water and rinse thoroughly in clean warm water. Dry off the jars in a cool oven and use while hot, so that they do not crack when the boiling jam is added.

Jar covers

Most stationers sell packets containing waxed discs, Cellophane covers, rubber bands and labels.

The fruit

This should be sound and just ripe; if necessary, it is better to have it slightly under- rather than over-ripe – at this stage, the pectin (see below) is likely to be most readily available.

Pectin and acid content

The jam will set only if there is sufficient pectin, acid and sugar present. Some fruits are rich in pectin and acid and give a good set; these include cooking apples, gooseberries, damsons, redcurrants and black-currants, some plums, also Seville oranges, lemons and limes. Those giving a medium set include plums, greengages and apricots, blackberries and raspberries. Fruits that are of poor setting quality include strawberries, cherries, pears, melon, marrow and rhubarb.

The pectin test

If you are not sure of the setting qualities of the fruit you are using, the following test can be made:

When the fruit has been cooked until soft and before you add the sugar, take 5 ml (1 tsp) juice, as free as possible from seeds and skin, put it in a glass and when cool add 15 ml (1 tbsp) methylated spirit. Shake. Leave for 1 minute; if the mixture forms a jelly-like clot, then the fruit has a good pectin content. If it does not form a single, firm clot, the pectin content is low and some form of extra pectin will be needed. Fruits that lack acid and pectin require the addition of a fruit or a fruit juice that is rich in these substances. Lemon juice is widely used for this purpose, since it aids the setting and at the same time often brings out the flavour of the fruit to which it is added. Allow 30 ml (2 tbsp) lemon juice to 1.8 kg (4 lb) of a fruit with poor setting properties. Alternatively, use an extract of apple or gooseberry (see below) or include the whole fruit, making a mixed fruit jam. Yet another method is to use a commercially bottle pectin – follow the manufacturer's directions.

Sometimes an acid only is added, such as citric or tartaric acid; these contain no pectin but help to extract the natural pectin from the tissues of the fruit and improve the flavour of fruits lacking in acid. Allow 2.5 ml ($\frac{1}{2}$ level tsp) to 1.8 kg (4 lb) fruit with poor setting properties.

Home-made pectin extracts

Apple: any sour cooking apples or crab-apples may be used for this purpose, also apple peelings and cores and windfalls.

Take 900 g (2 lb) fruit, wash it and cut it up without peeling or coring. Cover with 600–900 ml (1–$1\frac{1}{2}$ pints) water and stew gently for about $\frac{3}{4}$ hour, until well pulped. Strain

through a jelly bag. Make the pectin test to ensure that the extract has a high pectin content. Allow 150–300 ml ($\frac{1}{4}$–$\frac{1}{2}$ pint) of this extract to 1.8 kg (4 lb) fruit that is low in pectin.

Redcurrant and gooseberry: make in the same way.

Sugar

Granulated sugar is suitable and the most economical for jam making but less scum is formed with lump sugar and preserving crystals. There is no completely satisfactory substitute for sugar in jam making. If honey or treacle is used the flavour is usually distinctly noticeable. Glucose and glycerine do not have the same sweetening power as cane sugar. If any of these are used not more than half the sugar should be replaced.

Preparation and cooking

Pick the fruit and prepare according to type, then wash it quickly. Put the fruit into a preserving pan or large, strong saucepan, add water as directed in the recipe and simmer gently until it is quite tender. The time will vary according to the fruit – tough-skinned ones such as gooseberries, blackcurrants or plums, will take $\frac{1}{2}$–$\frac{3}{4}$ hour. Remove the pan from the heat and add the sugar, stir well until this has dissolved; add a knob of butter (this reduces foaming), then return the pan to the heat and boil rapidly, stirring constantly, until the jam sets when tested.

Testing for a set

Temperature test: this is the most accurate method. Stir the jam, put in a sugar thermometer and when the temperature reaches 105°C (221°F), a set should be obtained. Some fruits may need 1 degree lower or higher than this, so it is a good idea to combine this test with one of the following:

Saucer test: put a very little of the jam on a cold saucer or plate, allow it to cool, then push the finger across the top of the jam, when the surface should wrinkle. (The pan should be removed from the heat during this test or the jam may boil too long.)

Flake test: remove some jam with a wooden spoon, let it cool a little and then allow the jam to drop. If it has been boiled long enough, drops will run together to form flakes which break off sharply.

Potting and covering

The jars used for jam must be clean and free from flaws and they must be warmed before the jam is put in. As soon as a set has been reached, pour the jam into the jars, filling right to the necks. The only exceptions are strawberry and other whole-fruit jams and also marmalades – these should be allowed to cool for about 15 minutes before being potted, to prevent the fruit rising in the pots. Wipe the outside and rims of the pots and cover the jam whilst still very hot with a waxed disc, wax side down, making sure it lies flat. Either cover immediately with a damped Cellophane round, or leave the jam until quite cold before doing this. Label the jar and store in a cool, dark place.

Pickles and chutneys

For anyone with a productive garden these preserves are almost as important as jams and bottled fruit. In many of them bruised and poorly shaped fruits and vegetables can be used up, since their appearance is usually of no account in the finished product.

Equipment for pickles and chutneys
Choose enamel-lined, aluminium or stainless steel pans. Avoid brass, copper or iron, as they tend to impart an unpleasant metallic taste to the preserve. Avoid metal sieves for the same reason and use a nylon one. Jam jars or special pickle jars can be used. Cover them with one of the following:
(a) metal or Bakelite caps, with a vinegar-proof lining,
(b) greaseproof paper and then a round of muslin dipped in melted paraffin wax or fat,
(c) preserving skin (sold in rolls) or vinegar-proof paper,
(d) large corks (previously boiled), covered with a piece of greaseproof paper tied down with string.

If the jars are not adequately covered, the vinegar will evaporate, the preserve shrink and the top dry out.

Pickles

Vegetables
Choose crisp, fresh vegetables and wash and prepare them according to the recipe. They must then be brined (opposite) to remove surplus water, which would otherwise dilute the vinegar and render it too weak to act as a preservative for the vegetables.

Ordinary table salt is quite suitable to use for brining. Rinse the vegetables in cold water after brining, or the pickle may be too salty.

The vinegar

This is the preserving agent and is almost the most important factor. It should be of the best quality (especially for pickles), with an acetic acid content of at least 5 per cent. 'Barrelled' vinegars are usually of only 4–5 per cent acetic acid content and are not so good. Incidentally, the colour is no indication of strength; further distilling has the effect of rendering vinegar colourless. This 'white' vinegar gives a better appearance to light-coloured pickles such as onions and cauliflower, but malt vinegar gives a rather better flavour. The vinegar is normally given extra flavour by being infused with spices or herbs – see below.

Note: simmer chutney, uncovered, to permit evaporation.

Spiced vinegar

1 litre (1¾ pints) vinegar
30 ml (2 level tbsp) blade mace
15 ml (1 level tbsp) whole allspice
15 ml (1 level tbsp) cloves
18-cm (7-in) piece cinnamon stick
6 peppercorns

Put the vinegar and spices in a pan, bring to the boil and pour into a bowl. Cover with a plate to preserve the flavour and leave for 2 hours, then strain the vinegar and use as required.

An even better result is obtained if the spices are left to stand in unheated vinegar for 1–2 months.

Note: if the individual spices are not available, use 25–50 g (1–2 oz) pickling spice. Different brands of pickling spice will vary considerably, e.g. some contain whole chillies, and give a hotter result.

For aromatic vinegar see page 36.

Dry brining

For cucumber, marrow, tomatoes and French beans. Layer the prepared vegetables in a bowl with salt, allowing 15 ml (1 level tbsp) to each 450 g (1 lb) vegetables. Cover and leave overnight.

Wet brining

For cauliflower, cabbage and onions. Place the prepared vegetables in a bowl. Cover with a brine solution, allowing 50 g (2 oz) salt dissolved in 500 ml (1 pint) water to each 450 g (1 lb) vegetables. Put a plate over the surface, to ensure that the vegetables are kept under the liquid, cover and leave overnight.

Finishing

Pack the brined, well rinsed and drained vegetables into jars to within 2.5 cm (1 in) of top. Pour spiced vinegar over; take care to cover the vegetables well, giving at least 1 cm (½ in) extra to allow for any evaporation which may take place, but leaving a small space at the top of the jar to prevent the vinegar coming into contact with the cover. Cover securely.

Use the vinegar cold for crisp, sharp pickles – e.g. cabbage, onion – and hot for softer pickles such as plums and walnuts.

Chutneys

Chutneys should be simmered uncovered, to allow evaporation. The chutney is ready when no loose liquid remains and the mixture is the consistency of a thick sauce.

The best results are obtained when the ingredients are cut up in small pieces, thinly sliced or minced and then cooked very slowly for 1½ hours or longer; the cooking time depending very much on the depth of the contents of the pan. Sometimes the toughest ingredients, say onion, are cooked alone in a covered pan, then the other ingredients are added and the whole cooked without a lid.

Storing

Pickles and chutneys should be stored in a cool, dark, dry place and allowed to mature for 2–3 months before eating. The exception is red cabbage, which loses its crispness after 2–3 months.

Index